C000117890

DOMESTICATING VIGILANTISM IN AFRICA

DOMESTICATING VIGILANTISM IN AFRICA

EDITED BY
THOMAS G. KIRSCH
& TILO GRÄTZ

 JAMES CURREY

James Currey
www.jamescurrey.com
an imprint of
Boydell & Brewer Ltd
PO Box 9
Woodbridge
Suffolk
IP12 3DF
and of
Boydell & Brewer Inc.
668 Mt Hope Avenue
Rochester
NY 14620 USA
www.boydellandbrewer.com

All rights reserved. No part of this book may be reproduced in any form, or by electronic,
or mechanical means, including information storage and retrieval systems,
without permission in writing from the publishers, except by a reviewer
who may quote brief passages in a review.

Copyright © Contributors 2010
First published 2010

1 2 3 4 5 14 13 12 11 10

British Library Cataloguing in Publication Data
Domesticating vigilantism in Africa.
1. Vigilantes—Africa. 2. Crime prevention—Africa—
Citizen participation.
I. Kirsch, Thomas G. II. Grätz, Tilo.
364.4'3'096-dc22

ISBN 978-1-84701-028-5 (James Currey cloth)

Typeset in 10/11pt Photina with Castellar display
by Long House, Cumbria
Printed and bound in Great Britain by
CPI Antony Rowe, Chippenham and Eastbourne

Contents

Vigilantism, State Ontologies & Encompassment
An Introductory Essay

1

Domesticating Sovereigns
The Changing Nature of Vigilante Groups in South Africa

2

Ethnicity, Religion & the Failure of 'Common Law'
in Nigeria

3

Dévi & his Men
The Rise & Fall of a Vigilante Movement in Benin

4

Vigilantes in War
*Boundary Crossing of Hunters in Burkina Faso
& Côte d'Ivoire*

5

Bodies of Power
Narratives of Selfhood & Security in Nigeria

6

Violence in the Name of Democracy
Community Policing, Vigilante Action & Nation-Building in South Africa

Photographs

Notes on Contributors

RAY ABRAHAMS is a Fellow of Churchill College, Cambridge, and was a member of the Cambridge Department of Social Anthropology (1963-1998). He has carried out research in Tanzania, Uganda, Finland and Estonia and has written widely on relations between local communities and the state. His main publications include *The Political Organization of Unyamwezi* (1967), *The Nyamwezi Today* (1981), *A Place of Their Own* (1991), *Vigilant Citizens: Vigilantism and the State* (1998) and several edited books on eastern Africa and eastern Europe. He has also published many articles on vigilantism and other subjects.

LARS BUUR is senior researcher at the Danish Institute for International Studies and Research Associate at the Wits Institute for Social and Economic Research in Johannesburg and the Center for the Studies of Democracy and Development in Maputo. His research interests concern sovereignty, securitization and vigilantism in southern Africa and elite formation and productive sector development in Mozambique. He has co-edited *State Recognition and Democratization in Sub-Saharan Africa* (2007) and *The Security-Development Nexus* (2007).

TILO GRÄTZ studied social anthropology, history and African studies in Berlin at the Free University and Humboldt University. He holds a PhD from Bielefeld University (1998) and obtained his habilitation degree in Social Anthropology at the University of Halle-Wittenberg in 2008. Between 1999 and 2005, he was working as Senior Research Fellow at the Max-Planck Institute for Social Anthropology in Halle. At present, he is employed as a Senior Research Fellow at the University of Hamburg, doing research on electronic media in West Africa; he also works as an Associate Lecturer at the University of Halle-Wittenberg and the Alice Salomon University of Applied Sciences, Berlin.

STEN HAGBERG is Professor of Cultural Anthropology at Uppsala University. His research interests concern democracy, decentralization, development and the politics of belonging in Burkina Faso. Major publications include *Between Peace and Justice: Dispute Settlement between Karaboro Farmers and Fulbe Agro-pastoralists in Burkina Faso* (1998), *Poverty in Burkina Faso* (2001) and the co-edited books *Bonds and Boundaries in Northern Ghana and Southern Burkina Faso* (2000) and *Ethnographic Practice and Public Aid* (2009), together with several papers published in journals and books. He is currently the president of the Euro-African Association for the Anthropology of Social Change and Development (APAD).

JOHANNES HARNISCHFEGER studied social anthropology, political science, philosophy and literature. He has taught at universities in Kenya (1988-90), Nigeria (1993, 1994-96) and South Africa (1996-99), and is at present involved in a research project on northeast Nigeria, organised by the Institutes of African Studies at the Universities of Frankfurt and Cologne. His research focuses on witchcraft and spirit possession, Christianity in Igboland and the Biafra War. He has recently published *Democratization and Islamic Law* on the Sharia conflict in Nigeria (2008).

THOMAS G. KIRSCH is Professor and Chair of Social and Cultural Anthropology at the University of Konstanz. He received his Ph.D. from the European University Viadrina in Frankfurt/Oder and taught at the Department of Anthropology and Philosophy in Halle/Saale and then at the Department of Anthropology at Goldsmiths College, University of London, before coming to Konstanz in 2009. Between 1993 and 2001, he conducted fieldwork on African Christianity in Zambia, on the basis of which he has published two monographs and articles in the journals *American Anthropologist*, *Visual Anthropology* and *American Ethnologist*. Since 2003, he has conducted extensive fieldwork on violence, security and crime prevention in South Africa.

SYNA OUATTARA is a researcher in social anthropology at the School of Global Studies, University of Gothenburg. He received his PhD in 2006 from the University of Gothenburg. In 2008, he published the monograph *Deux sociétés secrètes dans des espaces publics: bois sacrés, initiations et rites de passage chez les Sénoufo de la Côte d'Ivoire et du Mali*. Since 1998, he has done extensive fieldwork on issues of environment, culture and development; indigenous knowledge; and traditional medicine in West Africa. Furthermore, he has been initiated into the hunters' association in Mali and Côte d'Ivoire. Currently, Ouattara is exploring initiated hunters' knowledge of traditional medicine in West Africa.

DAVID PRATTEN is Director of the African Studies Centre, University of Oxford, a Lecturer in the Social Anthropology of Africa and a Fellow of St Antony's College. He is author of *The Man-Leopard Murders: History and*

Society in Colonial Nigeria (2007), which won the 2007 Amaury Talbot Prize awarded by the Royal Anthropological Institute. He has also edited a volume of essays on vigilantism, *Global Vigilantes: Perspectives on Justice and Violence* (with Atryee Sen, 2007), and 'Perspectives on Vigilantism in Nigeria', a special issue of *Africa* (Vol. 78.1 2008). He is co-editor of *Africa: Journal of the International African Institute.*

Foreword
Some Further Thoughts on Comparative Study

RAY ABRAHAMS

'For it is the attempt both to generalise and at the same time take on board the intensity of the fieldwork experience, that is at the heart of anthropology. There is a middle ground which is not just a compromise, and which is absolutely central to the subject.'[1]

The study of vigilantism is a relatively recent development in social anthropology, and a substantial body of new fieldwork-based material has been amassed since my own (1987) and Suzette Heald's (1982, 1986) first discussions of the subject.[2] Prior to these, most accounts were by historians dealing with vigilante movements in North America, and especially those operating in San Francisco and Montana and the southern USA (the Ku Klux Klan) during the second half of the 19th century. This material became the subject of an important pioneer survey by Richard Maxwell Brown (1975), who had himself studied early vigilantism among South Carolina settlers (1963). My own book, *Vigilant Citizens* (1998), was a broader comparative study of such cases along with many others from South America, south-east Asia, Africa and Europe.[3]

In 2005 I was privileged to be invited to two conferences organised by younger social anthropologists at which an impressive body of new research on the subject was presented. The first meeting, held in West Sussex, was attended by anthropologists and other interested scholars, and its wide-ranging proceedings with material from several continents have now been published in the volume *Global Vigilantes* (Pratten & Sen 2007). The second meeting, which has resulted in the present book, was a workshop organised by the editors that formed part of the German Anthropological Association conference in Halle, and its focus was particularly African. In my contribution to the West Sussex volume, and in the spirit of its title, I was keen to clarify my approach to the identification and comparison of vigilantism as a geographically widespread and historically recurrent phenomenon. I want here to continue my discussion of these questions, and to explore in a preliminary way some of the questions that narrower comparison of local differences within a region appears to raise.

A regional approach?

I hope I will not be misunderstood if I say that I was particularly pleased to encounter so much work by Africanist anthropologists at both these events. At the same time, there is arguably some need for caution here, for one needs to ask, rather than to take for granted, what a close anthropological focus on a particular region has to offer.

Isaac Schapera (1953) was an early commentator on this issue. Like many others, he saw such study as a major task of social anthropology, and his stated preference for conducting at least the initial stages of such work within specific regions clearly has a common-sense plausibility. His main stress was on the possibility of complete coverage of an area, but it is also clear that many variables can be kept under control if the societies concerned have a common origin and are subject to investigable similar or different influences.[4] Despite some successes, however, it also appears that such a regional focus does not automatically lead to comparative enlightenment even when the ethnography itself is of the highest quality.

A detailed examination of the complex literature on these issues would be out of place here, and I merely venture some reflections on them stemming from my own research. The similarities and differences between neighbouring and/or related societies have a history which can be partly understood as a history of structural choices, including similar or different solutions to similar problems, made by the members of a society themselves and for them by others. Moreover, one can argue that many such problems are extremely widespread, occurring well beyond the confines of a region.

Vigilantism and the quest for order

In the present case of vigilantism, it is arguable that wherever people live within state structures, similar questions about the (un)satisfactory provision of law and order by the state frequently arise, as I hope is brought out by my own broader comparative study. I have suggested that 'taking the law into one's own hands' is a common response of citizens to such problems of order, and I have taken this as my focal concern. I am aware that this may seem to some an arbitrary choice and I acknowledge that it is possible to approach the same forms of behaviour from other perspectives, such as those of political hegemony or the economic interests of the actors, which are clearly often a part of the vigilante scene. I have, however, preferred to see these as common, interesting and sometimes influential adumbrations rather than the key comparative issue for analysis, while at the same time stressing that vigilantism is a highly labile phenomenon, whose practitioners may have multiple motives for their actions. I have tried to encompass much of the variability of real situations through the use of an 'ideal-type' approach to definition, as I have discussed in some detail elsewhere (1998, 2007). It is possible that there is something of myself in this decision and approach, but I would argue that it also has a strong empirical base. This is certainly the case in Nyamwezi and Sukuma culture and society, where I encountered the *Sungusungu* groups that formed the subject of my first analyses in this field, and I consider that a quest for order is also a much more widespread and more powerful force in society than 'hard-nosed' economic and political maximisation theories would suggest. One aspect of this point that struck me in the writing of my book was the regular tendency of vigilantes (and others) to seek legitimation of their activities through the assertion of such a quest, even when other, 'less noble' motives appeared to be present and perhaps dominant. While this makes it clear that a desire for order carries a risk of vulnerability to political manipulation, it also suggests that one dismisses such a desire from one's reckoning at one's intellectual peril. I might add – since it has not always been well understood – that this forms the general starting point for my own approach to definition and comparison in this field. By exploiting the flexibility of an ideal-type analysis I have tried to bring a wide variety of cases within a common frame by comparing the extent and form of their approximation to what I have seen as the 'type case'.

An anthropological approach?

There is a further question to confront, however, and this concerns the value of social anthropology itself as a discipline. A key point here is its ultimate fieldwork base, and the level of respect this implies for the cultures and social structures of the people whose lives we study at a local level. Much of my own work supports the view that this local level cannot be properly studied in isolation, but a proper balance needs to be achieved (cf. Englund & Leach 2000).

Turning this 'spotlight' on myself, I realise that I may have strayed from such a balance in my search for unifying features in the field of vigilantism and my emphasis upon relations between 'citizens' and 'the state', while at the same time documenting a range of slippage away from the ideal type I had constructed. Of course, my discussion of my Nyamwezi/Sukuma material pays considerable attention to the indigenous cultural and social structural background to the development of *Sungusungu*. However, partly for want of relevant detailed material, and also because of my interest in the spread of vigilante ideas and activities through migration and the influence of the press and other media, it is arguable that my book sometimes paid less attention than it ideally might have done to exploring the significance of local differences in ideas of citizenship and perceptions of the implications of state membership.

One returns here to the hope that the availability of increasing quantities of detailed local ethnographic data, as presented in the present book, might help to generate a more nuanced and differentiated comparative picture of the processes of the emergence of vigilante activity in various locations. I have already stressed that there is nothing automatic about this, but the mechanism of a focussed conference or workshop which has led to this volume and to Pratten and Sen's *Global Vigilantes* should offer as good a chance as any of the development of mutually well-informed quests for answers to a range of questions which the participants, and others inspired by their work, may go on to pursue.

An East African example: The Nyamwezi and Sukuma and the Kuria

I will close with a modest offering in this vein. Alongside my own and others' Nyamwezi and Sukuma work, Heald's (2006, 2007) and Fleisher's (2000a, 2000b) studies of *Sungusungu* among the Kuria of Kenya and Tanzania remind us that eastern Africa may also provide the possibility of enlightening comparison in this field. For it seems clear that despite the involvement of the people in question in broadly similar state structures, local differences of social organisation may illuminate significant differences in the development of this vigilante movement among them.

As I have discussed at length elsewhere (Abrahams 1987, 1989, 1998; see also Bukurura 1995 and Masanja 1992), so-called *Busalama* or *Sungusungu* groups originated among northern Nyamwezi and neighbouring Sukuma villagers in the early 1980s as a response to perceived high levels of robbery – especially cattle theft – and, in some areas, witchcraft. These groups appear to have developed spontaneously as a genuinely grassroots local initiative in a few communities near the borders of three adjoining administrative districts, namely Kahama, Nzega and Shinyanga.[5] The movement mushroomed rapidly, spreading from village to village throughout the region. Local leaders were invited by members of nearby communities to come and help establish similar groups.

Each village group has its own body of officers. These are led by a chief (*ntemi*) who is supported by a second-in-command (*ntwale*); the latter are often diviners and medicinal experts. Below them are several *makamanda* (this noun is derived from English 'commander') and a few other named officers, including a secretary (*katibu*) whose job is to keep records of proceedings and look after subscriptions. Ordinary members, and especially younger ones, are simply known by the term *askari* – the Swahili term for soldiers or other armed personnel. Although in some communities there was initially a women's wing, by the early 1990s the movement was predominantly if not wholly a male one.[6] Each member has a bow and arrows and a gourd-stem whistle to be blown only in emergencies. When a theft has been committed a hue-and-cry is raised and the thieves are to be followed by the young men of the village concerned. The whistles would be used to alert neighbouring villages, whose residents then forewarn others in the same way to look out for and try to intercept the criminals.

In my first paper on the movement (1987), I noted that this spontaneous development did not appear to be mirrored in some other areas of Tanzania, such as that of the Kuria in Tarime District, despite the reported presence there of a great deal of cattle theft. I noted that, despite some official encouragement to adopt *Sungusungu* forms, at that time Kuria villagers appeared to have done no more than take the law into their own hands sporadically when police action against rustlers had proved ineffective. My own response was to suggest that such official encouragement could well have been offputting and to note that alternative local arrangements might have been available. I also set out some of the features of Nyamwezi and Sukuma social structure which seemed highly favourable to the development of *Sungusungu* village vigilantism in that area, and I shall return to these shortly. Meanwhile, *Sungusungu* groups were in fact eventually established in the 1990s among both the Tanzanian and Kenyan Kuria, and a substantial literature is available about them (cf. Fleisher 2000a, 2000b; Heald 2007). Although this literature does not explicitly pick up on my arguments about the favourable local conditions for *Sungusungu*'s emergence among the Nyamwezi and Sukuma, it does provide some extremely valuable insights into the contrastingly less favourable environment that indigenous Kuria society appears to have offered for such a development.

During my initial Nyamwezi fieldwork I was much struck, especially in the northern part of the area, by what I referred to as 'neighbourhood organization' (cf. Abrahams 1965, 1967). My undergraduate studies had emphasised the often critical importance of lineage and other forms of kinship in the constitution of local African communities, and it came as a surprise for me to find that, despite earlier work by Wilson (1951) and Beattie (1957), Nyamwezi villages could not properly be described as kinship units. As I documented at the time, neighbourhood was one of several main structural and organisational subsystems of Nyamwezi society, along with chiefship, kinship and affinity, domestic grouping and a variety of voluntary associations, including so-called secret societies.[7]

Villagers collaborated in their capacity as neighbours in a wide range of social and economic activities, including agricultural work, housebuilding, the performance of specific roles in marriages and funerals, and – mainly in the north – operating a system of neighbourhood courts that dealt with a variety of offences including dereliction of these neighbourly duties, verbal abuse, ritual mistakes and failures to pay fines imposed for previous misdemeanours. Another important point in this context is that although villages recognised the independent status of each other's courts, they also acknowledged a clear responsibility to deal with relevant offences committed by their members in other villages. Much the same situation prevailed among the neighbouring and closely related Sukuma people. As I noted in 1987 (cf. also 1989), the presence of such groupings and the sometimes uneasy relations between them and the state in one form or another appears to have been a major persistent feature of the Nyamwezi and Sukuma political scene. It can be viewed as part of a continuously monitored and negotiated equilibrium between public service and authority, emanating from the 'centre', and freedom and authority at local level. The Nyamwezi and Sukuma polity has in this sense been persistently a 'dual' one. At the same time the chiefdom system itself predicated a universalist idea of citizenship over and above ethnic, kinship and other sectional divisions, and it remained a key feature of the political landscape until its constitutional downgrading after Tanzanian independence.[8]

In addition, the associations I have mentioned deserve some consideration here. They included dance societies, cultivation teams, spirit possession and other ritual associations, hunting groups, and threshing teams. Some of these, such as the Swezi spirit-possession associations, were part of a much wider network of such groups stemming ultimately from the interlacustrine area to the north and east, but the active groups, though not simply village-based, were typically local and relatively small in scale and not subject to higher administrative authority. They were not part of the formal chiefship system, though chiefs often felt it politic to become members of some of them, and their relation to kinship was typically one of complementarity rather than conflict, though potential for the latter is sometimes highlighted in their rituals of initiation.

Along with village neighbourhood organisation itself, involvement in such groupings has provided a continuous template and source of practical experience for villagers in the area in the organisation of their own affairs. Most of the groups had similar internal structures, largely drawing their original inspiration for these from the chiefdom model, with its chiefs, headmen, secretaries and messengers, as *Sungusungu* also did when it was started.[9]

Overall, it has not seemed too surprising that groups like *Sungusungu* should emerge in response to rising crime rates in an area where a sense of public order and responsibility (as opposed to private, sectional or segmentary interests) is well developed, and where much of the groups' basic organisation and structure follows templates provided by previously existing collaborative local groups which 'ordinary' villagers have long experience of running for themselves.

The situation that prevailed among the Kuria seems rather different, and a key issue that emerges from both Heald's (2006, 2007) and Fleisher's (2000a, 2000b) studies is the inhibiting influence exercised by the sectional activities of 'clans' and lineages which provide a basic framework for local organisation.[10]

Heald describes how *Sungusungu* has not 'naturally' sprung forth among the Kenyan Kuria. She notes that the development involved a 'decisive shift in . . . the *"moral economy"* of the area', and she tells us it 'did not emerge spontaneously, out of a Durkheimian uprising of the collective conscience, but was a conscious act of design' (2007: 184, 189). The beginnings and history of the movement more generally both among the Kenyan and Tanzanian Kuria have depended on an alliance between local organisers and the administrative wing of central government. This alliance was necessary to overcome indigenous problems in the local communities and also problems of opposition and harassment from the police and the judiciary. As Heald (2007) points out, and I and Bukurura (1993) have documented, there was also 'central-government' support for *Sungusungu* in the Nyamwezi and Sukuma area in the face of comparable hostility. However, this support largely came from influential party ideologists including Nyerere himself, and the main division involved was between such leaders and the bureaucracy more generally. Beyond this, the situation in the two areas was markedly different. Nyamwezi and Sukuma *Sungusungu* did emerge more or less spontaneously and enjoyed very high levels of local support. The best that central government and bureaucratic opponents of the movement could try to do was to claim it, rather lamely, as part of 'the Party', and to try to 'hijack' it for a variety of largely urban projects.

Among the Kuria, a serious part of the uphill struggles of the movement was that cattle-raiding was an endemic feature of life at the local level, and that raiders often themselves apparently operated in consort with the police and judiciary. This appears to have been less true of the Nyamwezi and Sukuma area, although police inefficiency, partly though not wholly due to corruption, was a common source of dissatisfaction there as elsewhere. It is important, however, not to see the endemically high rates of cattle-raiding and other predatory crime, and the problems of dealing with such activities, among the Kuria as simply a statistical phenomenon. A crucial concomitant was clearly the influential presence in the area of competing clans. As Fleisher (2000a, 2000b) has shown for Tanzanian Kuria, this sometimes worked in surprising ways, but the key factor in the present context was a deeply engrained particularistic tendency to see stealing cows from other clans in a seriously contrasting light to stealing them from one's own clan. Similarly, Heald (2007) also tells how lineage interests constituted a continuing source of sectional division in the Kenyan case that she analyses. Lineages held both long-standing and more recent grudges against each other, and there was suspicion, despite the apparent openness of proceedings, that some members of different lineages represented in the recently established committee of the local *iritongo* (wider socio-political community) were secretly providing help to accused kinsmen.[11] One can readily understand how such endemic attitudes and structures might hinder the indigenous development of a more universalistic ethic of pursuing Kuria-wide ordered relations, and the fact that central-government representatives were key elements in the eventual establishment of *Sungusungu* in both Kenya and Tanzania is of course consistent with this. So too is the background information that Heald provides on the local leaders of the Kenyan group, whom she describes as 'new men'. She notes that the founding prime mover and four others among the first officers of the group had histories of professional or public-sector employment, as did some of the rank-and-file members. This is in sharp contrast to the Nyamwezi and Sukuma situation where the movement began spontaneously in out-of-the-way and relatively 'traditional' communities, and where – as far as I can judge – such past experience of state and parastatal employment among leaders figured far less prominently.

This is not to say, however, that indigenous structures that cross-cut clan and lineage loyalties were altogether absent from Kuria society. Here I have particularly in mind the recognition of a wider community (*iritongo*) and the age-group system, which also seems to have played a role, though not a wholly positive one in the new development. At first, elements of traditional age-set organisation were exploited in enforcing attendance at meetings and the payment of fines for non-attendance. Later, however, when the age-sets started to use such fines for their own rather than wider community purposes, it was decided by the *iritongo* committee that their power 'had to be broken', and the age-sets' formal role in the organisation was abolished (Heald 2007: 191). Meanwhile, the previously relatively muted power of the *iritongo* itself was strengthened and developed to form the basis of the new organisation as lineage and age-set power were diminished.

Old debates and modern settings

I hope this brief exploration of local differences will encourage others to attempt more and hopefully better comparative analyses along broadly similar lines. I must confess that, having begun my anthropological career roughly 50 years ago and having seen so many theoretical fashions come (and sometimes go), I find a modicum of pleasant irony in the idea that something not too far away from Fortes and Evans-Pritchard's well-worn distinction between centralised and segmentary structures in *African Political Systems* (1940; see also footnote 10) may still have something useful to tell us about contemporary changes in modern states. At the same time, however, some of the (almost equally long-standing) riders to and criticisms of their model are also important if we wish to progress further.

One may usefully remember here both Southall's (1956) point that there are 'stations' in between these polar types and Leach's (1954) arguments that such systems may be in an unstable equilibrium and that indigenous peoples do not all believe that they are living in the best of all possible structural worlds. Also pertinent is Southall's claim that Alur subjects were prepared to forgo segmentary freedoms in favour of chiefly rule partly because of the escape this offered them from constant oppositional friction. Similarly, the Tiv are said by Bohannan (1957) to have 'welcomed' the courts of the colonial era despite their deeply entrenched segmentary lineage organisation.[12]

I consider that such material can throw further light on the Kuria scene and, perhaps, on the development of vigilante activity more generally. The segmentary tendencies in Kuria society worked against the emergence of community-wide vigilantism, but possible structural bases for such a development were not wholly lacking there, and change has proved possible even if its future is precarious. At the same time, I am naturally interested to see that, yet again, issues of order have been the main engine of such change.

I hope that this makes sense to the very able younger anthropologists whose work provides the main substance of this book. It has been a privilege to meet and work with them, and they leave me with confidence that the study of vigilantism in Africa, along with social anthropology more generally, is in safe hands.

Notes

1 Abbreviated from a comment I made at the 1988 'Manchester debate', reprinted in Ingold (1996).
2 Some valuable early work was also carried out by political scientists and sociologists such as Rosenbaum & Sederberg (1976) and Gitlitz & Rojas (1983).
3 For further detailed references see Brown (1975) and Abrahams (1998).
4 Schapera does not explicitly make this latter point in the paper in question but, not surprisingly, he touches on it in some of his other works. Later, however, he appears highly critical of all comparative work (cf Comaroff, Comaroff & Schapera 1986).
5 Cf. Abrahams (1987) and Bukurura (1994b). As I noted in 1987, it is probably significant that these communities were situated in a cattle-rich zone well away from district headquarters.
6 See Bukurura (1994a); Bukurura (1994b) also documents ways in which the movement became supportive of men's rights over women.
7 The label 'secret society' can be slightly misleading. The societies in question had their ritual secrets which were carefully guarded, but such groups' existence and the identity of their members were generally common knowledge.
8 While differing from a bureaucratic model in its paternalistic idiom, the universalistic nature of chiefdom citizenship in the area was clearly marked. Its nature is examined in detail in Abrahams (1967) and Cory (1955). A key feature in the present context was the recognition that all subjects of a chief should be equally entitled to justice from his court.
9 Such use of a 'chiefdom model' led some Tanzanian government officials to the misguided fear that *Sungusungu* was an attempt to regenerate traditional chiefship in the area.
10 For convenience, I use 'clan' here following Fleisher's and Heald's usage. Dr Malcolm Ruel, who also knows the area well, informs me that he prefers to use the term 'province' for the Kuria units (*ebiaro*; sing. *ekiaro*) concerned. He agrees, however, that

there are also lineages, while at the same time noting that they do not exhibit the classic patterns of systematic internal segmentation found among the Tallensi or Tiv. My own use of the term 'segmentary' here refers primarily to the sectionalism *vis-à-vis* each other that the groups in question exhibit.

11 The term *iritongo* is not easy to translate as its reference varies contextually. As Ruel (1962) points out, it relates to a variety of aspects of community within the larger Kuria territorial *ebiaro* subdivisions.

12 Early acrimonious attacks on Bohannan (cf. Gluckman 1965: 209–12) for excessive emphasis on the special nature of the Tiv situation might readily have been avoided if both sides had clearly recognised and stated that adult Tiv lived in and had been socialised into, a segmented society, which became encapsulated in a colonial state that they both resisted and in some ways found attractive.

References

Abrahams, Ray 1965 'Neighbourhood organization: A major sub-system among the Northern Nyamwezi' *Africa* 35, 2, 168–86.

—— 1967 *The Political Organization of Unyamwezi* (Cambridge: Cambridge University Press).

—— 1987 '*Sungusungu*: Village vigilante groups in Tanzania' *African Affairs* 86, 343: 179–90.

—— 1989 'Law and order and the state in the Nyamwezi and Sukuma area of Tanzania' *Africa* 59, 3, 354–68.

—— 1998 *Vigilant Citizens: Vigilantism and the State* (Cambridge/Malden MA: Polity Press).

—— 2007 'Some thoughts in the comparative study of vigilantism' in Pratten & Sen 2007: 407–30.

Abrahams, Ray & Bukurura, Sufian 1993 'Party, bureaucracy and grass-roots initiatives in a socialist state: The case of *Sungusungu* vigilantes in Tanzania' in Hann, Chris (ed.) 1993 *Socialism: Ideals, Ideologies and Local Practices* (London: Routledge): 92–101.

Beattie, John 1957 'Informal judicial activity in Bunyoro' *Journal of African Administration* 9, 4, 188–95.

Bohannan, Paul 1957 *Justice and Judgment among the Tiv* (Oxford: Oxford University Press).

Brown, Richard M. 1963 *The South Carolina Regulators* (Cambridge MA: Belknap Press of Harvard University).

—— 1975 *Strain of Violence* (Oxford: Oxford University Press).

Bukurura, Sufian H. 1994a 'Sungusungu: Vigilantes in west-central Tanzania' PhD dissertation, University of Cambridge.

—— 1994b '*Sungusungu* and the banishment of witches in Kahama' in Abrahams, Ray (ed.) 1994 *Witchcraft in Contemporary Tanzania* (Cambridge: African Studies Centre): 61–69.

—— 1995 'Combating crime among the Nyamwezi and Sukuma' *Crime, Law and Social Change* 24, 3, 257–66.

Comaroff, John; Comaroff, Jean & Schapera, Isaac 1986 'On the Founding Fathers, fieldwork and functionalism: A conversation with Isaac Schapera' *American Ethnologist* 15, 3, 554–65.

Cory, Hans 1953 *Sukuma: Law and Custom* (London: Oxford University Press).

—— 1955 *The Indigenous Political System of the Sukuma and Proposals for Political Reform* (Kampala: Eagle Press).

Englund, Harri & Leach, James 2000 'Ethnography and the meta-narratives of modernity' *Current Anthropology* 41, 2, 225–48.

Fleisher, Michael L. 2000a '*Sungusungu*: State-sponsored village vigilante groups among the Kuria of Tanzania' *Africa* 70, 2, 209–28.

—— 2000b *Kuria Cattle-Raiders: Violence and Vigilantism on the Kenya/Tanzania Frontier* (Ann Arbor MI: University of Michigan Press).

Fortes, Meyer & Evans-Pritchard, Edward 1940 *African Political Systems* (London: Oxford University Press).

Gitlitz, John & Rojas, Telmo 1983 'Peasant vigilante committees in northern Peru' *Journal of Latin American Studies* 15, 1, 153–97.

Gluckman, Max 1965 *Politics, Law and Ritual in Tribal Society* (Oxford: Blackwell).

Heald, Suzette 1982 'Chiefs and administrators in Bugisu' in Robertson, Alexander F. (ed.) 1982 *Uganda's First Republic* (Cambridge: African Studies Centre, University of Cambridge): 76–98.

—— 1986 'Mafias in Africa: The rise of drinking companies and vigilante groups in Bugisu, Uganda) *Africa* 56, 4, 446–67.

—— 2006 'State, law, and vigilantism in northern Tanzania' *African Affairs* 105, 19, 265–83.

—— 2007 'Controlling crime and corruption from below: *Sungusungu* in Kenya' *International Relations* 21, 2, 183–99.

Ingold, Tim (ed.) 1996 *Key Debates in Anthropology* (New York: Routledge).

Leach, Edmund 1954 *Political Systems of Highland Burma* (London: Bell).

Masanja, Patrick 1992 'Some notes on the *Sungusungu* movement' in Forster, Peter & Maghimbi, Sam (eds) 1992 *The Tanzanian Peasantry: Economy in Crisis* (Avebury: Aldershot): 203–15.

Pratten, David & Sen, Atreyee (eds) 2007 *Global Vigilantes: Perspectives on Justice and Violence* (London: Hurst & Co.).

Rosenbaum, Jon H. & Sederberg, Peter C. (eds) 1976 *Vigilante Politics* (Philadelphia: University of Pennsylvania Press).

Ruel, Malcolm 1962 'Kuria generation classes' *Africa* 32, 1, 14–37.

Schapera, Isaac 1953 'Some comments on comparative method in social anthropology' *American Anthropologist* 55, 3, 353–66.

Southall, Aidan 1956 *Alur Society* (Cambridge: Heffers).

Wilson, Monica 1951 *Good Company* (London: Oxford University Press).

Vigilantism, State Ontologies & Encompassment
An Introductory Essay

THOMAS G. KIRSCH
& TILO GRÄTZ

Bringing together ethnographic case studies of vigilantism from various parts of sub-Saharan Africa, this volume starts from the observation that, in many African countries, the question of who is entitled to formulate legal principles, to enact justice, to police morality and to sanction wrongdoings has increasingly become the subject of violent contestation and conflict.[1] Generally speaking, these conflicts arise out of tensions between the principles of sovereignty, empirical statehood and citizens' self-determination. More particularly, they concern the conditions, modes and means of the legitimate exercise of power. Consequently, in this volume these conflicts are seen as diagnostic of how social actors in sub-Saharan Africa debate, practice and reconfigure sociopolitical and socio-legal orders.

In order to understand the range and variability of these diagnostics, the contributions to the present volume take a broad approach to the phenomenon of vigilantism, conceptualising it as an ever-evolving and contested social practice that can be enacted by different types of social agencies and that takes diverse organisational forms. Accordingly, the volume incorporates the examination of vigilante action on the part of groups as varied as, for instance, bodies of night guards (David Pratten), community policing forums (Thomas Kirsch), hunters' associations (Sten Hagberg and Syna Ouattara), and ethnically and religiously based militias (Johannes Harnischfeger). Moreover, two contributions (Lars Buur and Tilo Grätz) look at how legal self-help groups transmogrify over time, morphing from one organisational form into another, while Ray Abrahams' foreword to this volume pursues a comparative examination of the correlations between the emergence of vigilante groups in sub-Saharan Africa and structural aspects of social organisation.

As a topic that has been dealt with only relatively recently in research on Africa, the subject matter of this volume opens important and illuminating windows into historical and contemporary processes of social transformation which involve the blurring of polticolegal boundaries. In doing so, the papers in this volume seriously contest what has long been assumed to constitute the (future) fabric of Africa in these terms, namely a continent composed of *sovereign states* that are endowed with a monopoly in the legitimate use of violence within their respective territories.

Assumptions can be wrong. States in sub-Saharan Africa are not – and probably never have been – what modernist ideal-type conceptions projected them to be (see, for example, Jackson & Rosberg 1982).[2] It is true that, apart from cases like Somalia, and despite the long farewell to the model of the modern state made by some analysts of processes of globalisation, state agencies have *not* disappeared from the African political scene. Nonetheless, scholars have not always found it easy to identify the characteristics of postcolonial states in Africa. This is arguably due to the fact that since their inception in Western colonialism such states have constantly been reconfigured, and in this process have taken on forms and appearances whose multifarious nature makes it 'hard to go back to easy generalisations about "the African state"' (Boone 1998: 129). In any case, there is always something ontologically elusive about states anywhere in the world, as is nicely summarised in Erik Ringmar's remark: 'If we give the state a transcendental status, it disappears *from* the world; if we see it merely as a set of empirical attributes, it disappears *in* the world' (1996: 439).

Against this background, while puzzling over the concomitant presence and absence of the state in Africa, 'scholars have been proclaiming the "crisis of the state in Africa" for so long ... that the phrase has become a cliché' (Huxtable 1998: 279).[3] It also seems that, through repetition, the invocation of this phrase on occasion escalates into an Afro-pessimistic mantra assuring us that states in Africa are in *permanent* crisis – invariably debased, fragmented, disingenuous, inoperable. This alleged crisis sees societies in Africa as in plight and distress, leaving space for the irruption of new politicolegal actors with disparate, often uncompromising moralities and at times dubious legitimacy – vigilantes included. Of course, as István Hont (1995) noted in his comparative discussion of what he wryly refers to as the '"contemporary crisis of the nation state" in historical perspective', the expression 'permanent crisis' represents a contradiction in terms. All the same, as inquiries into the phenomenon of vigilantism attest, including those collected together in this volume, the paradoxes involved in politicolegal life in sub-Saharan Africa play a consequential catalytic role in processes of rapid social transformation not *despite* but *because of* the fact that they are oxymoronic in respect of how power and meaning are constituted through them.

Spectacles of (organised) violence

On the face of it, vigilante action often has a breathtakingly blunt, brutal message. Take, for example, the following account of the 'execution' of alleged criminals by the Bakassi Boys, a notorious vigilante group in Nigeria (Baker 2002; Harnischfeger 2001, 2003; Meagher 2007; Reno 2002; Smith 2004, 2006; Ukiwo 2002). Those suspected of crimes

> are driven along the streets by a succession of blows, so that they have no time to turn to the bystanders, bewail their fate, or appeal to onlookers' feelings of compassion. Nor do the Bakassi Boys announce the sentence, or attempt to justify their actions. On arriving at the place of execution, they simply throw the bound victims to the ground and chop away at them for minutes on end with their blunt machetes – a silent bloodbath, because the victims do not scream, even though some are still writhing on the ground when the Bakassi Boys finish their task by tossing car tyres on top of them and dousing them in petrol. (Harnischfeger 2003: 24–25)

This example illustrates that, more often than not, the violence enacted by vigilante groups in sub-Saharan Africa has a performative dimension and is 'both instrumental and expressive' (Riches 1986: 11).[4] However, it would be misleading to suppose that the vigilantes' spectacles of violence always represent an expression of effervescent group aggression (Verkaaik 2003). Consider, for example, what happens *before* the Bakassi Boys drive the alleged criminals through the streets:

> In order to ensure a steady stream of new criminals arriving at the place of execution, victims are also brought in from other areas. At first … they remain for some days imprisoned in the Bakassi Centre, where they are interrogated by an investigation committee. Only once their guilt has been established are they taken out on to the street and then to a road junction that is sufficiently large for hundreds of spectators. (Harnischfeger 2003: 24)

Thus, what at first sight appears to be spontaneous mob justice (cf. Baker 2008: 78–81) is in this case being coordinated with almost managerial efficiency (see also Anderson 2002: 531–2) and follows a well-planned choreography involving a stage (the road junction), protagonists (Bakassi Boys and 'criminals'), and a projected audience.[5]

Sometimes these performances have recourse to long-standing symbolic repertoires whereby vigilante action becomes explicable and legitimised by association with other powerful domains and institutions – such as secret societies – and the moral dichotomies they espouse. For example, David Pratten has reported that in Annang villages in south-western Nigeria, thieves are 'stripped naked, painted with charcoal, necklaced with a palm frond and paraded, tied at the waist, around the village and neighbouring markets' (2008b: 74). He argues that the parading of thieves by the vigilantes resembles ancestral masquerades involving the masked figures of anti-social spirits who are likewise painted in black and who also have a rope around the waist by means of which the spirit's movement during the masquerade is controlled.

However, of course, it is not only vigilante groups who strive to establish or maintain power through public displays of violence and physical punishment. As is well known, in Nigeria and many other countries worldwide, violence 'symbolize[s] the capacity of the military to impose its will through control of the means of violence' (Smith 2006: 130). The persistence of such symbolism among state and non-state agencies that are struggling for power or a share of it endorses 'a view of sovereignty as a tentative and always emergent form of authority grounded in violence that is performed and designed to generate loyalty, fear, and legitimacy from the neighbourhood to the summit of the state' (Hansen & Stepputat 2006: 297).

Phenomenologies and conceptualisations

Vigilantism presents a picture of bewildering volatility and complexity. There is amazing variation and flexibility over time and space in, for instance, how vigilante groups in Africa are structured and organised. Vigilantes have borrowed elements from and aligned themselves with 'traditional' and 'modern' institutions as varied as secret societies,[6] community-oriented agencies of policing,[7] the military,[8] 'traditional' assemblies and courts,[9] private security companies,[10] non-governmental organisations,[11] sports associations[12] and hunters' associations.[13] There is considerable variety in terms of how their activities are provided with legitimacy, some vigilante groups having recourse to 'religion' or some form of esoteric knowledge,[14] others to 'tradition', 'ethnicity' or 'autochthony',[15] while still others create innovative combinations of these registers.[16]

In addition, vigilante groups differ in marked ways in terms of how they relate to state agencies and other politicolegal authorities, their reactions oscillating between different forms of resistance, disengagement, accommodation, containment and collaboration. Yet, as Lars Buur argues in his contribution to the present volume, and as will be discussed in detail below, the categories 'vigilantism' and 'state' should not be conceived of as 'two pure and discrete domains, clearly separated from and in opposition to one another' (Buur, this volume, 62). In line with this position, Buur's chapter deals with the historically changing relationships between vigilante groups and state agencies in South Africa, showing that periods of disjunction and outright confrontation have alternated with periods of entanglement and mutual support. And as Sten Hagberg and Syna Ouattara demonstrate in their comparative study of hunters' movements in Burkina Faso and Côte d'Ivoire, relationships between vigilante groups and states may also be influenced by processes of transborder mobility which allow vigilantes to emerge as a new type of sociopolitical actor in the space between two countries. Moreover, the chapter describes a fascinating example of the dynamic morphologies of vigilante action mentioned above: theirs is a case of a 'traditional' institution, namely a cult of hunters, which is transformed into a vigilante movement and whose members later became mercenaries, but use their experiences as religiously initiated hunters and vigilantes to do so.

But it is not just the variations in vigilantism which are remarkable: vigilantism also confronts the scholar with a set of paradoxes concerning the social construction of sociality and morality. One such paradox is that, in many vigilante groups, acts of violence and extrajudicial executions are paralleled by a 'desire for peace and order which led to their emergence and which genuinely seems to inform most of their activities' (Abrahams 1987: 196). In addition, much of what the members of vigilante groups seek to achieve *in principle*, such as justice or personal security, becomes subverted *in practice* through their concrete actions (see, for example, Hellweg 2004: 18–19; Smith 2006: 130, 144).

It is paradoxes like the above which have made the notion of 'states of exception', as employed in the writings on sovereignty of Carl Schmitt (2005) and Giorgio Agamben (1998, 2005), attractive to scholars recently working on vigilantism in sub-Saharan Africa. For instance Lars Buur, in his study of vigilantes in a township in South Africa, points out: 'The townships have become spaces of exception; spaces in which the law is, if not completely suspended, then, at least, enforced primarily by local justice structures that are governed by values and practices other than human rights and due process' (Buur 2003: 35). Here, a *state* of exception takes the form of a *space* of exception (see also Gregory 2006; Rhodes 2005). In politicolegal terms, the paradox is that the township lies within the territory of the South African state while also being an exception to it – or rather, *in* it. However, as Thomas Kirsch shows in his chapter in the present volume, the 'state of exception' not only tends to have a specific spatiality, it also represents a paradoxical principle of politicolegal practice that develops in *time*, namely the sanctioned temporary suspension of law which is constitutive of the law.

Given the complexities outlined so far, it comes as no surprise that a major challenge in any study of vigilantism is the conceptualisation of its object. In what has become a classic definition, the criminologist Les Johnston (1996) defines 'vigilantism' as a social movement constituted by 'private voluntary agents' who, on the basis of premeditation and in the face of what they perceive to be transgressions of institutionalised norms, aim to control crime and to provide security for the movement's members and for significant others by using or threatening to use violence. In developing this definition Johnston distinguishes between 'private voluntary activities' that are recognised by the state and those 'without the state's authority and support' (Johnston 1996: 226); only the latter is defined as 'vigilantism'. Further, in contrast to many other scholars who define 'vigilantism' as an activity of people who 'take the law into their own hands', Johnston is to be applauded for *not* making 'illegality' or 'extralegality' a feature of his definition.

However, a few caveats are in order here. First, as will be discussed in greater detail below, Johnston's use of the term 'the state' in the singular is problematic because it implies that 'the state' is a bounded and unified actor. Second, as Buur shows in his contribution to the present volume, police officers in South Africa 'know about and indeed rely on vigilantes breaking the law by using corporal punishment to discipline and extract information. But as long as it does not become public knowledge, [vigilantes] have *carte blanche* to continue their "good work"'. Similar findings have been made elsewhere on the African continent. However, this 'strategic ignorance' on the part of the police is empirically and conceptually different from what Johnston is referring to when he talks about 'state recognition'.

Third, as Jeff Weintraub has pointed out, 'the use of the conceptual vocabulary of "public" and "private" often generates as much confusion as illumination' (Weintraub 1997: 1–2). This is also partly true of Johnston's definition of vigilantism. For example, according to Johnston, violent off-duty actions by police officers do *not* represent vigilantism 'since, whether on duty or not, [police officers] continue to enjoy full police powers. In that respect, their off-duty actions cannot be demarcated from their public status, functions, and responsibilities' (1996: 224). Johnston does concede that, if 'police officers engage in "private enterprise", it is neither as mere private persons nor as mere public police, but as something altogether more complex' (*ibid.*). Nonetheless, these insights regrettably do not lead him to question the usefulness of the 'private'/ 'public' distinction for the definition of vigilantism (see also Clapham 1999).

Abrahams has rightly pointed out that vigilantism is 'not so much a thing in itself as a fundamentally relational phenomenon, which does not make much sense except in connection with and often in contrast to others' (Abrahams 1998: 7). He understands vigilante action to be 'part of a broad zone in the world of law and politics' (*ibid.*) which is protean and shifting, making the analytical demarcation of vigilantism difficult. Moreover, in previous publications as well as in his foreword to this volume, Abrahams states that he considers vigilantism to be, as he phrased it formerly, 'encapsulated within the state and yet conceptually and at times politically opposed to official governmental institutions' (*ibid.*). This understanding of 'vigilantism' as a relational opposite to 'the state' therefore brings out another difficulty in defining it, namely the problem of specifying what vigilantism is *not*. We will return to this point below.

What is particularly noteworthy about Abrahams' definition is that he subscribes to an ideal-type approach to 'vigilantism' (see Abrahams 2003: 26, 2007: 423) which provides useful analytical tools, and yet comes with the proviso that these may merely be approximations to what, in empirical worlds, unfold as complex and contingent phenomena. This contingency has to do with the fact that vigilantism tends to be enacted in 'frontier conditions' – that is, in zones of uncertainty and insecurity where power and social norms are, or have become, contested (cf. Abrahams 1998: 24–52). Such zones are marked by classificatory vagueness and volatility of social structurations. As a 'twilight institution'

(Lund 2006), vigilantism is both an agent in these zones and a *re*agent to what characterises them. On the one hand, in trespassing against social boundaries and shifting between different registers of self-organisation and self-legitimation, vigilantism regularly contributes to feelings of ambiguity and insecurity. On the other hand, vigilantes aim at disambiguation and security by (re)establishing boundaries, defining standards and authorising registers of legitimacy. Hence, taken together, here processes of destabilisation and stabilisation go hand in hand – which adds another paradox to those mentioned above and bears witness to 'the power of vigilantism to generate ambivalence' (Abrahams 1998: 3) for those who study it and, more particularly, of course, those who experience it in their life-worlds (see also Pratten 2008a: 3).

Taking up the metaphor of the 'frontier', David Pratten, in his contribution to the present volume, understands the Annang vigilantes in Nigeria whom he studied to be 'intermediaries' who are socioculturally productive yet politically precariously positioned and who act as 'brokers' in a 'legally pluralistic setting', thus bridging formal and informal domains of dispute settlement. The chapter by Kirsch, on the other hand, argues that the model of the community policing forum (CPF) in South Africa is situated both at the centre *and* at the social margins of the (envisioned) nation state. CPFs are at the centre because they form part of democratic strategies of post-apartheid nation-building, but by dealing with 'criminal activities' they also aim at the margins of what, in visions of the nation state, is defined as lawful and legitimate. Kirsch shows that, for those who try to act in the spirit of this model, the model entails dilemmas which, in turn, can lead to 'civic states of exception' – that is, to vigilante action through which attempts are made, paradoxically, to affirm South African principles of participatory democracy by temporarily suspending them.

Dichotomies in action

Given our considerations so far, attempts to reach a better understanding of what is involved in vigilante action in sub-Saharan Africa should aim, first, not at compiling lists of classificatory properties, but at identifying family resemblances. The latter approach is particularly helpful when assuming a comparative perspective in terms of historical (see, for example, Abrahams 1998; Fourchard 2008) or societal differences, the latter involving comparison on regional (Abrahams, this volume) or global (Pratten & Sen 2007) scales. Second, such an enterprise should also take account of the important fact, mentioned above, that vigilantism is lodged in paradoxical configurations where, for instance, acts of contradistinction provide evidence of mutual entanglements (see also Comaroff & Comaroff 2006: 5).

It appears that, on the most basic level and in light of the two preliminary remarks above, the actions of vigilantes all over the world rely on the idea of an essential, norm-based dichotomy ('right'/'wrong') which, through the practice of vigilantism, is translated into social dichotomies. On the one hand, it is translated into the distinction between 'malefactor' and 'non-malefactor', the term 'malefactor' being used here, in line with its Latin etymology, in the broad sense of 'someone who does wrong or does something bad'. Being broad, this term has the advantage of covering issues of both 'legality' and 'morality'.[17] On the other hand, vigilantism translates this norm-based dichotomy into a 'politics of belonging' (Hagberg 2004: 51) with two social boundaries: first, the boundary defining membership in the vigilante group that differentiates between 'insider' and 'outsider', and second, the boundary between those whose interests are being served by the vigilantes' activities ('the targeting group') and those whose interests are (at least potentially) impinged on by them ('the targeted group'). With regard to the latter, it is important to note that these social boundaries do *not* coincide. That is to say, in terms of social proportionality, vigilantism is a phenomenon in which – on a varying 'geographical scale' (Bassett 2003: 3, 2004; see also Pratten 2008b: 66–9) – a relative minority acts for and over a relative majority.

Lastly, it is important to consider what one means by saying vigilantes 'act for and over' others. Broadly speaking, vigilantes strive to give *validity* to the norm-based principles and regulations they propagate. Use of this term is not accidental. Of course, vigilantism revolves around the conjunctions of power and legitimation on the one hand, and of laws and morals on the other. But it also has to be recognised that, in many cases, vigilante groups do *not* institute truly new laws and moralities, but seek to support (or broaden the reach) of existing ones that are considered to be unduly neglected or counteracted in practice. One can accordingly say that the activities of vigilante groups represent attempts to 'validate' norm-based principles and regulations – that is, to corroborate them, give them force and authority and, in so doing, make them reality.

When examining how such validation unfolds, it is important to bear two aspects in mind. First, when considering empirical cases of vigilantism in sub-Saharan Africa such as those discussed in this volume, it becomes obvious that the moral and social dichotomies outlined above are not given or stable, but are subject to change and are objects of conflict and contestation. For example, comparative work has shown that the category of 'crime' as a sociolegal notion with moralistic underpinnings is a social construction, though one that has the ability to 'fracture and partition social nexuses and organize ways that groups interrelate' (Parnell 2003: 2). Therefore, whatever claims are made to the contrary in a given situation or sociocultural setting, there exist no universally shared criteria for deciding who is a 'malefactor'. Moreover, even in cases where the legitimacy of a given vigilante group is shared relatively ubiquitously by local people, documented empirical cases from various countries in Africa leave no doubt that 'vigilantism' and 'criminality' are often networked into each other via links of various kinds, leading to constellations in which 'the politics of protection and the violence of criminality are ... closely intertwined' (Anderson 2002: 541; see also Abrahams 1996: 45; Heald 2007: 6; Smith 2006: 133). Hence, taken together, it is important to recognise that the moral and social dichotomies that are essential for vigilantism are perpetually produced and reproduced in social practice.

Second, the same processuality applies to another dichotomy, mentioned above, which looms large in the debates on vigilantism in sub-Saharan Africa: the distinction between 'state' and 'non-state'. While some scholars have positioned vigilante groups in opposition to 'the state' or consider them to be critical of the state's performance, others have argued, with reference to South Africa, that 'although these organisations claim to be based outside and in opposition to an ineffectual, sometimes even immoral, state, they are involved in state-like performances such as security enforcement and in a perpetual renegotiation of the boundaries between state and society' (Buur & Jensen 2004: 144; see also Heald 2006; Smith 2006). Thus, when seen in comparative perspective, vigilante groups in sub-Saharan Africa have demonstrated versatility and flexibility in relating to state agencies and representatives of 'the state', sometimes putting up (or merely posing as) resistance to them, while at other times collaborating with or being instrumentalised by them.

Recapitulating a central aspect of the above, it can therefore be noted that vigilantism confronts us with paradoxical sociopolitical configurations in which, on the one hand, a set of dichotomies play a crucial role in how the action space of vigilantes is constituted while, on the other hand, the same dichotomies prove remarkably malleable when one looks at how vigilantism is acted out in practice.

The malleability of dichotomies imputes an ambiguous status to the units of analysis in studies of vigilantism. One consequence of this is that it is difficult to determine, despite the attempts of several political commentators, whether vigilantism should be regarded as either a cause or an effect of ongoing sociopolitical crises in sub-Saharan Africa. It is a debatable point, for example, whether the defiance of state-instituted law through vigilantes, their usurpation of force and acts of situated sovereignty should be interpreted as *contributing to the 'crisis of the state in Africa'*. This suggestion is usually made in light of evidence that vigilantes often undermine the politicolegal authority of state agencies like the police and people's confidence in that authority.[18] Alternatively, one can ask whether the existence of vigilantism should be seen as *an effect of 'failing' states*, whose (alleged) inefficiency in providing or failure to provide security, it has been argued, leaves a void that is filled by people's acts of popular justice.[19] It is in the latter sense that Abrahams remarked that 'the very existence of vigilante groups may be plausibly interpreted as a criticism of the state' (1987: 180). Or, to offer a further possible interpretation, would it be more correct to say that certain forms of vigilantism do not indicate state failure at all but, almost to the contrary, *a specific way of executing state power*, namely decentralised governance with vigilantism as a constitutive component?[20]

The great range of variation in vigilante action as exhibited in the contributions to the present volume suggests that these questions cannot be answered once and for all. The chapters demonstrate that what is needed in the analysis of vigilante action in sub-Saharan Africa is close attention to its embeddedness in social contexts, to the way state agencies and other sociopolitical actors deal with vigilante groups and in turn are dealt with by them, as well as to their performance, modes of organisation and sources of legitimacy. Moreover, when checking the chapters of this volume against each other and relating them to previous studies of vigilante groups in Africa, it becomes clear that answering questions such as the above requires reflection about the conceptual framing of 'vigilantism' as an object of study.

Besides prefacing the chapters that follow, the remainder of this introduction attempts to develop such reflections by starting from the assumption that, despite their differences, the case studies presented here share various features and conditions of their existence that become visible as soon as one views the discourses and actions of vigilantes as a *precarious analogue* of those of state agencies.

Vigilantism and the ontology of the state

Patrick Chabal once noted: 'To talk about politics in Africa is virtually to talk about the state' (Chabal 1992: 68). While this bold remark would not go uncontested among social scientists interested in the complexities and intricacies of everyday politics and 'the politics of politics', there is a strong sense in which the topic of this volume, namely vigilantism, can also only be talked about when talking about 'the state' (cf. Abrahams 2007: 423). This is because, whatever definition one subscribes to, vigilantism is an inherently relational concept, not only in terms of relations between different social groupings and moralities, but also with regard to what, in the wider context of vigilante action, is referred to, invoked as and practised in the name of 'the state'. However, as Chabal also points out in his influential discussion of the state in Africa, 'there is precious little agreement on its conceptual meaning or the interpretative implication of its analysis' (Chabal 1992: 68; see also Lund 2006: 673).

This lack of agreement is also reflected in how vigilantism in Africa is conceptually framed by social scientists. In fact, one can argue that the differences and disagreements in the much-debated question of whether vigilantes in Africa are resistant to or collaborate with 'the state' in part results from the interrelated facts that, first, scholars differ in how they position themselves towards 'the state', and second, that they hold different views about what has been called 'the ontological status of the state'.

To point out that divergences in scientific interpretation partly lie in the eye of the beholder is, of course, not to say that historical changes and differences between empirical cases are irrelevant. It does not need to be emphasised that states in Africa have undergone massive changes over time. In recent decades, for example, the consequences of democratic reforms and the strengthening of so-called civil society – influenced by pressure exerted by external political powers and the conditionality of development aid – have contributed to a diversification of African politico-legal structures. This process often involves a (partial) retreat and loss of legitimacy for the state, as well as the adoption of 'glocalised' (Robertson 1995) neo-liberal discourses and policies of decentralisation and state devolution. In this context, what can be witnessed is the appropriation of larger juridical competences by local actors, associations, political groups and social movements that frequently go together with, first, a discursive retraditionalisation of local spheres, and second, debates on the question of how the 'politics of public order' (Anderson 2002) relate to modern citizen-ship and communal authorities. But notwithstanding all these develop-ments, it is also important to take note of the fact that

> Rather than assuming that knowledge producers [e.g., social scientists] are located *a priori* outside the state – thereby confronting the state as an other – it is historically more appropriate and analytically more productive to take them as interested parties in the disputes surrounding the definition of the state and its role and the policies that it should carry out (De L'Estoile *et al.* 2005: 11).

We suggest that this self-positioning of social scientists towards the state – as, for instance, being in opposition to it or as acting in its service – has a crucial influence on how 'the state' is conceptualised and how the discourses and actions of state agencies are interpreted. For example, it influences whether 'the state' is represented in a particular scholarly work as desirable or undesirable, (too) weak or (too) strong, liberating or repressive.

Regarding the second point above, that concerning the ontological status of the state, Erik Ringmar has called upon social scientists to clarify 'what we mean when we talk about a "state" and [to] figure out in which sense notions like "existence" or "non-existence" can be applied to this kind of entity' (1996: 440). In his own attempt to tackle this issue, Ringmar distinguishes between realist and pluralist approaches. The realist approach considers 'the state' to be 'given *exogenously* to the analysis of it, and hence [to be] endowed with something akin to a transcendental ontological status' (*ibid.*: 441). The pluralist approach, by contrast, holds that concepts of 'the state' should emerge as a result of empirical studies and that 'the state is very far from a united, purposive, rational actor, but ... made up by a multitude of different subnational bureaucracies and organisations, each with its own agenda, its own set of goals and its own traditional ways of doing things' (*ibid.*: 442).[21]

In research on vigilantism in sub-Saharan Africa, the realist approach is exemplified in studies that accentuate the (allegedly) unified and encompassing nature of state structures and, consequently, invoke the singular ('the state') when dealing with state representatives and their interactions with non-state actors. This approach follows the Westphalian model of the sovereign state, also reflected in Max Weber's writings, in which international sovereignty – that is, the 'non-intervention and mutual recognition of juridically independent territorial entities' (Krasner 2001: 41) – is reckoned to be a precondition for a given state's domestic sovereignty. In this logic, conceptually putting 'the state' in the singular in relation to its *external* world allows scholars to put 'the state' in the singular in relation to its *internal* worlds. 'The state' here appears to be a unified agency in its own right – even 'a person writ large' (Mitchell 1991: 83) – which acts and is acted upon.

On the other hand, in research on vigilantism in sub-Saharan Africa the notion of the state as a pluralist assemblage of different agencies can be found in two different versions, one taking account of the fact that 'the state' is composed of different state sub-units, the other foregrounding the fact that 'the state' is practised by a combination of state and non-state units.

As regards the first version, sub-units of the state that have proved relevant in vigilantism research are – depending on the country under discussion and the analytical perspective adopted – defined in terms of either region, levels of government, or separation of powers. For example, with regard to the separation of powers, in her recent work on vigilantism Heald (2005, 2006, 2007) has convincingly argued that the state in Africa is 'far from being a unitary enterprise [but can be] shown to be at war with itself' (Heald 2006: 266). She demonstrates that different branches of the Tanzanian state apparatus reacted differently to the emergence of *sungusungu* vigilantism (see also, for example, Abrahams 1987, 1998; Bukurura 1994; Campbell 1989; Fleisher 2000a, 2000b, 2002; Paciotti & Mulder 2004). Broadly speaking, while the political and administrative branches tended to support vigilante groups in order to confront what was felt to be rampant social disorder, the police and the judicial branch remained mainly critical of such groups, partly because they were seen as undermining their institutional *raison d'être* and legitimacy. 'The emergence of *sungusungu*,' Heald points out, thus 'in effect drove a wedge through the state machinery of government, with the administration effectively aligned on one side and the police and judiciary on the other' (2002: 9).

But the idea of the unified nature of 'the state' is also challenged when taking account of, first, regional variations within state territories, and second, differences in the levels of government (local, regional, supraregional, nationwide). This is particularly evident in the case of Nigeria. As Johannes Harnischfeger shows in his chapter in the present volume, vigilante activities in contemporary Nigeria and the reactions of state agencies to them are informed by tensions between authorities within the federal states and the central government. He argues that since Nigeria's return to democracy in the late 1990s, 'the call for democratic self-determination did ... *not* unite the people, but set ethnic and religious groups against each other'. Vigilante activities accordingly reflect sectional interests and political tensions not only within Nigerian civil society, but also between different levels of government. Comparable tensions between different levels of government can be found in other African countries. For example, in Côte d'Ivoire state agencies reacted in contradictory ways to vigilante activities by Benkadi hunters, oscillating 'between their local approval of Benkadi and their national condemnation of it' (Hellweg 2004: 21). Similarly, in post-apartheid South Africa, the central state disapproves of vigilante practices, while the same practices are 'often accepted at local levels of the state and by local ANC structures' (Buur & Jensen 2004: 139).

The second version of the idea of 'the state' as a pluralist assemblage of different agencies – that is, where 'the state' is practised through a combination of state and non-state units – is based on a recognition that the 'notion that Africa was ever composed of sovereign states classically defined as having a monopoly on force in the territory within their boundaries is false' (Herbst 1996/97: 122). Historically speaking, this has to do with the fact that the 'colonial legal order was by its very nature a plural legal order' (Benton 1999: 563), which, over time, was transformed from 'a relatively fluid legal pluralism in which semi-autonomous legal authorities operated alongside state law, to a hierarchical model of legal pluralism in which state law subsumed in one way or another all jurisdictions' (*ibid.*). However, as has repeatedly been emphasised in studies of colonialism, this subsuming was certainly never as successful as colonial administrators would have liked it to be. In the British colonies this was partly due to colonial policies of indirect rule, which involved an outsourcing of politicolegal power and which frequently tolerated – *in practice if not in theory* – a plurality of monopolies of violence within one and the same territory (Killingray 1986, 1997; Mamdani 1996).

Meanwhile, as is increasingly recognised by political observers, decentralisation and 'fragmented systems of authority' (Hansen & Stepputat 2006: 306) are also salient features of the African postcolonial scene. Since the early 1990s, the emphasis on 'retraditionalisation' (Oomen 2000) in numerous countries in sub-Saharan Africa has led to a 'gradual resurgence and enlargement of the role of traditional authority in local governance, development, and national politics' (Buur & Kyed 2007: 2). The incorporation of vigilantes who seek legitimacy by drawing on 'tradition', 'culture' or 'authochthony' into the agendas of state agencies forms part of this process, although one that is characterised by a particular contradiction. In their contribution to this volume, Sten Hagberg and Syna Ouattara show how hunters' movements in Burkina Faso and Côte d'Ivoire have at times been co-opted by state representatives,

while at the same time many of them actually discard the ideological infrastructure of modern statehood by engaging in 'traditional' (i.e. 'pre-
modern') forms of spatial mobility that ignore the territorial boundaries of
modern nation-states (see also Heald 2006: 272, 2007: 8).

In recent years, scholars interested in politicolegal plurality of the kinds
outlined above have increasingly been influenced by Michel Foucault's
(1991) work on 'governmentality', understood as a form of power that is
performed as the 'conduct of conduct' in both state and non-state
contexts. In coining this term, Foucault linked the semantics of
'governing' (*gouverner*) with 'modes of thought' (*mentalité*) to stress the
nexus between technologies of (state) power, forms of reasoning and
subjectification. Most important for what is discussed here is the fact that
Foucault's approach has been considered useful in the examination of
forms of contemporary governance in Africa which, in line with global-
ised neoliberal policies, stress the fragmented and dispersed nature of
(state) power. In these forms of governance, the formal authority and
sovereignty of state government is relativised and qualified by proceeding
on the assumption that 'the state' is just one among a variety of different
agencies of governance, some of which form part of civil society.

In the context of the provision of protection and policing services, the
latter type of sociopolitical governance has been applauded for
strengthening democracy and increasing the involvement of civil society
in the fight against crime and the provision of human security (see, for
example, Wood & Shearing 2007; Loader 2000a; Johnston & Shearing
2003). In a similar vein, the concept of 'multi-choice policing', as elabor-
ated by Bruce Baker for African contexts, expresses the idea that there are
'multiple authorisers and providers [of policing who] form a complex set
of choices for Africans as they seek to negotiate a measure of protection
from abuse in their daily lives' (Baker 2008: 6). This approach takes as
its starting point the agency of people in selecting from a variety of
options, examining in an anthropologically appealing way 'security from
the point of view of the experience of the citizen rather than from the
governance perspective of the political authority' (*ibid.*: 27). In research
on popular justice in Africa, this agency-oriented and down-to-earth
perspective bears some resemblance to approaches that view vigilantism
as a 'form of local, everyday policing' (Buur & Jensen 2004: 140; see also
Jensen 2007: 48–9).

Yet, not surprisingly, such multiplicities in the realm of security have
also been seen in a negative light. On the one hand, this is because the
decentralisation of security has often meant a withdrawal of state
agencies and the privatisation of security provision, which in turn forces
citizens to become paying consumers of commodified security services – if
they can afford to do so (Loader 2000b; see also Sen & Pratten 2007:
2–5). On the other hand, the engagement of civil society actors in public
policing, as in vigilantism, can of course be problematic – or at least
considered ambiguous – because their operations tend to follow sectional

interests and moralities, thereby reflecting political divisions and infringing on the (human) rights of others. When seen in this light, the use of violence in the vigilantes' acts of popular justice, the exclusivism, judicial arbitrariness and lack of democratic accountability that is characteristic of many of their operations, makes vigilantism appear to be the ugly face of civil society (see also Allen 1997; Chambers & Kopstein 2001; Fatton 1995; Meagher 2007).

Studying vigilantism therefore means being confronted with troublesome, fundamental questions concerning the possibility of social consensus, the uses and abuses of power, and the politico-moral evaluation of social pluralism. It implies confronting the question of whether we live in a Hobbesian world, in which a strong centralised state is required to subsume citizens' (disruptive) plurality, or a Lockean world, in which the state's (rather modest) task is to preserve the natural rights of its citizens, who are conceptualised as a plurality of actors within civil society. These questions are vexing because they rely on deductive assumptions concerning the nature of human beings and sociability. And yet, whatever is deemed to be an answer to these questions is germane to any study of vigilantism in Africa because it more or less inadvertently determines whether politicolegal plurality and what have been called 'fragmented sovereignties' (Baker 2006) and 'overlapping sovereignties' (Randeria 2007) should be regarded as being part of the *problem* or of the *solution*.

Vigilantism and its opposites

As the latter remarks suggest, the governance perspective challenges the idea of clear-cut divisions between 'the state' and what are said to be its opposites or aspects of its opposites, such as 'society' or vigilantes' 'self-justice'. This also implies that the more the concept of 'the state' as a bounded and unified structure is questioned, the more difficult it is to differentiate the activities of vigilante groups from those of other ('state' and 'non-state') agencies. The aforementioned practice of outsourcing what have previously been the functions of state agencies to the 'private' sector is one reason for this. Another reason is that 'the state' not only represents an institutional reality, but – as several contributions to this volume exemplify – also a discursive and ideational reality.

The latter idea owes much to the writings of Philip Abrams who, in his well-known 'Notes on the difficulty of studying the state' (1988), distinguishes between 'state-system' and 'state-idea'. Comprising features of what has been addressed above with regard to 'realist' and 'pluralist' approaches in the study of states, the 'state-system', according to Abrams, is the 'palpable nexus of practice and institutional structure centered in government and more or less extensive, unified and dominant in any given society' (Abrams 1988: 58). His notion of the 'state-idea', on the other hand, aims at foregrounding the fact that 'the state' also represents an ideological project because it 'gives an account of political institutions in terms of *cohesion, purpose, independence, common interest and morality* without necessarily telling us anything about the actual nature, meaning or functions of political institutions' (*ibid.*: 68; emphasis added). For Abrams, the most significant question in the study of 'the state' is therefore how 'the idea of the existence of the state has been constituted, communicated and imposed' (*ibid.*: 69).[22]

Building on these insights, Timothy Mitchell has pointed out that 'state-system' and 'state-idea' should be seen as two aspects of one and the same process and that, in effect, 'the phenomenon we name "the state" arises from techniques that enable mundane material practices to take on the appearance of an abstract nonmaterial form' (Mitchell 2006: 170). Therefore, according to Mitchell, the boundary between 'state' and 'society' is not fixed and given, but is instead 'a line drawn internally, within the network of institutional mechanism through which a social and political order is maintained' (*ibid.*). This becomes particularly evident in the case of 'twilight institutions', such as vigilante groups, which on the one hand 'are intensely preoccupied with the state and with the distinction between state and society, [while] on the other hand, their practices constantly befuddle these distinctions' (Lund 2006: 673; see also Buur & Jensen 2004: 145).

The perspectives outlined so far have two important implications for the analysis of vigilantism in sub-Saharan Africa. First, they help us gain insights into the relationship between state agencies and vigilante groups. If the demarcation line between 'state' and 'non-state' is drawn *within* sociopolitical processes and institutions, shifting this boundary can either be an inclusive act, whereby vigilante groups are co-opted and enrolled to support the agendas and regimes of order of state agencies, or it can be an act of exclusion, whereby vigilantes come to impersonate the state's Other.

Second, these approaches allow for the idea that the reality of 'the state' is *not* bound by the institutional frameworks of state agencies, but rather that this reality can be narrated and enacted *outside* of them. In other words, 'the state' as a 'state-idea' can be invoked in the form of 'languages of stateness' (Hansen & Stepputat 2006) by social actors in *both public and private sectors* who 'speak like a state' when subscribing to the ideal that there exists (or should exist) in sociopolitical life a 'cohesion, purpose, independence, common interest and morality' (Abrams 1988: 58), that bridges variations between different sections of society.

Bringing together the considerations so far and developing them further, it can be argued that in its diverse forms, 'vigilantism as practice' (Sen & Pratten 2007: 6) is so contentious in sub-Saharan Africa not only because of the unsettling and dubiously legitimate violence involved, but also in certain regards because it constitutes a *precarious analogue* to what is represented and enacted in the name of 'the state' (cf. Buur & Jensen 2004: 144). It is an analogue to 'the state' because the actions and discourses of vigilante groups perform two basic operations which are characteristic of those of state agencies, namely 'verticality' and 'encompassment'. With regard to 'the state', James Ferguson and Akhil Gupta describe these operations as follows:

> *Vertically* refers to the central and pervasive idea of the state as an institution somehow 'above' civil society, community, and family. Thus, state planning is inherently 'top down' and state actions are efforts to manipulate and plan 'from above,' while 'the grassroots' contrasts with the state precisely in that it is 'below,' closer to the ground, more authentic, and more 'rooted.' The second image is that of *encompassment:* here the state (conceptually fused with the nation) is located within an ever widening series of circles that begins with family and local community and ends with the system of nation-states. (Ferguson & Gupta 2002: 982)

Ferguson and Gupta note that by performing these operations, states 'help to secure their legitimacy, to naturalise their authority, and to represent themselves as superior to, and encompassing of, other institutions and centres of power' (*ibid.*).

Vigilantism, we suggest, is based on similar operations. It can be understood as a social practice that, first, unfolds in the space between sociopolitical and sociolegal domains of life; second, engages in the creative enactment of dichotomies through which a relative minority attempts to establish and/or maintain the validity of certain legal and/or moral principles over a relative majority; and third, involves the invocation of some transcendent quality such as 'traditional' norms, autochthony, ethnicity and religion. The latter two features are essential for the vigilante groups' operation of 'vertical encompassment' in replacing or supplementing state functions.[23]

That the invocation of transcendent qualities is crucial for vigilantes' legitimacy becomes evident from the fact that in sub-Saharan Africa many people explicitly distinguish between 'right'/'proper' and 'wrong'/'improper' vigilantes. For example, Daniel Smith shows that in the case of the Bakassi Boys in Nigeria, over time there developed a 'disillusionment of the masses with vigilante groups because the vigilantes themselves were perceived as becoming political and therefore corrupt' (Smith 2006: 128). That the Bakassi Boys had previously enjoyed support was accordingly due to the perception that they were *in*corruptible and *a*political. And as Hellweg describes in the case of *dozo* (hunters') movements in Côte d'Ivoire, people assumed that there existed 'fake *dozos*' who 'donned *dozo* uniforms for criminal ends without the proper initiation' (Hellweg 2004: 9; see also Bassett 2003: 20–21). These empirical examples indicate that vigilante groups are often expected to be (in a manner of speaking) 'different' – that is, to stand apart and to strive for the (relatively) higher moral ground; such examples also provide some explanation for why vigilantism tends to have a short lifespan.

The precariousness of the analogy between the operations of 'the state' and vigilantism is due to the latter's ambiguity: it is precisely those features of vigilante groups which – under certain circumstances – can make them subsidiary consociates of state agencies that, if not accommodated by being enrolled in state agendas, under other circumstances pose the biggest threat to the state agencies' authority. And it is for this reason that state agencies in sub-Saharan Africa have at times been *fighting* and at other times been *courting* or even *hijacking* (Meagher 2007) vigilante groups.

Given this background, Tilo Grätz's chapter in the present volume raises questions concerning the conditionality of vertical encompassment by vigilante groups. Grätz looks at the case of the vigilante group led by Dévi Zinsou Ehoun – known as 'Colonel' Dévi – which operated in south-western Benin between 1999 and 2002. This group tried to substantiate its existence by gradually expanding its range of activities. Struggling to gain legitimacy by demonstrating effectiveness, this group constantly developed new modes of action: it started with night patrols on a small scale, and later set up road-blocks on transit routes; it began by meting out 'traditional' punishments, and later held public tribunals that mimicked the state courts. However, as regards the state, initial tacit governmental consent for small-scale encompassment turned into confrontation when the group expanded its range and modes of action, and in doing so threatened governmental authority on a higher level. Today, what remains of this group are vivid memories and a cement statue in a village in southern Benin, as described in Grätz's chapter in this volume. The statue portrays 'Colonel' Dévi in military boots and trousers, stripped to the waist, equipped with a state-of-the-art pump-action shotgun, a plethora of magical amulets and talismans, and what appears to be a fierce look in his eyes. It is a statue that speaks graphically to the disturbing creativity and ambiguity of vigilantism.

The contributions

The chapter by Lars Buur combines the historical analysis of vigilantism in apartheid and post-apartheid South Africa with the vivid ethnographic description of present-day vigilantes and their interactions with policemen. Buur examines changes in the relationships between state agencies and various types of legal self-help groups and makes two arguments. First, he suggests that studies of vigilantism should consider the vigilantes' relationship with the political order that prevails at the time. Second, he shows that perceptions of vigilante action in post-apartheid South Africa reflect apartheid discourses concerning 'mob violence' and 'ungovernability', even though much present-day vigilantism exhibits differences from previous vigilante practices in being generally supportive of the ANC-led government.

Taking account of wider political developments in Nigeria after 1999, Johannes Harnischfeger pursues a detailed comparison between the Oodua

People's Congress (OPC) in southwest Nigeria and Islamist *Hisba* vigilantes in northern Nigeria. His chapter shows that these groups reject the politicolegal authority of the Nigerian central government and that both frame their activities as struggles for (democratic) self-determination. Pointing out that 'self-policing' is crucial for these groups 'to constitute themselves as political communities', and tracing their development over time, Harnischfeger analyses how their respective sectional interests are linked with other politicolegal authorities on different levels, legitimised and violently enacted by using ethnic (OPC) and religious (*Hisba*) idioms.

As noted, Grätz's chapter discusses the vigilante group led by 'Colonel' Dévi. Grätz reconstructs the origins of this group, its strategies, its changing relationships with local communities and state agencies, and especially the conditions of its initial success and later failure. The group emerged as a local response to growing terror perpetrated by 'criminals', but soon transformed itself into a regional policing movement that prosecuted and penalised 'criminals'. The chapter also shows that although Dévi's group came into conflict with the state, some of its procedures concerning adjudication resembled those of state institutions.

The chapter by Sten Hagberg and Syna Ouattara discusses the multifaceted evolution of hunters' movements in Burkina Faso and Côte d'Ivoire, demonstrating how, over time, initiates into the 'traditional' cult of hunters (*donsoya*) became involved in vigilante activities and more recently as mercenaries in the civil war in northern Côte d'Ivoire. Hagberg and Ouattara show, first, that the hunters' specific skills and knowledge in matters of religion *and* vigilantism *and* warfare provided them with lucrative economic opportunities, and second, how the idea of their supra-ethnic and transnational identity helped them become new sociopolitical actors in the politically unstable space between the two countries.

David Pratten's chapter deals with Annang vigilantism in southeast Nigeria, which has its historical origins in night-guards and watch committees and, since the late 1980s, has been enacted by the members of officially endorsed youth associations. Examining biographies of these vigilantes and how they construe their modes of action narratively, Pratten emphasises the significance of 'cultural registers of violence'. The violence exercised by the vigilantes represents a way of satisfying 'a sense of the categorical self' while also marking spatial and social boundaries and demarcating the (male) moral community by inflicting bodily inscriptions through punishments. Pratten encourages us to see vigilantism as a productive force involved in the formation of 'self' and 'other'.

The chapter by Thomas Kirsch is framed by a general discussion of the relationship between 'democracy' and 'vigilantism' and focuses on the inadvertent blurring of boundaries between citizens' participation in crime prevention and vigilante action in present-day South Africa. Kirsch combines a critical analysis of policy documents with the examination of an ethnographic case study and shows, first, that South African principles of participatory democracy in community policing occasionally produce dilemmas for those who engage in it; and second, that these dilemmas can have problematic consequences when 'idealists' start to employ violence in order to resolve such dilemmas. Kirsch's contribution thus shows that vigilante action is often nested in paradoxical configurations.

Notes

1   This volume originates in a workshop held in October 2005 as part of the biennial conference of the German Anthropological Association (GAA) in Halle/Saale, Germany, which was organised by the editors in collaboration with Katja Werthmann, who at that time was acting as chairperson of the GAA's African Studies Group. We would like to thank all participants in this workshop; the Max Planck Institute for Social Anthropology in Halle/Saale, which made holding the workshop possible; and also the Center for Excellence at the University of Konstanz, which provided the financial support for copyediting this volume.

2   It is in this sense that Pierre Englebert gave his review article on political-science studies of African states the provocative title 'The contemporary African state: Neither African nor state' (Englebert 1997).

3   In different renderings, the theme of what we call the 'concomitant presence and absence of the state in Africa' also forms the background to Jean Bayart's distinction between the 'visible' and 'invisible' realms of the state (e.g. Bayart 1993), as well as to Patrick Chabal's and Jean-Pascal Daloz's suggestion that 'politics in Africa is not functionally differentiated, or separated, from the socio-cultural considerations which govern everyday life' (1999: 148).

4   The violent nature of vigilantism means that any attempt to study it as an ethnographer raises methodological concerns and ethical dilemmas. Since participant observation of vigilante action is ethically problematic and often not practicable, much of the ethnography of vigilantism in Africa relies on people's second-hand accounts. At the same time, however, as Lars Buur points out in his contribution to this volume, if methodologically we were to confine ourselves to second-hand accounts, anthropologists would remain empirically ignorant and most probably reproduce popular stereotypes and biased explanations of what actually happens in the course and context of vigilante action.

5   The coordinated nature of much vigilante action can also be seen in the well-documented fact that many vigilante groups in Africa have (at least temporarily) adopted certain central features of bureaucratic institutions.

6   See, for example, Nolte (2004); Gore & Pratten (2003: 203); Pratten (2007: 180–92).

7   See, for example, Fourchard (2008: 17); Hansen (2006: 288–9); Kirsch (2006).

8   See, for example, Abrahams (1987: 184).

9   See, for example, Fleisher (2000a, 2000b, 2002); Heald (2006, 2007: 7–13).

10   See, for example, Oomen (2004); Von Schnitzler et al. (2001).

11   See, for example, Bassett (2003: 15); Hellweg (2004: 14–15).

12   See, for example, Anderson (2002: 549).

13   See, for example, Bassett (2003); Hellweg (2004).

14   See, for example, Adamu (2008); Bangstad (2005); Bassett (2003: 3–7); Harnischfeger (2003: 31–5); Hellweg (2004: 11); Last (2008: 50-5); Le Roux (1997); Pratten (2008b: 71–2).

15   See, for example, Hagberg (2004: 53); Nolte (2008: 84).

16   See, for example, Anderson (2002: 533-4); Casey (2007); Higazi (2008).

17   Use of the term 'malefactor' also does justice, first, to the situation in African societies

where, as Heald has noted for East Africa, 'theft and witchcraft [are] bracketed together' (1986: 65) and second, to the fact that many vigilante groups in Africa not only hunt down those accused of 'crime' but also those accused of 'witchcraft' (see, for example, Abrahams 1998: 31–3). For South Africa, Buur has suggested that vigilantism 'deals with a range of inchoate moral concerns related to the well-being of the individual and the community. It places itself somewhere between what is formally known as criminal justice, on the one hand, and civil justice, on the other, and it deals with different kinds of disputes and crimes, not all of which correspond to those dealt with by the judiciary. These include petty crimes such as family-related disputes (gender, matrimonial, inheritance), generational conflicts (sexuality, schooling, use of respectful language), theft by known relatives or neighbours, disputes around money-lending and between neighbours, and conflicts related to distribution of scarce resources such as jobs, land, cattle, and so on. A list of serious crimes might include witchcraft, murder, rape (of both women and children), burglary, and so on' (Buur 2005: 200).

18 See, for example, Buur (2006: 748, 750); Jensen (2007: 47–8).

19 See, for example, Abrahams (2003: 26); Bassett (2003: 1); Buur & Jensen (2004: 139); Harnischfeger (2003: 26–7); Heald (2006: 279); Hellweg (2004: 5).

20 See, for example, Abrahamsen & Williams (2007: 131); Buur (2005); Fourchard (2008: 27–32); Hansen & Stepputat (2006: 308); Kyed (2007); Pratten (2006; 2008a: 4).

21 Yet, as briefly mentioned above, Ringmar maintains that social scientists are caught in a dilemma when opting for either of these approaches because it 'seems that we need to take the state for granted in order to be able to analyse whatever goes on in world politics, yet the very same state mysteriously disappears once we start looking for it' (Ringmar 1996: 442).

22 See also Joel Migdal's definition of the state as 'a field of power marked by the use and threat of violence and shaped by (1) the image of a coherent, controlling organization in a territory, which is a representation of the people bounded by that territory, and (2) the actual practices of its multiple parts' (Migdal 2001: 15–16).

23 In his analysis of vigilante activities by *dozo* hunters in Côte d'Ivoire, Joseph Hellweg also employs the concept of 'encompassment', but in a different way from that in which we are using it here. Referring to Louis Dumont's idea of hierarchy as the 'encompassment of the contrary' (Dumont 1980: 243), Hellweg argues that hunters 'encompassed the domain of state security within their hunting roles to stabilize, rather than subvert, the nation-state' (2004: 3).

References

Abrahams, Ray 1987 '*Sungusungu*: Village vigilante groups in Tanzania' *African Affairs* 86, 343, 179–96.

—— 1996 'Vigilantism: Order and disorder on the frontiers of the state' in Harris, Olivia (ed.) 1996 *Inside and Outside the Law: Anthropological Studies of Authority and Ambiguity* (London: Routledge): 41–55.

—— 1998 *Vigilant Citizens: Vigilantism and the State* (Cambridge: Polity Press).

—— 2003 'What's in a name? Some thoughts on the vocabulary of vigilantism and related forms of "informal criminal justice"' in Feenan, Dermot (ed.) 2003 *Informal Criminal Justice* (London: Ashgate): 25–40.

—— 2007 'Some thoughts on the comparative study of vigilantism' in Pratten & Sen 2007: 419–42.

Abrahamsen, Rita & Williams, Michael C. 2007 'Introduction: The privatisation and globalisation of security in Africa' *International Relations* 21, 2, 131–41.

Abrams, Philip 1988 'Notes on the difficulty of studying the state' *Journal of Historical*

Sociology 1, 1, 58–89.

Adamu, Fatima L. 2008 'Gender, Hisba and the enforcement of morality in northern Nigeria' *Africa* 78, 2, 136–51.

Agamben, Giorgio 1998 Homo sacer: *Sovereign Power and Bare Life* (Stanford CA: Stanford University Press).

—— 2005 *State of Exception* (Chicago: University of Chicago Press).

Allen, Chris 1997 'Who needs civil society?' *Review of African Political Economy* 24, 73, 329–37.

Anderson, David M. 2002 'Vigilantes, violence and the politics of public order in Kenya' *African Affairs* 101, 405, 531–55.

Baker, Bruce 2002 'When the Bakassi boys came: Eastern Nigeria confronts vigilantism' *Journal of Contemporary African Studies* 20, 2, 223–44.

—— 2006 'Beyond the state police in urban Uganda and Sierra Leone' *Afrika Spectrum* 41, 1, 55–76.

—— 2008 *Multi-Choice Policing in Africa* (Uppsala: Nordic Africa Institute).

Bangstad, Sindre 2005 'Hydra's heads: PAGAD and responses to the PAGAD phenomenon in a Cape Muslim community' *Journal of Southern African Studies* 31, 1, 187–208.

Bassett, Thomas J. 2003 'Dangerous pursuits: Hunter associations (*donzo ton*) and national politics in Côte d'Ivoire' *Africa* 73, 1, 1–30.

—— 2004 'Containing the *donzow*: The politics of scale in Côte d'Ivoire' *Africa Today* 50, 4, 31–49.

Bayart, Jean-Francois 1993 *The State in Africa: The Politics of the Belly* (London: Longman).

Benton, Lauren 1999 'Colonial law and cultural difference: Jurisdictional politics and the formation of the colonial state' *Comparative Studies in Society and History* 41, 3, 563–88.

Boone, Catherine 1998 '"Empirical statehood" and reconfigurations of political order' in Villalon, Leonardo A. & Huxtable, Philip A. (eds) 1998 *The African State at a Critical Juncture* (Boulder CO: Lynne Rienner): 129–42.

Bukurura, Sufian Hemed 1994 'The maintenance of order in rural Tanzania: The case of Sungusungu' *Journal of Legal Pluralism and Unofficial Law* 34: 1–29.

Buur, Lars 2003 'Crime and punishment on the margins of the postapartheid state' *Anthropology and Humanism* 28, 1, 23–42.

—— 2005 'The sovereign outsourced: Local justice and violence in Port Elizabeth' in Hansen, Thomas Blom & Stepputat, Finn (ed.) 2005 *Sovereign Bodies: Citizens, Migrants, and States in the Postcolonial World* (Princeton NJ: Princeton University Press): 192–217.

Buur, Lars & Jensen, Steffen 2004 'Introduction: Vigilantism and the policing of everyday life in South Africa' *African Studies* 63, 2, 139–52.

Buur, Lars & Kyed, Helene Maria 2007 'Introduction: Traditional authority and democratization in Africa' in Buur, Lars & Kyed, Helene Maria (eds) 2007 *State Recognition and Democratization in Sub-Saharan Africa* (New York: Palgrave Macmillan): 1–30.

Campbell, Horace 1989 'Popular resistance in Tanzania: Lessons from the *Sungu Sungu*' *Africa Development* 14, 4, 5–43.

Casey, Conerly 2007 '"Policing" through violence: Fear, vigilantism, and the politics of Islam in northern Nigeria' in Pratten & Sen 2007: 93–124.

Chabal, Patrick 1992 *Power in Africa: An Essay in Political Interpretation* (New York: St Martin's Press).

Chabal, Patrick & Daloz, Jean-Pascal 1999 *Africa Works: Disorder as Political Instrument* (Oxford: James Currey).

Chambers, Simone & Kopstein, Jeffrey 2001 'Bad civil society' *Political Theory* 29, 6, 837–65.

Clapham, Christopher 1999 'African security systems: Privatisation and the scope for mercenary activity' in Mills, G. & Stremlau, J. (eds) 1999 *The Privatisation of Security in Africa* (Johannesburg: South African Institute of International Affairs): 23–45.

Comaroff, John L. & Comaroff, Jean 2006 'Law and disorder in the postcolony: An introduction' in Comaroff, Jean & Comaroff, John L. (eds) 2006 *Law and Disorder in the Postcolony* (Chicago: University of Chicago Press): 1–56.

De L'Estoile, Benoît; Neiburg, Federico & Sigaud, Lygia 2005 'Introduction: Anthropology and the government of "Natives"' in De L'Estoile, Benoît; Neiburg, Federico & Sigaud, Lygia (eds) 2005 *Empires, Nations, and Natives: Anthropology and State-Making* (Durham NC: Duke University Press): 1–29.

Dumont, Louis 1980 Homo hierarchicus: *The Caste System and Its Implications* (Chicago: University of Chicago Press).

Englebert, Pierre 1997 'The contemporary African state: Neither African nor state' *Third World Quarterly* 18, 4, 767–75.

Fatton, Robert 1995 'Africa in the age of democratization: The civic limitations of civil society' *African Studies Review* 38, 2, 67–99.

Ferguson, James & Gupta, Akhil 2002 'Spatializing states: Toward an ethnography of neoliberal governmentality' *American Ethnologist* 29, 4, 981–1002.

Fleisher, Michael L. 2000a '"*Sungusungu*": State-sponsored village vigilante groups among the Kuria of Tanzania' *Africa* 70, 2, 209–28.

—— 2000b *Kuria Cattle Raiders: Violence and Vigilantism on the Kenya/Tanzania Frontier* (Ann Arbor MI: University of Michigan Press).

—— 2002 '"War is good for thieving!" The symbiosis of crime and warfare among the Kuria of Tanzania' *Africa* 72, 1, 131–49.

Foucault, Michel 1991 'Governmentality' in Burchell, Graham; Gordon, Colin & Miller, Peter (eds) 1991 *The Foucault Effect: Studies in Governmentality* (London: Harvester): 87–104.

Fourchard, Laurent 2008 'A new name for an old practice: Vigilantes in south-western Nigeria' *Africa* 78, 1, 16–40.

Gore, Charles & Pratten, David 2003 'The politics of plunder: The rhetorics of order and disorder in southern Nigeria' *African Affairs* 102, 407, 211–40.

Gregory, Derek 2006 'The Black Flag: Guantánamo Bay and the space of exception' *Geografiska Annaler, Series B* 88, 4, 405–27.

Hagberg, Sten 2004 'Political decentralisation and traditional leadership in the Benkadi hunters' association in western Burkina Faso' *Africa Today* 50, 4, 51–70.

Hansen, Thomas Blom 2006 'Performers of sovereignty: On the privatization of security in urban South Africa' *Critique of Anthropology* 26, 3, 279–95.

Hansen, Thomas Blom & Stepputat, Finn 2006 'Sovereignty revisited' *Annual Review of Anthropology* 35, 1, 295–315.

Harnischfeger, Johannes 2001 'Die Bakassi-Boys in Nigeria: Vom Aufstieg der Milizen und dem Niedergang des Staates' *KAS–AI* 12, 13–46.

—— 2003 'The Bakassi Boys: Fighting crime in Nigeria' *Journal of Modern African Studies* 41, 1, 23–49.

Heald, Suzette 1986 'Witches and thieves: Deviant motivations in Gisu society' *Man* 21: 65–78.

—— 2005 *Domesticating Leviathan:* Sungusungu *Groups in Tanzania* (London: Crisis States Research Centre).

—— 2006 'State, law, and vigilantism in northern Tanzania' *African Affairs* 105, 419, 265–83.

—— 2007 *Making Law in Rural East Africa:* Sungusungu *in Kenya* (London: Crisis States Research Centre).

Hellweg, Joseph 2004 'Encompassing the state: Sacrifice and security in the hunters' movement of Côte d'Ivoire' *Africa Today* 50, 4, 3–27.

Herbst, Jeffrey 1996/97 'Responding to state failure in Africa' *International Security* 21, 3, 120–44.

Higazi, Adam 2008 'Social mobilization and collective violence: Vigilantes and militias in the lowlands of Plateau State, central Nigeria' *Africa* 78, 1, 107–35.

Hont, István 1995 'The permanent crisis of a divided mankind: "Contemporary crisis of the nation state" in historical perspective' in Dunn, John (ed.) 1995 *Contemporary Crisis of the Nation State?* (Oxford: Blackwell): 166–231.

Huxtable, Phillip A. 1998 'The African state toward the twenty-first century: Legacies of the critical juncture' in Villalón, Leonardo A. & Huxtable, Phillip A. (eds) 1998 *The African State at a Critical Juncture* (Boulder: Lynne Rienner): 279–93.

Jackson, Robert H. & Rosberg, Carl 1982 'Why Africa's weak states persist: The empirical and the judicial in statehood' *World Politics* 35, 1, 1–24.

Jensen, Steffen 2007 'Policing Nkomazi: Crime, masculinity and generational conflicts' in Pratten & Sen 2007: 47–68.

Johnston, Les 1996 'What is vigilantism?' *British Journal of Criminology* 36, 2, 220–36.

Johnston, Les & Shearing, Clifford D. 2003 *Governing Security: Explorations in Policing and Justice* (London: Routledge).

Killingray, David 1986 'The maintenance of law and order in British colonial Africa' *African Affairs* 85, 40, 411–37.

—— 1997 'Securing the British Empire: Policing and colonial order, 1920–1960' in Mazower, Mark (ed.) 1997 *The Policing of Politics in the Twentieth Century* (Oxford: Berghahn Books): 167–90.

Kirsch, Thomas G. 2006 'Paradoxes of democracy in crime prevention'. Paper presented at the University of Cape Town/University of the Western Cape Anthropology Seminar Series, Cape Town, South Africa.

Krasner, Stephen D. 2001 'Rethinking the sovereign state model' *Review of International Studies* 27, 5, 17–42.

Kyed, Helene Maria 2007 'State vigilantes and political community on the margins in post-war Mozambique' in Pratten & Sen 2007: 393–415.

Last, Murray 2008 'The search for security in Muslim northern Nigeria' *Africa* 78, 1, 41–63.

Le Roux, Cornelius J. B. 1997 'People Against Gangsterism and Drugs (PAGAD)' *Journal for Contemporary History* 22, 1, 51–80.

Loader, Ian 2000a 'Plural policing and democratic governance' *Social Legal Studies* 9, 3, 323–45.

—— 2000b 'Consumer culture and the commodification of policing and security' *Sociology* 33, 2, 373–92.

Lund, Christian 2006 'Twilight institutions: An introduction' *Development and Change* 37, 4, 673–84.

Mamdani, Mahmood 1996 *Citizen and Subject: Contemporary Africa and the Legacy of Late Colonialism* (Princeton NJ: Princeton University Press).

Meagher, Kate 2007 'Hijacking civil society: The inside story of the Bakassi Boys vigilante group of south-eastern Nigeria' *Journal of Modern African History* 45, 1, 89–115.

Migdal, Joel S. 2001 *State in Society: Studying How States and Societies Transform and Constitute One Another* (Cambridge: Cambridge University Press).

Mitchell, Timothy 1991 'The limits of the state: Beyond statist approaches and their critics' *American Political Science Review* 85, 1, 77–96.

—— 2006 'Society, economy, and the state effect' in Sharma, Aradhana & Gupta, Akhil (eds) 2006 *The Anthropology of the State: A Reader* (Malden MA: Blackwell): 169–86.

Nolte, Insa 2004 'Identity and violence: The politics of youth in Ijebu-Remo, Nigeria' *Journal of Modern African Studies* 42, 1, 61–89.

—— 2008 '"Without women, nothing can proceed": Yoruba women in the Oodua People's Congress (OPC), Nigeria' *Africa* 78, 1, 84–105.

Oomen, Barbara 2000 '"We must now go back to our history": Retraditionalisation in a Northern Province chieftaincy' *African Studies* 59, 1, 71–95.

—— 2004 'Vigilantism or alternative citizenship? The rise of Mapogo a Mathamaga' *African Studies* 63, 2, 153–71.

Paciotti, Brian & Mulder, Monique Borgerhoff 2004 '*Sungusungu*: The role of preexisting and evolving social institutions among Tanzanian vigilante organizations' *Human Organization* 63, 1, 112–24.

Parnell, Philip C. 2003 'Introduction: Crime's power' in Parnell, Philip C. & Kane, Stephanie C. (eds) 2003 *Crime's Power: Anthropologists and the Ethnography of Crime* (New York: Palgrave Macmillan): 1–32.

Pratten, David 2006 'The politics of vigilance in southeastern Nigeria' *Development and Change* 37, 4, 707–34.

—— 2007 'Singing thieves: History and practice in Nigerian popular justice' in Pratten & Sen 2007: 175–205.

—— 2008a 'The politics of protection: Perspectives on vigilantism in Nigeria' *Africa* 78, 1, 1–15.

—— 2008b '"The thief eats his shame": Practice and power in Nigerian vigilantism' *Africa* 78, 1, 64–83.

Pratten, David & Sen, Atreyee (eds) 2007 *Global Vigilantes: Perspectives on Justice and Violence* (London: Hurst & Co.).

Randeria, Shalini 2007 'The state of globalization: Legal plurality, overlapping sovereignties and ambiguous alliances between civil society and the cunning state in India' *Theory, Culture & Society* 24, 1, 1–33.

Reno, William 2002 'The politics of insurgency in collapsing states' *Development and Change* 33, 5, 837–58.

Rhodes, Lorna A. 2005 'Changing the subject: Conversation in Supermax' *Cultural Anthropology* 20, 3, 388–411.

Riches, David 1986 'The phenomenon of violence' in Riches, David (ed.) 1986 *The Anthropology of Violence* (Oxford: Blackwell): 1–27.

Ringmar, Erik 1996 'On the ontological status of the state' *European Journal of International Relations* 2, 4, 439–66.

Robertson, Roland 1995 'Glocalization: Time–space and homogeneity–heterogeneity' in Featherstone, Mike; Lash, Scott & Robertson, Roland (eds) 1995 *Global Modernities* (London: Sage): 25–44.

Schmitt, Carl 2005 *Political Theology: Four Chapters on the Concept of Sovereignty* (Chicago: University of Chicago Press).

Sen, Atreyee & Pratten, David 2007 'Global vigilantes: Perspectives on justice and violence' in Pratten & Sen 2007: 1–21.

Smith, Daniel Jordan 2004 'The Bakassi Boys: Vigilantism, violence and political imagination in Nigeria' *Cultural Anthropology* 19, 3, 429–55.

—— 2006 'Violent vigilantism and the state in Nigeria: The case of the Bakassi Boys' in Bay, Edna G. & Donham, Donald L. (eds) 2006 *States of Violence: Politics, Youth and Memory in Contemporary Africa* (Charlottesville VA: University of Virginia Press): 125–47.

Ukiwo, Ukoha 2002 '*Deus ex machina* or Frankenstein monster? The changing roles of Bakassi Boys in eastern Nigeria' *Democracy and Development* 3, 1, 39–51.

Verkaaik, Oskar 2003 'Fun and violence: Ethnocide and the effervescence of collective aggression' *Social Anthropology* 11, 1, 3–22 .

Von Schnitzler, Antina; Ditlhage, Goodwill; Kgalema, Lazarus; Maepa, Traggy; Mofokeng, Tlhoki & Pigou, Piers 2001 *Guardian or Gangster? Mapogo a Mathamaga: A Case Study* (*Violence and Transition Series* 3) (Johannesburg: Centre for the Study of Violence and Reconciliation). Available online at: <www.csvr.org.za/docs/vigilantism/guardian organgster.pdf> (last accessed 22 July 2008).

Weintraub, Jeff 1997 'The theory and politics of the public/private distinction' in Weintraub, Jeff & Kumar, Krishan (eds) 1997 *Public and Private in Thought and Practice* (Chicago: University of Chicago Press): 1–42.

Wood, Jennifer & Shearing, Clifford 2007 *Imagining Security* (Portland OR: Willan) .

1

Domesticating Sovereigns
The Changing Nature of Vigilante Groups in South Africa

LARS BUUR

Introduction

For years, South African media reports on vigilantism have been full of images of criminals who have been necklaced, flogged or *sjambokked*;[1] of angry mobs and kangaroo courts that have set thieves alight; and of supposed criminals who have been stabbed or stoned to death.[2] The targets of attack have belonged to the generic category of 'criminals', predominantly young men who are caught and accused of or somehow linked to a 'polyvalent category of crime' (Buur 2003: 23–24) encompassing both criminal and civil transgressions (see also Buur & Jensen 2004, Buur 2005a).

Crime, it has been suggested, has in many ways become the new unifier of the South African nation, to the extent that it has become the main preoccupation of both the poor and the rich, and this long before the 2010 Football World Cup brought crime and preoccupations with crime to the attention of global audiences. Two researchers of elite perceptions of poverty have conveyed the panic surrounding crime in South Africa as follows: 'Indeed, it is difficult to over-state the alarm on this issue, especially among white and Asian elites ... crime has come close to replacing apartheid as *the* national problem. It is perceived as damaging the economy, by deterring tourism and discouraging investment, thus hindering growth' (Kalati & Manor 2005: 163, emphasis in the original).

Kalati and Manor's research focused on elites and how they perceive poverty. These researchers acknowledge that in most cases crime affects poor or relatively poor black (and coloured) township dwellers. They conclude that one factor that structures elites' perceptions of poverty is physical distance. Yet why do members of the black elite not emphasise crime as the national problem in the same way that members of white and Asian elites do? Today hardly any members of the black South African elite live in townships; many maintain 'ancestral' and/or symbolic township family homes, but most have moved to suburbs where security provision can be bought. That the black elite downplays the importance of crime may therefore seem illogical because its members occupy the same geographical space as the white and Asian elites. However, it is precisely because crime has taken on the role as *the* national problem that the black elite has done everything it can to downplay its importance because crime is seen as a derogative judgement of African National Congress (ANC) rule. In other words, for the black elite it is a problematic coincidence that crime emerged as *the* national problem in South Africa at exactly the time when the country's first black-dominated government took power.

An illustrative incident was the June 2006 response of the then Minister for Safety and Security, Charles Nqakula, to opposition MPs who claimed a 'tsunami of crime' was rolling over the country (see Quintal & Du Plessis 2006). The Minister responded angrily to the suggestion, insisting there was 'no crime tsunami':

> Those who whinge can leave the country ... Those ones can continue to whinge away, they can continue to attack everything that we do, they can continue to be as negative as they want, in the end it is the many people out there who for many years have been crying for peace and stability in South Africa who determine who rules this country ... They can continue to whinge until they're blue in the face, they can continue to be as negative as they want to or they can simply leave this country so that all of the peace-loving South Africans, good South African people who want to make this a successful country can continue with their work. (Quintal & Du Plessis 2006)

But for black township dwellers with no possibility of escape, crime has the same significance as described above for Asian and white elites: anxiety about crime is everywhere, and anyone is potentially a criminal or victim (Steinberg 2001; Buur 2003). For the media, police and politicians, the prevailing explanation for people taking the law into their own hands and using excessive violence in doing so is that township residents have run amok, that they are undisciplined, irrational and irresponsible. That township residents are prone to spontaneous violent action seems to be a common belief. Consider, for example, this news article about crime and responses to police action:

> Mob 'frees' vigilante suspects. Angry community members stormed a court near Nelspruit on Monday and 'released' eight suspects facing charges of mob justice, said Superintendent Benjamin Mtsholi Bhembe ... eight people had appeared in the Kabokweni magistrate's court to face three charges of murder. The case arose from the burning to death on August 9 of three men accused of criminal activity in Kabokweni, near Nelspruit ... While ... remanding them, the community stormed the court and overwhelmed the police members and the court orderlies and they released the eight ... 'It's something which happened spontaneously,' said Bhembe. (News24 2006a)

In order to change this situation, many analysts of non-state forms of ordering have called for the presence of larger numbers of more efficient police officers, as well as a justice system that caters for the needs of poor township residents. According to this way of thinking, if only the state would get it right there would be no problem. What vigilantism in its present form seems to be reacting to, these analysts suggest, is the ineffectiveness, unresponsiveness and ultimately failure of the police and justice system (Dixon & Johns 2001; Schärf & Nina 2001). It is systemic failure that has caused people to act on their own.

In the nomenclature of criminology, those who act on their own are vigilantes in one form or another because they take the law into their own hands, sometimes in spectacularly violent ways. In the nomenclature of the ruling party, the ANC, they are 'anti-state' and therefore also 'anti-ANC', and are trying to undermine the present black-majority government: they are people acting without leadership, or worse, people who have been 'misled', 'misguided' and '(mis)used' by *somebody* taking advantage of their ignorance. Exactly who this '*somebody*' is, is never explained, as if we all know, but a 'third force', 'reactionary forces', 'counter-revolutionary forces' and 'unknown forces' have been highlighted over the years as the *forces* that are trying to undermine the South African miracle (see Buur 2005b).

That vigilantism is constituted outside the law or the legal framework of the state is relatively uncontroversial: vigilantes break the formal state law, whatever the argument for doing so. But, as I will argue in this chapter, vigilantes are not necessarily 'anti-state' or even 'non-state', nor, by implication, 'anti-ANC' for that matter. For example, the history of the 1980s suggests that not all vigilantes in South Africa were non- or anti-state: while one type of vigilante that emerged from the ANC-aligned United Democratic Front (UDF) was understood as being opposed to the political order of the apartheid regime (Nina 1995), other vigilantes were considered 'conservative' because they were more concerned to defend their way of life against the UDF-aligned vigilantes (see Mamdani 1996; Jensen & Buur 2007).[3]

I therefore suggest that approaching the categories of 'state' and 'vigilante' as two pure and discrete domains that are clearly separated from and in opposition to one another makes little sense. How vigilantes are related to state agencies and political orders is an area that needs to be explored. This chapter deals with vigilantism in South Africa over time, starting out from the present in order to trace some salient features of its evolution. In doing so I pay particular attention to the ways in which changing relationships between vigilantes, state agencies and political orders have been construed. I argue that when vigilantism is approached from the perspective of its relationship to a given political order (whether it challenges and contests a political order, or works with it in defence of it), it becomes clear that the relationship is often an intimate one characterised by what Mbembe (2001) calls 'conviviality'. This is less an open disjunction than a form of tension, with the relationships being characterised by 'the dynamics of domesticity and familiarity, inscribing the dominant and the dominated within the same *episteme*' (Mbembe 2001: 110). As pointed out in the introduction to this volume, therefore, vigilantism as a sociological phenomenon needs to be explored in the context of its relationship to the state agencies and political orders that it either collaborates with or challenges.

To suggest that vigilante groups have had a long history of relationships, often ambivalent ones, with state agencies and political orders is to insist on a certain trans-historicity. Groups and organisations have been called vigilantes, and vigilante members have been identifying themselves with the concept, for well over 100 years in South Africa. Even though ascription to and identification with the concept have changed over time, the types of relationships that have evolved have been remarkably stable. However, whereas conventional approaches have associated vigilantism with challenges to the state's monopoly of the use of legitimate violence, I suggest that when we shift the focus to how vigilantes relate to state agencies and political orders, although we may still find opposition to these orders, such relationships are not necessarily structured by stark contrasts.

In the same vein, to insist on a degree of trans-historicity to this phenomenon is *not* to deny that current perceptions and discussions concerning vigilantism emanated from the anti-apartheid township struggles of the 1980s and early 1990s. Indeed, I will argue that the 1980s were constitutive of current perceptions of vigilantism in South Africa. Nonetheless a seemingly radical shift has taken place in how vigilantism is perceived and acted upon. Ideas and anxieties from the 1980s have stuck, particularly the fear that 'people's courts' and 'people's power' might return, along with the 'ungovernability' mode of struggle associated with the township revolt against apartheid. Such fears are seldom if ever raised in public today, but they have endured as an unpleasant reminder of the violent foundations of the present democratic order. What has changed is the fact that most vigilante groups today have emerged in order to protect the ANC-dominated state and its agencies from the 'onslaught of crime', to use the phraseology often employed by vigilantes, ordinary township residents and police officers.

However, to insist that one of the main historical origins of contemporary vigilantism was the township struggle of the 1980s would be an oversimplification, because here we are talking about two converging aspects of the township struggles. On the one hand were the 'people's courts' that emerged in tandem with the mode of anti-apartheid struggle enforced by groups of young (primarily male) activists known as 'Young Lions' or *Amabutho* (Seekings 1993). On the other hand, there were the 'conservative vigilantes' or 'reactionary forces', some of whom were supported by the apartheid regime in order to fight ANC- and UDF-aligned youth movements. Thus, the apartheid era's perceptions of vigilante activities were intimately related to how the apartheid state defended itself. This should be borne in mind as we explore how vigilantism manifested itself during 2001 in the township of KwaZakhele, on the outskirts of Port Elizabeth.

Vigilantism Anno 2001 in KwaZakhele

We had been sitting in on a two-day workshop for community policing forum (CPF) members, hosted by a non-governmental organisation and looking at how to exercise human-rights-friendly policing. The workshop was financed by a foreign donor. The presentation and initial discussions concerned themselves with such issues as how to make a citizen's arrest, who has the right to use violence, how the relationship between CPFs and the South African Police Service should be articulated, and so forth. However, the proceedings of the workshop were constantly interrupted by questions from CPF members who were also active in the various Safety and Security (S&S) structures operating at ward level. These CPF members wanted to know how they could discipline criminals and young people without being sent to prison or 'kicked out' of the CPF; how they could protect themselves against the 'onslaught of crime' when they were not allowed to obtain guns from the police or bullet-proof vests; why they should risk their lives for the sake of communities and politicians when they were constantly harassed by the police; how it was possible to apprehend criminals without means of transport; and other, similar questions relating to their everyday engagement in the CPF. These questions proved difficult for the workshop organisers, police community liaison officer and CPF board members to answer, in large part because there were no simple answers. The CPF board and police relied on the S&S structures to deal with everyday crime, but they could not formally or officially endorse the *modus operandi* or techniques that CPF-aligned groups used to deal with criminals in the townships.

Despite the free meals offered on the second day, my two fellow-participants, Sipelo and Pitso – from the 'D-Man' section of KwaZakhele township and both members of an S&S structure – became more and more impatient.[4] Soon they wanted to go home, saying they had more serious business to deal with. We left during the last session on women's rights and domestic violence because, as Sipelo told me in the car, 'there is no woman in our house who's got rights, only grandmothers' – alluding to their own economic straits and the fact that households often survive on their grandmothers' monthly pensions. Neither Sipelo nor Pitso have paid jobs that would enable them to pay *lobola* (bride-price) for women of whom they had 'broken the breasts' (made pregnant). Because they could not pay *lobola* they could not marry and set up their own households, and therefore they felt they had no women to respect except for their grandmothers. As such, both young men and women were socially stuck as 'youth' with little chance to marry and become 'adults'.

When we arrived at the S&S office, three other members of the crime-fighting group were waiting. Each wore an identification card bearing the CPF logo, laminated 'in town' at a white-owned shop which had cost them some money. This money was 'earned through our good work' – primarily by settling money-lending cases, in which case the group members deduct for themselves ten percent of each sum paid back. With the CPF logo and the 'town' lamination, the identification cards are as formal as they can get. The men were also carrying their ANC and ANC Youth League membership cards, just in case anyone challenged them for operating outside the law. Only one group member had a licensed gun, but I knew they also had at least three illegal guns for protection. As they explained many times, 'because the criminal elements know who we are, we are known and have many enemies, and they can come back and try to take you out'.

I was then briefed on the operation. We would, they said, be 'hunting' two young men accused of stealing two doors and a large window frame two nights ago. The victim was a female S&S member who was building her own house in the back yard of her family's house. Two young men seen hanging around the house had since disappeared. For the next two hours we went on a hunt through informal settlements in the adjoining township. As the S&S members went through the township searching shacks, they showed great respect for elderly inhabitants, always greeting them using the appropriate Xhosa expressions and then asking their permission to enter their property. We visited several *shebeens* (unlicensed drinking places) where the owners were told to notify the S&S structure immediately if the two men, who had been elevated to the status of 'gangsters' as the afternoon progressed, tried to exchange the doors and window frame for liquor. But the two men had disappeared.

We returned to the office, where we found the two suspects waiting outside. They were clearly nervous. They said they had been told by family members that the S&S structure was looking for them. 'We don't know why we are being looked for,' they explained, 'because we have not done anything.' They were ordered to wait outside while we went into the tiny office to discuss how to proceed. It was decided that the two should receive 'some treatment because of what they had done, letting us run around like fools'.

Meanwhile, an older woman had arrived. She introduced herself as the mother of the two men. She was then asked to go home and wait there while we questioned the suspects. After she left the two young men entered and the door was closed. They were told to 'tell everything', but they insisted they had nothing to do with the doors or the window frame or 'anything criminal at all – we don't do that kind of thing'. It was then explained to me that 'they need to get warmed up', at which point the two youngsters were ordered 'to stand on their heads up against the wall'. After careful instruction not to use their hands to protect their heads from the coldness of the concrete floor, a pack of cards was taken from the drawer and we began to play, ignoring the young men's moaning. From time to time, one of the S&S men went over and spoke quietly to them, telling them how they could make the floor as 'comfortable as possible'.

Once in a while people knocked on the door, older women and men making payments on money they had borrowed, in which cases a receipt was written out, or raising 'new cases' for the S&S structure to attend to. In these cases an S&S member would write a brief summary in 'the book register', the complainant would 'sign in' and in some cases pay transport money, depending on how far members of the S&S would have to travel to 'subpoena' or 'trace' people. When people noticed the young men standing on their heads, they were informed simply that 'we have work going on, it is soon finished'.

After having to stand on their heads for 40 minutes, the two men began repeatedly toppling onto the concrete floor, each time promptly being put back again. After almost a full hour of this treatment I was told that if they stayed there much longer, they 'could be damaged'. Well 'warmed up', they were told to get up. Then, as they stood swaying and confused, the S&S members fired a barrage of questions at them. The men's eyes showed how dizzy and dazed they were. They still maintained that they knew nothing about the doors and window frame. They insisted they had 'the right to be in the street' and that 'we have done nothing – this is a mistake'.

Now the two young men were abruptly placed face to face, with about half a metre between them. They were ordered to take turns slapping each other's faces with open hands, ten slaps each time. This continued for three rounds, with tears springing from the men's eyes and their faces becoming flushed. When one of the men gave only a weak slap an S&S member told him off and gave him instructions on how to slap properly: 'Do you want to be a man? Ag, man, you better learn to do it properly!' Just then came a knock on the door. A policeman half-opened it, looked around inside and smiled. 'Oh, you are working! What is it about?' S&S members explained and the policeman laughed, ending the conversation by saying: 'Good work! When you have cracked the case, bring the criminals to the station. The victim needs to make an official complaint. Can you send them to the office so the formalities are done?'

After the policeman had left the office the two men were ordered to face each other again, this time with more distance between them. A thin *sjambok* emerged. One of the female S&S members illustrated how it should be used, slapping it on the backside of one of the standing men. Visibly nervous, he tried to protect himself. She laughed at him and admonished him to behave 'like a man'. One of the young men was then handed the *sjambok* and told to hit the other young man ten times, five on each side. After the first round the men were made to exchange places and the other man did the striking. If a man's slaps were 'too mild – this is for kids, behave like a man', the suspect was ordered to repeat the blow with more force. By this time tears were flowing freely from the young men's eyes, but they still maintained their innocence. They did explain about thefts they had committed 'in town', of clothes and 'tackies' (sports shoes), but insisted they had never 'stolen from the community'. During this time the children of S&S members entered the office to ask for 'supper money', and members set up appointments with 'girlfriends' for the evening, as if this was all business as usual. My face must have shown my bewilderment, because one the oldest male group members, Ayanda, took me to one side and explained:

> Lars, it is better this way, you must understand. Why should we go to prison for helping the community and the police, can you tell me that? You see, when the police ask them: 'So who beat you?' he would point finger at the other criminal. And when they ask him: 'So who beat you?' he will tell him that it was the other one. The police will laugh at them. We get our information, police are happy, the community is happy, and we have done our work without going to prison. It's this that the workshop was all about ... tell me, Lars, isn't this what it was about, human-rights-friendly policing?[5]

Even though Ayanda had not been at the workshop that day, he had been at other such meetings. He stressed the point that the vigilantes had to be careful in order not to embarrass the CPF or the police. 'Minimal force', as the group members called it, should be used so that nobody was harmed and no complaints could be laid against them. 'We don't want to be part of the statistics,' they said, referring to police statistics on 'vigilantism', which by mid-2001 had risen sharply to become one of the top police priorities, along with murder, car hijacking and so forth, because it exposed the hollowness of the state's claim to sovereignty in the townships (see Buur 2005a, 2006).

For S&S members violence was considered necessary, but in this case it became clear that they had caught the wrong people. The two men were released with the words: 'Go home and tell your parents that you are ready to go to the bush [a reference to Xhosa initiation rites] – you can keep secrets, you have taken it like a man'. Both the male and female members of the S&S now expressed admiration for the young men's capacity to 'take a hiding', as they put it. 'The bush will be easy for them,' they said. The two young men stayed for another 30 minutes, now chatting and asking questions about the S&S structure, and clearly impressed by the male members' constant need to talk to 'girlfriends' who came to see them at the office.

When I returned the next day around 11 o'clock the previously missing two doors and window frame were standing against the office wall and the 'crime fighters' were all hanging around the office. They were in a celebratory mood. 'We cracked it, can you believe our luck? Just after you left, on our way home we met these two criminals [pointing towards the office door]. They were carrying the window frame and the doors. They were going to sell them at one of the *shebeens*, can you imagine?' The two young 'criminals' were from another township, so 'it is not one of our own'. They had hidden the doors and the frame, and had returned to sell them 'but we stopped them'. The two 'criminals' had then been handed over to the two young men who had been erroneously beaten the day before 'so they could get their anger out – anger can be bad, you know'. The S&S members were now waiting for the police to arrive. The female S&S member had left early that morning to make a formal complaint at the police station so that the case could be formally closed.

When the policemen arrived with the female S&S member they greeted the group with: 'Well done! This looks good in the stats – another crime solved. It's been a good week.' As the two 'criminals' were taken to be locked in the back of the old Toyota truck, one of the policemen grasped one of them by the head, turned it to face him and asked: 'Who beat him?' Silence among the S&S members. After a while, one of them said: 'It is not us, we don't know.' However, he then pointed reluctantly towards the two young men who had been beaten wrongly the day before. The police wanted to arrest the two for 'vigilantism', but the officers were now gently taken aside to have it explained to them how this would 'not be right – they helped us'. When the police realised what had happened, they laughed. 'Okay, okay, but be more careful next time. You know the district commissioner has told us to get rid of this vigilantism. He is very worried. We can't have people who take the law into their own hands, can we? This is not like before.'

I will return to this story towards the end of this chapter, because the intimate relationships that appear to have developed between the S&S structure and police are based on certain principles of what I tentatively call 'strategic ignorance'.[6] The police know about and indeed rely on vigilantes breaking the law by using corporal punishment to 'discipline' people and extract information. But as long as this does not become public knowledge – that is, knowledge that must be represented in the official statistics on vigilantism (see Buur 2005a on statistics and public secrets), the vigilantes have *carte blanche* to continue their 'good work.'

Here it is sufficient to point out that, as the last comment by the policeman indicates, the conditions under which vigilantes operate and relate to the state authorities have undergone a significant change. In contrast to the media representations of 'out-of-control mob violence' described in the introduction to this chapter, the sense one acquires of vigilantism in the D-Man section of KwaZakhele township is one of engagement, control, negotiation and premeditation. However, as I have described elsewhere (Buur 2008), the S&S structure in this area emerged from exactly the kind of extreme violence and stark opposition that characterised the earlier relationships of vigilante groups with state agencies. Therefore, something must have taken place to 'domesticate' this particular group. In order to understand this process we will need to explore South African vigilantism historically and in greater detail. This will foreground the contesting forces and changing political contexts at play in South African townships.

Vigilantism from 1880 to the 1980s

In South Africa, forms of non-state self-regulation and community discipline have their roots in rural African communities where chiefs and headmen held court or *makgotla* and imposed various sentences and punishments (Seekings 2001; Nina & Schärf 2001; Mangokwane 2001).[7] With migration to urban areas, some of these practices were carried over and reproduced in various forms in the three main urban environments where black Africans lived, namely migrant-worker hostels, informal settlements/ squatter camps and 'locations' (the latter term was used for black urban areas until around 1960, when 'townships' became the dominant term).

While it is generally recognised that it was the failure of official judicial systems to address conflicts in black urban environments that led to the development of the *makgotla* as informal systems of social control in the urban context,[8] what is often overlooked is how non-state self-regulation and *makgotla* developed in tandem with what, in a limited sense, can be termed the 'political mobilisation' of African urban and peri-urban dwellers. Self-regulation, and with it vigilantism, can be seen in this particular sense as inherently 'recognizable "modern" organisational forms' (Bundy 2000: 30), as they emerged along with the colonial state and its various modes of production. Thus, the black civic organisations that rose to prominence during the 1980s were not 'created in an institutional vacuum' but based on a long tradition of township organisation in which different types of representative bodies had, since at least the 1880s, used non-state self-regulation and boycotts and other forms of grievance-based protest as their organisational platforms (*ibid.*: 26–7).

One distinctive feature of the evolution of these forms of self-representation was the parallel development of state-stipulated representative bodies and less formal non-state bodies. The two forms of organisation, which mirrored each other in different constellations and articulations (see Bundy 2000 for an analysis of early forms of this parallel development) and have been present ever since (allowing for some twists and turns), strikingly resemble structures in South African townships today. On the one hand, in the townships official representative bodies initially known as 'location committees' became 'advisory boards' under the 1923 Urban Areas Act. These advisory boards consisted of members of the educated elite, such as teachers, clerks and clergymen; they were drawn from among registered municipal leaseholders, with roughly one-fifth of male black urban inhabitants claiming to be the representatives of informal urban black populations. On the other hand, in close tandem with official representative bodies emerged *iliso lomzi* – Xhosa for 'eye of the house', or what became known more generically as 'vigilante formations' by both state agencies and township residents.

The *iliso lomzi* that emerged – first in the Eastern Cape, but later more widely around the country under different names – were usually managed by educated residents, but had a broader representational foundation, including non-registered leaseholders. The *iliso lomzi* and their equivalents often formed in opposition to weak or 'soft' advisory boards, but were not always in competition with them; indeed, they shared platforms on numerous occasions over issues such as depressed living standards, material deprivation, violence and social disorder (Bundy 2000: 34; Seekings 2001: 85–6). Both forms of organisation addressed issues of security and the maintenance of peace and order in the face of generational tensions, delinquency and the disruption of family and community ties that resulted from intensified urbanisation. However, their popular appeal was not the same, as I explain below.

Over time, official 'committees' and 'boards' came under increasing 'popular suspicion' (*ibid.*) due to their collaboration with the various white regimes. By contrast, vigilante associations always seemed able to attract large followings through what later became the dominant form of popular and political mobilisation, 'mass meetings' (*ibid.*: 35). While the earlier formations, with their rural links, attempted to control people who came from a particular ethnic group and area, so that they were kept in contact with the norms and values of their areas of origin, the urban *makgotla* courts often attempted to transcend ethnic divides. Some of the urbanised courts, such as those in the migrant-worker hostels, were permanent, but others – particularly the more *ad hoc* emerging vigilante courts – tended to be ephemeral institutions that originated as a response to specific needs, cases of crime or crime waves that were causing panic. They were primarily geared towards maintaining a particular social order and focused on the punishment of criminals and the redress of social grievances or communal disturbance (pregnancy or property disputes, husband-and-wife relations). In the urban context these courts were in the main geared towards compensation – that is, they were restorative rather than simply punitive – but fines and flogging were accepted forms of punishment and discipline. It was older men who generally ruled over these processes, so that this form of social control exhibited a distinctive age and gender profile. This traditionalist and patriarchal tendency received the approval of the apartheid state and was often supported; indeed, it formed part of the complex ways in which the internal boundaries between citizens (whites), quasi-citizens (registered leaseholders) and subjects (non-white unregistered dwellers) were policed.

Given this background, Mamdani is not totally correct when he argues that as a general rule in Africa the colonial state was organised as a dual, 'bifurcated state' apparatus, with modern power in urban areas and traditional 'native authorities' in rural areas (1996: 16–23). Migration – both intra- and inter-state – had long blurred the boundary between urban and rural, thus transcending this system of governance (see Jensen & Buur 2007). What the colonial regime did first and the apartheid regime later on was to constrict the lives of huge sections of the black, coloured and Indian populations through a range of urban forms of subjectification, each with hybrid forms of political organisation and authority. However, Mamdani is right in his depiction of the logic of bifurcation, which the apartheid regime refined to its extreme in racial terms so that civil laws guaranteed civil rights to (white) citizens while 'customary' law, endorsed by the state, governed the indigenous (black) population. In this configuration, civil power was defined in racial terms and custom defined in ethicised cultural terms.

One consequence of this was that earlier forms of civic township struggle were, at least initially, ideologically self-limiting (Adler & Steinberg 2000a, 2000b). This was true for both 'formal' and 'informal' vigilantes who challenged the South African state and political system. Public involvement in local and national political struggles, in both written and spoken terms, was by and large avoided and contestation was limited mainly to non-participation in state structures on the one hand, and to non-violent engagement and civil disobedience on the other (Seekings 2000: 54). However, the situation changed considerably during the 1983–86 period, when organised and less-organised forms of judicial inter-vention were incorporated into the political resistance to apartheid, using both the language and the practices of the internal liberation movement that was rapidly developing. The different forms of organisation became reconceptualised as partners of the UDF, which emerged during this period of insurrection. The UDF became the embodiment of the South African masses, a vanguard for the ANC. Here, the notion of people's power (explored below) gives a retrospective sense to insurrectionary activities in primarily black townships.

These changes were rooted in the general strike of 1973 and the 1976–77 black-consciousness-inspired Soweto uprisings, which triggered a collective awareness and saw new organisational forms emerge within certain strata of the urban black population (Swilling 1997: 218; Bundy 2000: 28). These events led to the establishment in 1977 of a new governance system of community councils, replacing the former 'urban Bantu councils'. This devolution of central powers to self-governing councils for urban black populations can be seen as a thinly veiled attempt 'to stave off underclass protest through the provision of resources ("upgrading")' (Bundy 2000: 28). Or, described in stronger language, it represented a move to replace the direct administration of township dwellers by apartheid-government bureaucrats with indirect rule by 'black surrogates' (Mayekiso 1996). In 1982, reforms expanded the councils' powers under the Black Local Authorities Act to include the allocation of housing, business licences, business sites and student bur-saries and the collection of rents and service fees.

The Janus faces of 1980s vigilantism

The UDF – formed partly in response to the 1983 promotion of separate black local authority (BLA) elections and becoming, over time, the organisation under whose banner many civic and resident organisations struggled – tried vigorously to undermine the collaboration of black authorities with the apartheid regime by organising election 'stayaways' and consumer boycotts, and by employing various forms of intimidation, including petrol-bomb attacks on councillors' homes. Triggered by the apartheid programme for constitutional reform, and responding to the state's violent reaction, the period of insurrection engendered a particular political ethos in the black townships. In many ways, the form and ethos of the 1985–86 township struggles have become iconic and have had a lasting effect on subsequent civic and political contestations in South Africa.

In 1984, UDF-aligned organisations initiated rent and service-charge boycotts in order to undercut the financial basis of the new BLAs. The first recorded rent boycott was undertaken by residents of the Vaal Triangle and Evaton in September 1984 (TRC 1998, 2: 382). Similar boycotts and responses spread throughout the country, and militarised youths took it upon themselves to monitor and enforce boycotts. By the mid-1980s residents were calling for consumer boycotts to support both national and local political demands. While these boycotts were initially aimed at white- and Indian-owned business, they later targeted businesses owned by perceived 'collaborators', such as black businesspeople and township residents who cooperated with the government-established local authorities. Government buildings were burned and looted, and anyone defying the consumer boycott was forced to eat inedible grocery items like soap powder and candles. Some were even killed. The death toll escalated as attacks on 'informers' by residents increased. Methods of attack included burning and 'necklacing', as well as beating, stabbing, shooting and sexual assault. After 1985, UDF-aligned organisations established their own 'people's courts' in most townships as an alternative to the apartheid-legislated 'community guards', many of whom were under the guidance and protection of BLA councillors.

These developments were one of the ironies of the situation whereby the apartheid state transformed direct governance into indirect governance through the BLAs, which converted 'physically distant agents of the state into identifiable individuals who lived and operated among those whom they ruled' (Bundy 2000: 29). Beginning in 1984, and particularly from 1985 onwards, councillors became prime targets of routine attacks by ANC- and UDF-aligned vigilante youths, the 'Young Lions' or *Amabutho* organised in the people's courts. More importantly, as symbols of state power the councillors brought the frontier of apartheid into township neighbourhoods. The upheaval soon targeted all figures of authority, while at the same time the leadership of the struggle was being targeted and repressed by the authorities. The dual face of 'ungovern-ability and organisation',[9] as described in Nina's sympathetic account of the people's courts, created a parallel authority that 'was seen as part of a process of organising the future society' (Nina 1995: 7). The 'alternative sovereign' established in the name of the people was soon construed as a 'quasi-governmental' institution (Adler & Steinberg 2000b: 6) that assumed rudimentary administrative and service functions.

The form the township struggle took cannot be understood without considering the other side of the apartheid state's 'awkward ambi-dexterity' (Bundy 2000: 28). It is clear from the state's introduction of the 'Winning the Hearts and Minds' campaign in the mid-1980s – part of President P. W. Botha's 'Total Strategy' – that South Africa's rulers saw the conflict as a low-intensity one that called for 'counterinsurgency warfare', according to the military theories that emerged out of the experiences of General André Beaufrès of France in North Africa and Colonel J. J. McCuen of the United States in Vietnam (Hayson 1989: 2–7). The South African apartheid regime institutionalised the logic of these theories, first in its Total Strategy and later in its 'Joint Management System' approach, which dissolved the boundaries between the military and civil society. On the one hand, civic and union organisers and leaders were considered legitimate combat targets and physically 'eliminated' (killed, arrested, chased away or forced underground), while on the other hand, target populations were 'pacified' by the provision of housing, water, electricity, school bursaries and so on. Thus, in neither the choice of targets nor the particular way in which the 'war' was fought was there a distinction between military and civic codes of conduct. Following the mass mobilisation of young people in schools by UDF-aligned organisations, peaking in 1985 and 1986, thousands of these individuals were arrested, tortured and kept in solitary confinement for extended periods.

The monist ethos of singular politics that characterised township youth, and particularly the UDF-aligned Young Lions, should be understood in relation to the apartheid regime's strategies, as they created a need to protect and 'immunise' township structures against state repression. It should be noted, however, that the monist ethos was equally directed against the 'clandestine creation of surrogate armed forces', which appeared to 'emerge "spontaneously" from "the people" themselves' (Hayson 1989: 3). In response to the Young Lions, the apartheid regime assisted or directly instigated the emergence of con-cerned residents' groups or 'conservative vigilantes', as the South African Truth and Reconciliation Commission (TRC) and most com-mentators call them, such as *Inkatha* (on the Witwatersrand – now Gauteng – and in KwaZulu-Natal), *AmaAfrika* (in Port Elizabeth), and the *Witdoeks* (in Cape Town).

The emergence of these groups was seen by most commentators and analysts of the township struggle as the product of a state-sponsored 'third force', which also provided the conservative vigilantes with weapons, legal protection and even financial support. Indeed, the TRC later produced ample evidence for a range of endorsement, support and management mechanisms for vigilante groupings on the part of different clandestine apartheid security agencies (see, for example, TRC 1998, 3: 369). But importantly, as the TRC cautiously stated, 'not all vigilante activity was a product of state engineering. Intolerant actions and coercive campaigns of the UDF and its adherents mobilised genuine disaffection and anger amongst black residents, forming the basis for retaliatory actions by so-called "vigilantes"' (TRC 1998, 2: 302).

It is nevertheless interesting that neither the people's courts nor the more *ad hoc* activities of the *Amabutho* were actually described as vigilantism by the commission. The term 'vigilante' was used by the TRC almost exclusively to refer to 'state endorsed, supported and managed' vigilante groupings, with only two references to people's courts and *Amabutho* as 'UDF-aligned vigilantes' to be found in the final report from 1998. Both references were made in the context of human-rights violations committed in the Port Elizabeth area (TRC 1998, 3: 97–99).

I suggest that the two entwined trajectories described above became partly disentangled after 1990. The vigilantism of the first part of the 1990s has been seen as intrinsically related to anti-state or anti-government activities, but this time in the context of the new democracy. This concerns particularly the emergence of two organisations, People Against Gangsterism and Drugs (PAGAD) in 1996 and *Mapogo a Mathamaga* (see, for instance, Von Schnitzler *et al.* 2001; Buur 2005b, Buur & Jensen 2004; Oomen 2004). As this anti-state conception of vigilantism faded, media reports increasingly represented vigilante activities as spontaneous and volatile, carried out by mobs that were out of control, undisciplined and irrational, and drawing more clearly on the stereotypes of the people's courts and Young Lions outlined in the introduction to this chapter. I examine this stereotyping in more detail below.

Political deliberation

Images of 'people's power' captured the imagination of both the South African public and the international community. They became iconic expressions of a certain stereotype of the behaviour of township residents in general and of young black crowds in particular as inherently explosive, disorganised, immature, easy to provoke, liable to violent outbursts and especially vulnerable to political agitation. These images were at least partly created by media controlled by the apartheid state. According to the final report of the TRC, the media sector 'assisted in promoting the view that a crowd of black people equated a "mob," and a mob of black people was by nature barbaric and likely to engage in violence' (TRC 1998, 2: 181). In an irony of history, the images emerging from the TRC's amnesty hearings came to resemble those created by the state-controlled media under apartheid. For example, amnesty hearings such as that devoted to the Amy Biehl case evoked the image of undisciplined black township youths who were easy to manipulate through political slogans, such as 'One settler, one bullet' and 'Kill the farmer, kill the *Boer*,'[10] associated with Pan-Africanist Congress and Azapo – African nationalist organisations that took a harder line than the ANC (see TRC 1998, 3: 279, 510).[11]

The leadership of the various strands of the liberation struggle later acknowledged before the TRC that they did not have control over young people. For example, at the hearing on UDF activities held in Cape Town in May 1998, Patrick 'Terror' Lekota – a former UDF leader, later chairperson of the National Council of Provinces and at the time of writing Minister of Defence – had the following to say about 'necklacing' by UDF activists: 'We accept political and moral responsibility. We cannot say these people have nothing to do with us. We organised them; we led them. When we were taken into prisons, they were left without leadership and many of them, angry even at our arrest, did things which were irrational' (TRC 1998, 5: 383).

The commission's documented encounters with the former leadership of the UDF and present ANC leadership are ambiguous, as the leaders of the struggle tried to maintain that they did have control over young people while at the same time acknowledging that the various groupings acting in their name did things that were deeply disturbing and outside their control (see, for example, Mayekiso 1996). Simply to say that the young people had acted on their own would have been to reject key elements of the internal struggle as organised around the UDF. The ambivalence arises because ANC and UDF leaders needed to appropriate a domain of the struggle against apartheid that they never fully controlled in order to maintain their political image within their constituency, while at the same time they had to distance themselves from this very domain in order to maintain their stance on human rights in the eyes of the international community.

However, the image of people's courts, based on fear, that was dominant among the political class in the apartheid state, as well as the leadership of the ANC, has not been dispelled entirely. TRC chairperson Archbishop Desmond Tutu summed up the consequences of the past conflict in this way, in the foreword to the final report: 'We know that the liberation movements were not paragons of virtue and were often responsible for egging people on to behave in ways that were uncontrollable. We know that we may, in the present crime rate, be reaping the harvest of the campaigns to make the country ungovernable' (TRC 1998, 1: 17).

Handing back the sovereign to the 'new' state

During the early 1990s the street and area committees around which the Young Lions had formed – the cornerstones of 'people's power' – ceased to function in a systematic way in most townships (Seekings 1996; Cherry 2000). At the same time township-based civic bodies also declined, for several interconnected reasons. The most important of these was the struggle for political power between the ANC and the civic movement of the 1980s, the remaining elements of which came together in 1993 under the umbrella of the South African National Civic Organisation (SANCO). In the first years after the end of apartheid, SANCO saw its role in the new South Africa as a continuation of the popular tradition of direct democracy, now forming part of a critical but constructive civil society. While aligned to the ANC, it saw its role as a watchdog, ensuring that the ANC kept its promises (see Mayekiso 1996). Related to these developments was SANCO's attempt to organise the field of law enforcement at the local level. However, this initiative was put down by the ANC as the ruling party, which saw it as a challenge to the government's attempts to gain control over society. After SANCO fell out with the ANC in 1996, the former organisation largely disappeared from the political landscape as a co-ordinated entity (see Cherry *et al.* 2000). But in Port Elizabeth – one of the most important places, if not *the* most important place for the civic movement's development during the 1980s – the Port Elizabeth People's Civic Organisation (PEPCO) continued to play a significant role in a variety of ways until the end of the 1990s (Cherry 2000).

From 1991, PEPCO tried to organise and monopolise street committees in order to carry on the work of the people's courts in the name of 'anti-crime committees' (ACCs; see Nina 2001: 107–14). According to Nina (1995), 'crime-fighting' as an important domain of township sovereignty has continued to evade the control of both the state and the ANC. Nina, who did his fieldwork in Port Elizabeth's townships between 1991 and 1993, is perplexed by the ACCs' unwillingness to give up the 'investigative' dimension of crime-fighting, in which their use of physical violence continually brought them into conflict with the police. Nina generally judged citizens' arrests to be acceptable, but not the 'investigations': for him, investigations were the proper task of the police. However, while Nina anticipated that the exercise of violence would disappear from the ACCs' work as they gradually gained recognition from the state – in terms of his rather idealised understanding of 'crime-fighting' – in fact the violence did not disappear.

Although the ACCs constituted a well-structured and systematic attempt to organise local crime-fighting, during the 1990s their impact and role gradually diminished in Port Elizabeth's townships. ACCs would seem to emerge at times when crime in a particular township was perceived as out of control. In reality, however, rather than initiating enforcement efforts civic organisations arose and aligned themselves with already emerging vigilante groups that were attempting to control crime. But none of these attempts lasted, partly because of the violence, which caused the civic organisations embarrassment.

In 1995, in a bid to gain control over vigilante formations and regulate the relationship between the state and the wider public in the field of security provision, the ANC-led government formally established 'community policing forums' (CPFs). The CPFs were officially introduced through the Interim Constitution (CRSA 1996; Section 221, Act 200 of 1993) which allowed for a network of CPFs to be established at police-station level throughout the country. That this role would be played by CPFs and not by people's courts was not predestined in 1993. As a matter of fact, the ANC-led government had initiated a lawmaking process towards the recognition of people's courts and their incorporation into the official security apparatus of the new state, with green papers and white papers (the initial steps in the legislative process) being issued during the constitutional process running from 1993 to 1996. This was done under the leadership of Wilfried Schärf of the University of Cape Town's Institute of Criminology (personal communication; see also Schärf 2001). However, the ANC-led government remained ambivalent towards the people's courts and feared not being able to control them. The idea of incorporating the people's courts continued to be discussed right up to the turn of the millennium. However, as Schärf makes clear, after the release of the findings of the TRC and the public exposures of uncontrolled violence exerted in the name of or in the context of the people's courts, incorporating the latter may have been possible in principle but politically unthinkable.

The community policing forum is the most visible expression of the South African state's community policing policy. It became the main instrument for the state (and the ANC) to domesticate and defuse potential antagonisms in the areas of security and local justice. The CPF can be interpreted as an attempt to contain the energies of the people's power in state and dominant party practices – what we can understand, in line with Elias Canetti (1988), as a move from 'open' to 'closed' masses. In this sense, the CPF can be seen as an attempt to achieve a form of democratic socialisation by engaging township residents in participatory forums that compel citizens, in a variety of ways, to act according to standards of democratic behaviour.

From the beginning, the law regulating CPFs also stipulated that they could form 'safety and security structures' ('S&S structures'), bringing access to justice and conflict mediation down to the lowest level in the local-governance hierarchy. Generally, S&S structures work under the jurisdiction of the local CPF and are formally accountable to them. Officially made up of locally elected or appointed members, S&S structures are organised around the lowest level of local governance: the ward. They usually emerge when crime is perceived to be out of control and come to work closely with the police, as my time with the S&S structures in the D-Man section of KwaZakhele township illustrates. This brings us back to where we started, to KwaZakhele, where S&S members became everyday sovereigns.

The return of people's power

The events that brought into being the type of S&S structure described in the KwaZakhele example, explored in the first part of this chapter, involved a series of excessively violent acts committed by a group of young armed criminals, many of whom had served prison sentences. After several years terrorising the neighbourhood, this group of criminals broke into an elderly couple's house, stole everything and shot the wife dead when she tried to stop them raping her daughter. After the incident, a group of young men resident in KwaZakhele's Ward 21, most of them unemployed, decided that 'enough was enough'. They resolved to call a group of trusted former Young Lions to confront the criminals. This group managed to track down one of the assailants of the elderly couple, who was then tortured for five consecutive days in the most gruesome manner by the Young Lions. One witness said: 'It was bad. I think in the end his mother could not recognise him if she had seen him.' After forcing the group member to reveal the identity of his accomplices, the vigilantes managed within a week to capture the whole group, except for the leader, whom they apprehended three months later.

Despite the risks associated with confronting armed criminals, the former Young Lions decided to stay together and patrol the streets. In proceeding with this they engaged not only in endless battles with criminals, but also in struggles with the police, whom they did not trust – they felt the police were protecting the criminals. The reconstituted Young Lions were initially hailed as the saviours of the township for their vigorous action against crime. However, before long they came to be seen as part of the problem – preying on the vulnerability of the community for whose good they claimed to be working. The police, who felt threatened by the Young Lions, tried to arrest some of them. When this happened, a group of elders led by a prominent ANC member, a former Robben Island prison-mate of Nelson Mandela's, called a public meeting in order to end the impasse that threatened to rob the community of its protectors. At the meeting, 12 young men were elected as the community's 'concerned residents against crime'.

Having first being approached by the South African National Civic Organisation (SANCO) to form an 'anti-crime committee', the new elected structure was later contacted by the ANC through the local community policing forum to set up an S&S structure in a drive to curb crime and co-ordinate responses to it. Later the group was re-elected at another public meeting held under the auspices of New Brighton township police station, under which Ward 21 falls. Since then the S&S structure has worked, in its members' own words, 'hand-in-glove with the police in fighting crime', co-ordinating their respective activities and together conducting patrols and raiding shebeens at weekends to search for illegal firearms.

Conclusion

This chapter has attempted to trace the relationships over time between the state and political orders on the one hand, and vigilantes on the other, arguing that none of these phenomena should be approached as pure and separate domains, or necessarily as in opposition to each other. Instead, I have suggested that this relationship has been intimate and remarkably stable in the specific sense that vigilantism has continually challenged and contested the state and political order(s), while sometimes working together with or defending them. That is, vigilantism as a sociological phenomenon in South Africa does not exist separately from political order(s) and engagement with state agencies. This exploration of vigilantism over time brings to the fore the changing contexts in the South African townships and in the political field that structure the nature of the relationships of vigilantes with the state and with political order(s).

I have suggested that the vigilante structure on which I have focused in this chapter had an intimate relationship with the police, based on what I call 'strategic ignorance'. The police knew that the vigilante group was breaking the law, but at the same time relied on the vigilantes' illegal use of corporal punishment to enforce discipline and extract information. As long as the violent means used did not become 'public knowledge', the group had a relative *carte blanche* to continue its 'work'. As we have seen, this relationship differed in nature from the confrontational type of inter-action between the police and Young Lions just a few years previously. This indicates that the conditions under which vigilantes operate and that the way they relate to the state authorities have both changed. The sense one has in KwaZakhele is one of engagement, control, negotiation and premeditation, with the state remaining officially 'ignorant' as long as corporal punishment is exercised in a manner that suits it.

What does the intimate relationship between vigilantes and the state and political order(s) do to our understanding of the state as having a monopoly on violence and, therefore, of the state as the ultimate sove-reign authority more generally? Does this mean the concept of the sovereign state as the primary locus of political and symbolic authority needs to be replaced by a totally new understanding of political life and national community? I do not think so because the empirical configuration of *de facto* states and political order(s) has always been a messy affair. States have always been closely aligned with a variety of forces on the thresholds of their jurisdictions, where the 'indivisibility and discreteness' (Bartelson 2006: 464) that characterise the modern notion of sovereignty are challenged in practice. There is therefore a permanent tension between the indivisibility and discreteness of sovereignty and the concrete conditions of statehood on the one hand, and the political orders that political processes give rise to on the other. A tension arises when the actual dispersal of political power and legal authority is fractured in practice. Perhaps it is at least partly because of the messiness of statehood in practice that the idea of 'the indivisibility and discreteness' of sovereignty has been so successful.

This begs the question: how can it be that, despite overwhelming evidence that many states align themselves closely to vigilante groups, usually it seems quite easy to draw the line between the state and what is constituted outside its purview? Part of the answer may be that, in the nomenclature of both criminology and the law, those who act on their own are 'vigilantes' in one form or another because they take the law into their own hands, often in extremely violent and spectacular ways. In other words, the separation of powers – the lawmaking legislature, the law-enforcing executive and the judiciary – makes it possible to maintain the idea of 'vigilantism' as constituted outside the law or the legal framework, even if in practice the threshold is constantly transgressed.

A further issue is that when vigilante groups do emerge this seldom involves a rejection of the idea of a state or political order; rather, it represents an attempt to reconstitute or redefine a political order in a 'purer' form. Maybe this was why the 'struggle vigilantes' of the 1980s formed such a challenge – not just to the apartheid state, but also to the new political order of the ANC. The people's power and people's courts promised a different political order. However, the new order that resulted did not turn out in the way expected by many commentators. Nevertheless, as I have pointed out, since 1994 the ruling ANC has tended to construe vigilantes as 'anti-ANC forces' that are trying to undermine the present black-majority government, even when vigilantes are in a way defending the ANC state against the perceived crime wave. Present-day vigilantes work partly in the name of 1980s people's power and base their *modus operandi* partly on the way things were done during that period, but they have to do this, as I have illustrated elsewhere (see Buur 2005b, 2006), by de-politicising their claims so that competition with the ANC is downplayed. But even when vigilantes are defending the ANC government's work in the name of and in a way based on the one-time organisational features that actually brought the ANC to power, but from which the party now wants to distance itself due to the violent history associated with those events, vigilante groups inevitably become a painful reminder to the political order of the contingency of the postulated unity of the political community.

Notes

1 A *sjambok* is a whip, originally of dried animal hide but nowadays typically of plastic.
2 To mention just a few of the hundreds of news features I have gathered over the years, see Hosken (2003, 2006), IOL (2006a, 2006b), Jasson da Costa (2006), M&G (2006), News24 (2006a, 2006b, 2006c, 2006d), Quintal & Du Plessis (2006).
3 The UDF was an umbrella movement that during the 1980s was supposed to act for the then-banned ANC. It was a loose federation bringing together a large number of social, civic and political organisations of differing class backgrounds, ethnic constituencies and political orientations.
4 The 'D-Man' section of KwaZakhele township is named after a corner shop of that name.
5 I am aware that one might have reservations about conducting participant observation during instances of 'torture' and 'investigation' such as described here, but as Wilfried Schärf of the Institute of Criminology, University of Cape Town, argued in 2002 when he defended my research at a departmental seminar: 'Who is ethical here? The anthropologists that don't go to the townships any longer because of fear and ethical dilemmas, but still speaks about what is going on out there without knowing and with a great danger of romanticising township life out of political correctness, or Lars, who actually go there and know what is going on?' (personal notes, 2002). Schärf's point is that just because one actually sees and experiences something, this does not mean one necessarily endorses what one sees and experiences. Sometimes the best way of speaking up against something is by describing it so that others can make their own judgements.
6 Possibly the closest other term to 'strategic ignorance' is Taussig's (1999) concept of 'public secrets' – that is, things we all know but do not talk about.
7 *Makgotla* were originally 'elders' courts in the rural areas', which over time became part of urban life (Seekings 2001: 81–82; see also Mangokwane 2001). *Makgotla* is a Tswana word, but is now used more broadly in South Africa to describe local courts, just as the Zulu and Xhosa word *indaba* for an important conference has entered the South African English vocabulary more generally.
8 The official judicial system included both the ordinary ('white') Western system of courts and magistrates, and the special courts developed with a view to the application of ('black') indigenous law and custom. The official systems were generally seen as ineffective, corrupt and inaccessible, so other systems developed over time.
9 The term 'ungovernability' was coined by the ANC National Executive on 25 April 1985 via its slogan 'Make apartheid unworkable! Make the country ungovernable!' presented in a paper entitled: 'ANC call to the nation: The future is within our grasp' (TRC 1998, 2: 346). In this regard, the call by the ANC for 'ungovernability' can also be seen as a reaction to the launch of the UDF in August 1983.
10 The term *Boer*, Afrikaans for 'farmer', has historically been used to refer to Afrikaners (white Afrikaans-speakers); however, in this context it is being used in a derogatory way.
11 Amy Biehl was an American Fulbright exchange scholar at the University of the Western Cape Community Law Centre. On 25 August 1993 she was driving three black colleagues back to Cape Town's Guguletu township. A group of youths pelted her car with stones and forced it to stop, and Biehl was killed.

References

Adler, Glen & Steinberg, Jonny (eds) 2000a *From Comrades to Citizens: The South African Civics Movement and the Transition to Democracy* (London: Macmillan)
—— 2000b 'Introduction: From comrades to citizens' in Adler & Steinberg 2000a: 1–25
Bartelson, Jens 2006 'The concept of sovereignty revisited' *European Journal of International Law* 17(2): 463–74
Bundy, Colin 2000 'Survival and resistance: Township organizations and non-violent direct action in the twentieth century' in Adler & Steinberg 2000a: 26–51
Buur, Lars 2003 'Crime and punishment on the margins of the post-apartheid state' *Anthropology and Humanism* 28, 1, 23–42
—— 2005a 'The sovereign outsourced: Local justice and violence in Port Elizabeth' in Hansen, Thomas Blom & Stepputat, Finn (eds) 2005 *Sovereign Bodies: Citizens, Migrants, and States in the Postcolonial World* (Princeton NJ: Princeton University Press): 192–217
—— 2005b 'Sovereignty and democratic exclusion in the new South Africa' *Review of African Political Economy* 104, 5, 253–68
—— 2006 'Reordering society: Vigilantism and expressions of sovereignty in Port Elizabeth's townships' *Development and Change* 37, 4, 735–57
—— 2008 'Democracy and its discontent: Vigilantism, sovereignty and human rights in South Africa' *Review of African Political Economy* 35, 118, 571–84
Buur, Lars & Jensen, Steffen 2004 'Introduction: vigilantism and the policing of everyday life in South Africa' *African Studies* 63, 2, 139–52
Canetti, Elias 1988 *Crowds and Power* (New York: Farrar, Straus & Giroux)
Cherry, Janet 2000 'Hegemony, democracy and civil society: Political participation in KwaZakkele township, 1980–93' in Adler & Steinberg 2000a: 86–113
Cherry, Janet; Jones, Kris & Seekings, Jeremy 2000 'Democratization and politics in South African townships' *International Journal of Urban and Regional Research* 24, 4, 889–905
CRSA 1996 = Republic of South Africa 1996 *Constitution of the Republic of South Africa*, Section 221; Act 200 of 1993; Act 106 of 1996
Dixon, Bill & Johns, Lisa-Marie 2001 *Gangs, Pagad and the State: Vigilantism and Revenge Violence in the Western Cape* (*Violence and Transition Series* 2) (Johannesburg: Centre for the Study of Violence and Reconciliation)
Hayson, Nicholas 1989 *Vigilantes: A Contemporary Form of Repression* (*Seminar Series* 4, 1989) (Johannesburg: Centre for the Study of Violence and Reconciliation)
Jensen, Steffen & Buur, Lars 2007 'The national imperative: South Africanization, regional integration and mobile livelihoods' in Buur, Lars; Jensen, Steffen & Stepputat, Finn (eds) 2007 *The Security-Development Nexus: Expressions of Sovereignty and Securitization in Southern Africa* (Uppsala/Cape Town: Nordic Africa Institute/Human Sciences Research Council): 63–84
Kalati, Noushin & Manor, James 2005 'Elite perceptions of poverty and poor people in South Africa' in Reis, Elisa & Moore, Mick (eds) 2005 *Elite Perceptions of Poverty and Inequality* (Cape Town/London/New York: David Philip/Zed Books): 156–81
Mamdani, Mahmood 1996 *Citizen and Subject: Contemporary Africa and the Legacy of Late Colonialism* (Princeton NJ: Princeton University Press)
Mangokwane, Andries Mphoto 2001 '*Makgotla* in rural and urban contexts' in Schärf & Nina 2001: 148–68
Mayekiso, Mzwanele 1996 *Township Politics: Civic Struggles for a New South Africa* (New York: Monthly Review Press)
Mbembe, Achille 2001 *On the Postcolony* (Berkeley/Los Angeles/London: University of California Press)
Nina, Daniel 1995 *Rethinking Popular Justice: Self-Regulation and Civil Society in South Africa*

(Cape Town: Community Peace Foundation)

—— 2001 'Popular justice and the "appropriation" of the state monopoly on the definition of justice and order' in Schärf & Nina 2001: 98–120

Nina, Daniel & Schärf, Wilfried 2001 'Introduction: The other law?' in Schärf & Nina 2001: 1–13

Oomen, Barbara 2004 'Vigilantism or alternative citizenship? The rise of *Mapogo a Mathamaga*' *African Studies* 63, 2, 153–71

Von Schnitzler, Antina; Ditlhage, Goodwill; Kgalema, Lazarus; Maepa, Traggy; Mofokeng, Tlhoki & Pigou, Piers 2001 *Guardian or Gangster? Mapogo a Mathamaga: A Case Study* (*Violence and Transition Series* 3) (Johannesburg: Centre for the Study of Violence and Reconciliation). Available online at: <www.csvr.org.za/docs/vigilantism/ guardian organgster.pdf> (last accessed 22 July 2008)

Schärf, Wilfried 2001 'Policy options on community justice' in Schärf & Nina 2001: 39–70

Schärf, Wilfried & Nina, Daniel (eds) 2001 *The Other Law: Non-State Ordering in South Africa* (Lansdowne, Cape Town: Juta & Co)

Seekings, Jeremy 1993 *Heroes or Villains? Youth Politics in the 1980s* (Johannesburg: Ravan Press)

—— 1996 'The decline of South Africa's civic organizations, 1990–1996' *Critical Sociology* 22, 3, 135–57

—— 2000 *The UDF: A History of the United Democratic Front in South Africa 1983–1991* (Cape Town: David Philip)

—— 2001 'Social ordering and control in the African townships of South Africa: An historical overview of extra-state initiatives from the 1940s to the 1990s' in Schärf & Nina 2001: 71–97

Steinberg, Jonny (ed.) 2001 *Crime Wave: The South African Underworld and Its Foe* (Johannesburg: Witwatersrand University Press)

Swilling, Mark 1997 'Building democratic local urban governance in southern Africa' in Swilling, Mark (ed.) 1997 *Governing Africa's Cities* (Johannesburg: Witswatersrand University Press): 211–71

Taussig, Michael 1999 *Defacement: Public Secrecy and the Labour of the Negative* (Stanford CA: Stanford University Press)

TRC 1998 = Truth and Reconciliation Commission 1998 *Final Report of the South African Truth and Reconciliation Commission* Vols 1–5 (Cape Town: Juta & Co)

News media

Hosken, Graeme 2003 'Gruesome death for youth at mob's hands' *IOL* 20 January. Available online at: <www.int.iol.co.za/index.php?set_id=1&click_id=15&art_id=vn20030120 130749856C238675> (last accessed 22 July 2008)

IOL 2006a 'Alleged robbers stoned by angry villagers' *IOL* 23 June. Available online at: <www.int.iol.co.za/index.php?set_id=1&click_id=15&art_id=vn20060623005745516 C807610> (last accessed 22 July 2008)

—— 2006b 'I sjambokked trio to stop mob killing them' *IOL* 21 June. Available online at: <www.int.iol.co.za/index.php?set_id=1&click_id=15&art_id=vn20060620232508117 C730421> (last accessed 22 July 2008)

Jasson da Costa, Wendy 2006 'Crime whingers can leave, says Nqakula' *IOL* 2 June. Available online at: <www.int.iol.co.za/index.php?set_id=1&click_id=13&art_id=vn2006060 2104812572C523307> (last accessed 22 July 2008)

M&G 2006 'Outraged residents beat rapist to death' *Mail and Guardian* 7 November. Available online at: <www.mg.co.za/articlePage.aspx?articleid=289244&area=/breaking_news/ breaking_news__national/> (last accessed 22 July 2008)

News24 2006a '"Child rapist" stoned to death' *News24* 30 January. Available online at:

<www.news24.com/News24/South_Africa/News/0,6119,2-7-1442_1872298,00.htm l> (last accessed 22 July 2008)

News24 2006b 'Mob kills man, dumps body' *News24* 11 July. Available online at: <www.news24.com/News24/South_Africa/News/0,,2-7-1442_1966058,00.html> (last accessed 22 July 2008)

News24 2006c 'Mob "frees" vigilante suspects' *News24* 15 August. Available online at: <www.news24.com/News24/South_Africa/News/0,,2-7-1442_1982767,00.html> (last accessed 22 July 2008)

News24 2006d 'Angry mob stone robbers' *News24* 30 October. Available online at: <www.news24.com/News24/South_Africa/News/0,9294,2-7-1442_2022936,00. html> (last accessed 22 July 2008)

Quintal, Angela & Du Plessis, Janine 2006 'Nqakula: no crime "tsunami"' *IOL* 3 June. Available online at: <www.int.iol.co.za/index.php?set_id=1&click_id=594&art_id=vn2006060 3082818368C881609> (last accessed 22 July 2008)

2

Ethnicity, Religion & the Failure of 'Common Law' in Nigeria

JOHANNES HARNISCHFEGER

Introduction

With Nigeria's return to democracy in 1999 after 15 years of military rule, violence between different ethnic and religious groups 'exploded' (Ukiwo 2003: 115; Agbu 2004: 5, 13). Tensions had already built up under the military regime, but the security forces had been able to suppress most conflicts. When the generals returned to barracks and a more liberal and restrained government took over, the number of vigilante groups and militias in operation rose dramatically (Agbu 2004: 5; Pratten 2008: 1; Guichaoua 2007: 92). Many of these organisations claimed to be fighting for 'true democracy', by which they meant, above all, the right of ethnic or religious communities to control 'their' territory and resources, to live according to their own ideas of law and justice, and to be free from the 'internal colonialism' of other ethnic groups. In a deeply divided society like Nigeria's the call for democratic self-determination accordingly did *not* unite the people, but set ethnic and religious groups against each other, with devastating results: as Kukah (2002: 23) notes, 'fewer people died in the entire period of military rule than ... have now died in the first two year[s] of our democracy'. In mid-2005 it was estimated 'that at least 50,000 people have been killed in various incidents of ethnic, religious and communal violence since the return to civilian rule' (Economist Intelligence Unit 2005: 13).

With the transition to democracy, under which citizens could express their loyalties more openly, it became obvious that central control was widely resented. As many Nigerians no longer aspire to live under common laws, the project of nation-building has come to an end. In the Muslim-dominated north of the country, the parliaments of 12 federal states have rejected the secular traditions of Nigeria's constitution and introduced strict forms of Shari'a law. The government of Zamfara state was the first to implement an Islamic penal code, in January 2000. It plastered posters throughout the capital informing readers that the constitution has been suspended and that 'God's law is supreme' (Maier 2000: 180). And since the police force, which is a federal institution, is not prepared to enforce local religious laws, Islamist vigilantes have emerged who mete out 'instant justice'.[1]

In southern Nigeria vigilante activity is often undertaken by groups attempting to achieve ethnic self-determination. The 1999–2007 government of President Olusegun Obasanjo tried to ban and disarm some of these groups, invoking the constitution which rules that only the federal government is allowed to operate a police force. A series of raids on vigilante members led to hundreds being killed and many more being arrested; however, the central government was not able to enforce its monopoly on violence. Consequently, it reversed its strategy: in an attempt to regulate vigilante groups' activities it offered to cooperate with them. However, again there was little success. The state lacks the moral authority and institutional capacity to supervise local crime fighters. Faced with a multitude of rival groups that defy state laws, Nigerians have to find new ways to contain the use of violence.

Recent studies on 'multi-choice policing' in Africa assume that the distribution of security services will be regulated, more than before, on the basis of commercial transactions: 'once security ceases to be guaranteed to all citizens by a sovereign state, it tends to become a commodity' (Baker 2008: 173). There are many non-state actors willing to sell security, so it seems a sensible option to let market mechanisms decide in the competition between them. This allows customers to choose, according to their needs, what type of policing they want and how much they are willing to pay for it. In Nigeria, a considerable amount of protection and surveillance is organised on a commercial basis (Abrahamsen & Williams 2007: 137): Urban businesses employ private security companies, while villages tend to hire night guards, often recruited from outside the community. However, in many parts of Nigeria people have no choice. They are policed by groups that do not accept competition, but try to dominate local and regional security markets.

The two organisations examined in this chapter, the Oodua People's Congress and *Hisba*, do not work on the basis of supply-and-demand. Their interests go far beyond offering security services: their vigilante activities are shaped by the political, cultural and spiritual goals they pursue. Unlike neighbourhood watches, night guards or commercial security firms that provide equal security for all citizens living within their area of operation, the organisations examined protect the rights and privileges of particular communities. Many, if not '[m]ost Nigerian vigilante groups [are] linked to religious, ethno-regional and other sectional interests' (Nolte 2007: 219). Accordingly, these groups have very diverse notions of citizenship, crime and social control.

The Oodua People's Congress (OPC), named after the mythical ancestor of the Yoruba people in southwest Nigeria, claims to be a sociocultural organisation with four to five million members.[2] The group is open to men and women, Muslims and Christians, businessmen, intellectuals and jobless youth. There is only one condition: members have to be sons and daughters of the mythical Yoruba ancestor, and they are expected to profess so, saying 'I am the personification of Oduduwa, body and soul' (Akinyele 2001: 626).[3] By positing a common genealogy that binds all Yoruba, the OPC assumes a historical unity that never in fact existed: the ethnic category 'Yoruba' was introduced by Christian missionaries in the mid-nineteenth century to designate people who had previously not perceived themselves as a community. Yoruba identity was formed under conditions of (post)colonial competition for state power, and has remained precarious (Peel 2000: 278–88; Falola 2006). For a group like the OPC, which emerged out of violent confrontation with the state and was declared illegal, it has been advantageous to presuppose the existence of an ethnic 'nation' that authorises the group's activities. According to the OPC, a nation has the right to self-determination and is entitled to develop institutions to execute its will. By acting on behalf of this (imagined) polity, the OPC can claim functions of sovereign rule analo-gous to a state. It may (re)create order by defining standards of right and wrong and by marking the boundary with outsiders.[4]

Some OPC members who have undergone initiation as *eso* ('warriors') have formed an armed militia that has repeatedly clashed with members of other ethnic groups. These 'warriors' are involved in vigilante activities, patrolling the streets and chasing down supposed criminals. Combining vigilante work with the struggle for ethnic self-determination makes it difficult for group members to cooperate with the police. The federal security forces are perceived as ethnic outsiders because for decades they have been dominated by northern Nigerians, particularly Hausa and Fulani. Attacking this 'army of occupation' by killing policemen or by exposing the involvement of the police in crime has gained the OPC popularity among the 'indigenous' population in Yorubaland (Guichaoua 2006: 11; Nolte 2007: 223–5). The confrontation with police and army units was especially fierce during the period of transition – that is, in the final year of military rule and while the new democratic order was established. The antagonism receded when President Obasanjo, himself a Yoruba, acted to reduce the influence of northern politicians on the security forces.

In principle, however, OPC's vigilante activities are still embedded in a strategy that seeks to free Yorubaland from outside control. By assuming responsibility for public security, the OPC has tried to displace the police, the judiciary and other federal authorities in order to establish a new ethnically-based form of governance. Self-policing helps ethnic (and religious) groups to constitute themselves as political communities and to demonstrate sovereignty. Yet since this sovereignty is partial, fragile and contested it has to be asserted again and again 'through resolute violence' (Hansen & Stepputat 2005: 29). The OPC, like its rival, the federal government, claims to rule the land, so has to demonstrate it is in control:

'indigenous warriors' patrolling the streets force members of other ethnic groups to show deference, day by day, and thus to recognise the prerogatives of the 'sons of the soil'. In this context, the spectacle of punishing criminals is often more a display of power than of justice (Hills 2000: 162).

Sending militia members on crime patrol has further advantages for ethnic militias. It keeps the fighters mobilised even during periods when ethnic tensions are low, and gives them a pretext to carry arms. It generates income for individual members as well as for the organisation, and it boosts their popularity, at least initially. Combining vigilantism and ethnic militancy can also be advantageous from the perspective of vigilante groups which have not been aligned with ethnic organisations. By affiliating with the dominant militia in their area, these vigilante groups may be better protected from the police and from rival gangs. Moreover, they gain additional legitimacy when they enforce law and order on behalf of the 'autochthonous' population, the 'owners of the land'. In the late 1990s already existing groups of vigilantes, neighbourhood watches and night guards joined the OPC (Nolte 2008: 101; Fourchard 2008: 34–35), confirming a trend that has also been identified in other parts of Nigeria: in times of communal crisis, vigilantes merge with ethnic and religious militias (Higazi 2008: 119, 132).[5]

The second type of vigilantism explored in this chapter – religious policing as currently practised by Shari'a implementation groups in 12 states of northern Nigeria – 'differs fundamentally' (Last 2008: 41) from vigilantism in the predominantly Christian south. Hisba vigilantes, believing themselves to be guided by God-given laws, see policing in a more comprehensive way: as a mission to 'sanitize society against all social vices'.[6] As Shari'a law is meant to regulate all spheres of public and private life, it gives vigilantes wide scope to interfere and to arrest offenders against the law. The vigilantes may prosecute adulterers, restrict the movement of women and girls and enforce a strict dress code. However, most Nigerians in the south, who have different concepts of crime and delinquency, reject the idea of the existence of such a 'morality police'. Another contentious issue raised by Islamist vigilantes is the legal status of infidels. Is it acceptable for Islamic authorities to forbid Christians to build churches and impose the death penalty on practitioners of 'pagan' forms of worship?[7]

Religious and ethnic vigilantes such as Hisba and the OPC are authorised by *exclusive* communities, so they are obsessed with spatial and cultural boundaries – staking claims over territory and guarding it against 'alien influences' (Abrahams 2007: 414–15). However, they diverge fundamentally in terms of how they draw these boundaries. Among the Yoruba and other peoples of the south there is wide consensus that territorial control should be divided up between ethnic groups. For example, the 'Yoruba Agenda' – a blueprint for a new constitution signed by prominent Yoruba from all walks of life, including the OPC leaders Gani Adams and Dr Frederick Fasehun – declares that sovereignty, including the right to police, lies with 'the original indigenes of the land' (Yoruba Agenda 2005: 8, 32). Recognising such claims for autonomy has far-reaching consequences, since it leads to a 'pluralist idea of citizenship' (Ejobowah 2000: 32; see also Jinadu 2004: 15; Bach 1997) which divides the population into two broad categories and gives full citizen rights only to the 'original' inhabitants of a place. 'Indigenes' living in the land of their ancestors are regarded as the rightful owners who can ultimately decide how their territory is governed, whereas members of other ethnic groups which 'do not belong' to that area are given the status of settlers who have to accept the hegemony of the 'sons of the soil'.[8]

Shari'a supporters in the north reject ethnic autonomy in favour of religious self-determination. For orthodox Muslims the laws of God are supreme, and are the same in every society, so they override claims of indigeneity. Nevertheless, the implementation of Shari'a similarly leads to a stratified concept of citizenship, though a different, conflicting one: full citizenship rights are only given to true believers, whether they are 'indigenous' or not. Such individuals are entitled to define law and order and to enforce their sacred norms by means of Shari'a guards, thereby 'reasserting the right of Muslim dominance' (Last 2008: 47).

Given these differences, it is unlikely that Nigerians will reach an agreement on how to contain vigilante violence. Leaders of vigilante groups and militias defy the federal constitution, yet have no other set of rules available with which to settle their disputes. At the end of this chapter I will look at suggestions for restructuring Nigeria by creating a legal basis for ethnic and religious policing.

But before discussing possible scenarios, I shall compare the vigilante activities of the OPC and Hisba. For both groups policing is embedded in a strategy to gain hegemony, so they have directed their violence not only against criminals, but also against rival law enforcers. As they have to assert their claims in a hostile and competitive environment, shaped by oligopolies of violence, they cannot afford to stick to legal principles that would make their use of force even-handed and calculable. Vigilante groups are 'unstable' organisations, with shifting aims and strategies (Abrahams 2007: 410). Even the Hisba groups handle matters of justice in an arbitrary and opportunistic way, even though most such groups are currently supervised and funded by state governments. Unlike the OPC, Hisba groups operate on the basis of a clear and comprehensive religious law, enacted by state parliaments, yet they are unable to create legal security.

Like other vigilantes, OPC and Hisba crime-fighters claim to execute the will of 'their communities'. As these groups are recruited locally, often at ward level, they are indeed closer to the people than the police forces, yet they are not under popular control. In northern Nigeria, where the introduction of Shari'a was greeted by a wave of enthusiasm, it soon became obvious that Shari'a enforcers targeted mainly the weak and the poor. Nigeria's 'Shari'a of the whip' has antagonised large segments of the population and created bitter divisions among Muslim activists – between those who collaborate with state governors and others who act on behalf of the 'masses' (Gwarzo 2003: 301). In the case of the OPC, the organisation has split into 'militants' and 'moderates'; the rival factions took sides in local disputes and competed, sometimes violently, for their share in the security market (Guichaoua 2006: 15).

When comparing the OPC and Hisba, I will address specific questions. Can these organisations establish legitimate authority? Are there limits defining their sphere of operation and the scope of the law? How do they relate to ethnic and religious outsiders? And do they cooperate with local authorities and state institutions?

The OPC in southwest Nigeria

Asserting ethnic hegemony

Founded in 1994, the Oodua People's Congress initially functioned as the armed wing of a pro-democracy movement, led by human-rights activists who opposed the military regime and its annulment of the presidential election in June 1993. After the generals withdrew and Nigeria became democratic, the OPC had to find a new mission. It shifted its focus to present itself as a 'socio-cultural organization',[9] defending the interests of 'the Yoruba people'. In the words of Dr Fasehun, a founder member of the organisation and its uncontested leader until it split in 1999, the OPC is 'a completely non-violent organisation ... It is made up of the best elements of the Yoruba race; and the Yoruba nation is the best nation in Africa'.[10]

According to its leaders the OPC is pursuing two main goals. The first is 'flushing out criminals from Yorubaland',[11] which is done, as in other parts of Nigeria, with the help of machetes, petrol and tyres. The second goal is 'the protection of Yoruba interests anywhere in the world'.[12] So far OPC units have not operated outside Nigeria, however: their main area of operation is the southwest of the country, and here, in the OPC's home territory, the struggle for Yoruba interests goes quite a long way. When dockworkers in the port of Apapa in Lagos elected some ethnic Ijo as their trade-union leaders, an OPC commando stormed the port, shooting members of the rival faction, all to ensure that a Yoruba candidate would end up heading the union. Dr Fasehun defended this intervention: 'we felt that our fatherland was being taken away from us. The OPC had to invade the ports to show solidarity and assert the rights of the marginalized Yoruba' (Adekson 2004: 122; see also Akinyele 2001: 627; Human Rights Watch 2003: 23).

It is mainly in the city of Lagos, at the centre of OPC activities, that Yoruba nationalists see their political and economic position as being threatened. Nigeria's former capital has attracted millions of citizens from other parts of the country, including many Muslim Hausa from the north and Christian Igbo from the southeast. Although this mass migration started generations ago and many non-Yoruba Lagos residents were born in the city, the 'indigenes' generally still see non-Yoruba residents as 'settlers', 'tenants' or 'guests'. Like other Yoruba patriots, Gani Adams, leader of the more militant OPC faction, 'claimed that Lagos belonged solely to the Yoruba and ... he vowed to forcefully resist any attempts by the Igbo to "infiltrate" Yorubaland' (Adekson 2004: 133). OPC gangs attacked Igbo traders who were accused of having monopolised parts of the Alaba electronics market, and they clashed with militias raised among the ethnic-Ijo community in Lagos. However, the OPC's main targets were Hausa, members of the biggest ethnolinguistic group in the north, whose leaders had dominated Nigeria's politics for nearly four decades. The Yoruba 'warriors' were not willing to accept that the biggest abattoir in Lagos was managed by Hausa butchers, and they also intervened at the Mile 12 market when Yoruba traders clashed with the Hausa Yam Sellers' Association; the Hausa traders were given an ultimatum 'to cede control of the market'.[13] Another target was a radio station, Raypower, that rebroadcast BBC news in Hausa, the lingua franca of the north. The OPC 'accused the management of Raypower of cultural imperialism which undermine[s] the culture of Yoruba people' (Adekson 2004: 122), and 'threatened to deal with them if the broadcast were not stopped within two weeks' (Ikelegbe 2005: 500).

As 'sons of the soil', OPC members claim control over the land of their ancestors, and this territorial control is demonstrated by policing it. But when patrolling in quarters with a large proportion of 'non-indigenes' they sometimes met with fierce resistance. In October 2000 a major clash erupted in Ajegunle, a multi-ethnic slum in Lagos, after vigilante members pursued an alleged thief who happened to be a Hausa. The man on the run seized his only chance to evade instant justice by hiding among fellow Hausa, who declined to hand him over to his prosecutors. However, the Yoruba fighters insisted on their right to secure law and order in all parts of their hometown. They called in reinforcements and embarked on a 'kill-and-burn operation'[14] against the Hausa. The violence spread from Ajegunle to other parts of Lagos, so that eventually the city governor had to call in the army and impose a curfew. After three days of fighting journalists who could finally inspect the 'war zones' saw the streets 'littered' with corpses.[15]

In November 1999, after the killings at Mile 12, President Obasanjo had declared the OPC illegal and sanctioned the authorities to shoot at any member who resisted arrest. In order to enforce the ban Obasanjo deployed riot police and army units, which unleashed a 'reign of terror'.[16] Scores of OPC members were killed and at least 2,000 were detained (Human Rights Watch 2003: 1, 41, 43–44); however, the security forces did not manage to regain control over Lagos with its 10–15 million inhabitants. The OPC enjoyed considerable support among the ethnic-Yoruba population, and it had the backing of prominent Yoruba politicians. The governor of Ondo state referred to OPC members as 'freedom-fighters', and his colleague in

Lagos wanted to entrust them with official police functions.[17] There was also considerable support from the intellectual elite. Dr Beko Ransome-Kuti, who enjoyed much respect in Western human-rights circles as the long-term chairman of the Campaign for Democracy, also functioned as national treasurer of the OPC.[18] Gani Fawehinmi, Nigeria's most prominent human-rights lawyer, was allied to the more militant faction led by Gani Adams, which later became notorious through kidnappings and acid attacks on policemen. When asked about his involvement, Fawehinmi claimed that until 1999 he did not know about violent acts, but rather mistook the organisation for a 'human rights group'.[19]

Personal ties between the OPC and other segments of 'civil society' may explain why the Civil Liberties Organisation defended the group against attempts to ban it: 'Banning the OPC ... will lead to an increase in crime rate. The group has instilled fears in the mind of criminals'.[20] Sunday Mbang, a bishop in the Methodist church and president of the Christian Association of Nigeria, also pleaded against a ban, and Nobel-laureate author Professor Wole Soyinka stated that the OPC was a 'legitimate organisation'.[21]

Reacting to OPC activities, leaders of the Hausa community threatened 'to ruin Lagos if any Hausa resident is killed again'.[22] Given that the Hausa are a minority in Lagos, Hausa fighters had no chance to gain the upper hand. However, in the north they could strike back massively. Consequently, whenever ethnic clashes erupted in the southwest, members of the Yoruba minority in the north had to fear for their lives. After killings of Hausa in Sagamu, some 60km northeast of Lagos, Yoruba migrants living in Kano found they had to pay. Hundreds of the latter were killed, and endless convoys of refugees headed south, back to their 'homeland' where they could feel safe.[23]

However, after peaking in 2000, ethnic violence in southwest Nigeria abated. With the election of a Yoruba president there was more of a shift in power to the south, so the call to resist Hausa 'colonialism' lost its urgency. Moreover, in the course of ethnic clashes the local balance of power changed in favour of the Yoruba. Since the Hausa diaspora was no longer as self-assured as it had been during the rule of the northern generals, Hausa in the south were forced, at least in some contested areas, to acknowledge the hegemony of their 'host' community – a process observed by Nolte in Sagamu. Here, the Hausa 'settlers' have had to accept that an annual masquerade, organised by a Yoruba secret society, passes through their (Muslim) quarter of town. In addition, the local Hausa have had to give up their monopoly on the kolanut trade, and their community representative, the *Seriki Hausawa*, has had to show submission to the traditional ruler of the town by undergoing an installation ceremony in which he received his insignia of authority from the hands of the Yoruba chief (Nolte 2004: 77).

Vigilante activity, which began on a large scale in 1999, helped consolidate OPC control over disputed areas, but also came about as a response to popular demand. In the beginning, crime rates fell drastically as OPC members pursued criminals into zones where the police did not dare to operate (Human Rights Watch 2003: 8; Guichaoua 2006: 13–14).[24] Observers reported that the 'freedom-fighters' acted with much self-discipline. When they entered an area and began to search it house by house, they did not steal from local inhabitants.[25] In July 2002 Nigeria's Inspector-General of Police offered to cooperate with the vigilantes on condition that they hand over suspects to the police. OPC fighters complied to some extent, but then accused the police of releasing criminals in exchange for money.

In late 2005, after the leaders of both OPC factions had been arrested again, the organisation declared that it would cease vigilante operations in southwestern Nigeria in order 'to put an end to frequent confrontation with the police'.[26] However, many members have since become involved in the security business, on the basis of private contracts. Their employers are community associations, landlords or traders' associations, bank managers and businessmen. In principle these clients are free to decide how much security they need and where to buy it. However, very often they will contact local OPC officers in order to hire security staff. Such an arrangement is advantageous for both sides. The OPC receives a share of the salaries paid to the guards, and if any of the latter misbehave the employer may turn to the OPC zone coordinator to demand disciplinary measures. Erring members may be expelled or beaten up; however, disciplining them is actually difficult as they can easily join the rival OPC faction or some other gang (Guichaoua 2006: 12–13).

Factionalism and cultural unity

Clashes with the police were not the only reason why in 2005 OPC leaders decided to distance themselves from vigilantism. By then the organisation had lost much of its popular support, because too many real or fake members were involved in criminal activities. They would accept jobs from politicians, acting 'as mercenaries for political violence', or extort money so that the security services they offered sometimes resembled a protection racket (Guichaoua 2006: 14). Among non-Yoruba, OPC vigilantes had evoked fear right from the beginning as they were perceived as 'hostile towards other tribes' (Human Rights Watch 2003: 8). To disillusioned Yoruba who had initially supported the move-ment it seemed as if the organisation had been hijacked by 'hoodlums', 'miscreants' and 'illiterates' (Adekson 2004: 111).[27]

Two former members explained to me that things began to go wrong after the organisation split in early 1999 and the rival factions recruited new members indiscriminately in order to swell their ranks.[28] The controversy that initially divided the OPC leaders revolved around their relationship with the state. Gani Adams, a 29-year old youth leader with little formal education, accused the OPC president, Dr Fasehun, of participating in the transition towards Nigeria's Fourth Republic and taking bribes from Obasanjo during the presidential election campaign. Dr Fasehun then expelled his opponent from the organisation, citing 'hooliganism' and 'unnecessary terrorism' (Nolte 2004: 78), and he decried that Adams recruited his supporters among the 'rabble' (Adebanwi 2005: 349).

However, the rank-and-file of both factions, despite their bitter enmity, share a similar social background, and when they clash it is usually not about programmatic differences. Adams, of course, does have a reputation for militancy, but in his political demands he is not far away from Dr Fasehun and the mainstream of Yoruba politics. Adams was even appointed a member of the committee that drafted the 'Yoruba Agenda', which may be seen as a position paper intended to function as a common platform of the Yoruba elite in their negotiations with representatives of other ethnic groups. A large part of the Yoruba establishment acknowledges Adams as a legitimate leader of Yoruba youth. The militancy of his 'boys' appears acceptable, in principle, as it can be used by the elders in their competition with other ethnic elites: 'Yoruba elders, politicians and traditional rulers ... are persuaded that the OPC will help in instituting a "balance of terror" against the North' (Adebanwi 2005: 351, 350).

This tacit or open support of youth militancy seems to indicate that the rich and powerful have little fear that the angry young men might rebel against them. Most OPC activists come from poor backgrounds and are 'very conscious of the economic and social deprivations which they suffer. But they put all of these down to political marginalisation caused centrally by the Hausa–Fulani elite' (ibid.: 349). Ethnic nationalism has helped to play down class antagonisms within Yoruba society. Nevertheless, the OPC has in fact been used to articulate popular anger against the elite. During the national elections of 2003 both OPC factions mobilised voters against the corrupt incumbent Yoruba governors (Nolte 2007: 226–8).

According to the OPC's constitution, the Oodua Bill of Rights, the organisation is striving for an 'absolutely unflinching unity' by propagating an 'Oodua worldview' and by inducing their compatriots to 'identify with Yoruba history and cultural origin' (Adekson 2004: 113–14). On behalf of the Yoruba nation the OPC has revived cultural festivals and restored historic sites, including the shrine of a water-goddess in Lagos.[29] Many OPC members are staunchly religious Muslims or Christians, yet they do not protest against 'idol worship' – as implied by the shrine restoration – because the ancient gods are key symbols of Yoruba unity. At meetings of Afenifere, the most influential association of Yoruba politicians, members swear by Ogun, Sango and other deities. The situation is similar within the OPC. Dr Fasehun is a Christian while Adams is a Muslim, but their organisation is not divided along religious lines. When new members are initiated they swear by their common gods and they receive protective charms fashioned according to the 'ancient wisdom of our forefathers' (Adebanwi 2005: 354).[30]

In Yorubaland there are probably as many Muslims as Christians; the fault-line between the two faiths runs through the majority of families. A religious confrontation would be the worst disaster that could occur. No elected Yoruba governor has ever advocated the introduction of Shari'a, not even in a limited form, even though in northern Nigeria Shari'a courts with restricted jurisdiction existed for decades. Muslims in the north could approach Islamic courts to seek rulings in civil proceedings involving questions of inheritance, divorce and other family matters. However, even such a limited application of Islamic law would have brought strife to Yorubaland because Shari'a demands that a Christian may not inherit from a Muslim and *vice versa*. Despite the risks of religious polarisation, some Yoruba Muslims have joined the recent Shari'a campaign, and the governor of Lagos, himself a Muslim, came 'under immense pressure' to introduce Islamic law.[31] But so far ethnic solidarity among the Yoruba has proved stronger than religious loyalties. As a Muslim chief put it: 'I'm a Yorubaman first and foremost ... I have a duty to my race' (quoted in Ado-Kurawa 2000: 194).

Religious authorities in the north have accused their Yoruba co-religionists of not taking their faith seriously. However, both sides are aware that the call by Hausa–Fulani Muslims to join the Shari'a campaign and establish Islamic courts in Yorubaland is not meant to bring peace. After decades of religious conflicts in the north, Hausa–Fulani politicians would benefit if the 'Shari'a virus'[32] spread to other parts of the country. A northern periodical that favoured Shari'a commented: 'Yoruba have enough Muslim population to adopt their own mode of Shari'a and create their own fratricide'.[33] Faced with such attempts to deepen internal divisions, many Yoruba assume that only nationalism can contain religious passion. This may explain why a number of Yoruba intellectuals have supported the OPC despite its record as an 'extremely illiberal nationalist group' (Reno 2003: 296; see also Adekson 2004: 109). Critics in the north branded Soyinka an 'apostle of ethnic hatred',[34] but it seems his nationalism was calculated to save his people from a religious confrontation. To him, the Shari'a campaign looked like 'a prelude to civil war' (Freedom House 2002: 9, 56), as it spread southward from the Muslim-dominated regions in the far north into religiously mixed states.[35]

Hisba vigilantes in the Muslim north

Piety and control over territory

Muslim reformers in northern Nigeria reject ethnicity as basis for self-determination. Instead of reviving African traditions, they want to remodel their society according to a set of universal rules. By submitting to Shari'a, Nigerians would adopt a common identity which 'eliminate[s] tribalism and all other primitive chauvinistic ideologies' (Ado-Kurawa 2000: 271).

When practised strictly, Islamic law would overcome all man-made boundaries:

> all Muslims, irrespective of race, language or nationality, must constitute a single brotherhood, one *Umma* ... the *Umma*, from one end of the world to the other, is but one single nation, its diverse peoples sharing but one faith, one law, one culture and one destiny. (Sulaiman 1986: 11)

However, the fight for Shari'a in Nigeria has always been linked with ethnic hegemony. After Usman dan Fodio, a Fulani preacher, declared a Muslim holy war in 1804, his followers toppled the Hausa kings, whom they accused of apostasy and corruption, and replaced them with a Fulani aristocracy. Since the new rulers were drawn from a small minority of the population, they used Islam to unite the subjugated peoples and keep the disparate empire together. As custodians of the 'true religion', the rulers of this caliphate were especially keen to impose the external manifestations of the faith, such as the observation of Ramadan, Friday prayers and other rites; all this helped spread a uniform culture.

When Nigeria became independent in 1960 the premier of the Northern Region, Ahmadu Bello, embarked on a conversion campaign. As a direct descendant of Usman dan Fodio he frequently used the imagery of the *jihad* and stressed the continuity between his government and the old caliphate (Reynolds 1997: 56–60). The targets of his campaign were mainly the ethnic minorities in the Middle Belt, which had managed to defend their independence during the time of the *jihad*. Many members of these minorities had adopted Christianity as a way of distancing themselves from the advancing Hausa culture, so they saw the Islamisation policy as a component of 'internal colonisation'.

In recent years, when a new wave of Islamisation has been spreading south, representatives of these minorities have protested at the introduction of Shari'a law: 'The indigenous ethnic groups ... will not want to lose their ethnic identity due to the Islamization' (Gombe State 2000: 47, 17). However, the Hausa–Fulani leaders who dominate the north see the Middle Belt as within their sphere of influence and they are not willing to respect the principle of ethnic autonomy. Where Hausa–Fulani Muslims are strong enough to control state governments they have pushed for Islamic legislation as a means to override the rights of 'indigenous' groups that are mainly Christian or 'pagan' (Harnischfeger 2004).

While Islamic law is well suited to use for challenging claims of indigeneity, it can also be used for the opposite function: to consolidate the superior position of native populations. In Kano and other urban centres of the far north, where Hausa–Fulani Muslim culture has been entrenched for generations, the Shari'a campaign has supported 'an autochthonous, ethnic, religious exclusionism, backed by the often violent "policing" of *'yan daba* and *'yan hisba*' (Casey 2007: 92–3). The 'indigenous' population, by elevating its own sacred law to the status of state law, has asserted its hegemony *vis-à-vis* Christians from the south who have been migrating there since colonial times. Alhough these 'settlers' or 'aliens' often live apart from the rest of the population in so-called 'strangers' quarters', they have managed to bring parts of the local economy under their control. By passing Shari'a laws in the face of massive Christian protests, the 'original' inhabitants have presented themselves as the lords of the land who can force the state apparatus to do their bidding. Their sovereign power to determine public life is also manifested by an increased 'symbolic presence of Islam' (Alli 2005: 66), by public prayers and dress codes, and by strict fasting requirements and food taboos. Wherever Christian migrants turn their gaze, they are reminded that they are living in a foreign land and that they will remain outsiders as long as they resist assimilation. For those who want to overcome this marginal position and assimilate, the decisive step is conversion to Islam (Albert 2001: 293).

In this context of entrenching religious dominance, Islamic vigilantes serve a dual function. First, they make visible the boundary between believers and infidels by urging the faithful to discharge their ritual obligations and to abstain from 'un-Islamic behaviour'. Second, they force non-Muslims to acknowledge the supremacy of the 'indigenous' popula-tion. Though the minorities have not been reduced to *dhimmi* status (that is, the status of a subordinated population subject to Muslim protection and legal supervision), they have to respect at least some laws of the dominant religion: in a number of Shari'a states they may not drink alcohol, they have to observe some form of gender separation, and they are not allowed to build churches, not even in strangers' quarters.

For the majority of the population Kano, Zamfara and Sokoto are 'Muslim states that wish to see their state apparatus organized in con-formity with their faith' (Tabiu 2001: 10).[36] So they claim the right to govern their land without regard to the largely secular constitution and its catalogue of 'universal' rights. In debates with Western critics Shari'a has been presented as a 'defense against unwanted cultural globalization' and as a means to protect 'cultural diversity' and preserve the 'authentic' culture of northern Nigeria.[37] However, the recent Islamisation movement has rather served to reduce cultural diversity, particularly in rural areas where the Islamic majority has long coexisted with small 'pagan' com-munities. By banning music, dancing and the brewing of traditional beer, some governments have criminalised important elements of 'pagan' rituals. The height of the piety campaign saw busloads of urban-based Hisba members raiding villages in a bid to suppress un-Islamic forms of worship (Casey 2007: 106; Last 2008: 51). In this way they accelerated a process of social transformation which appeared to Western observers to be a 'de-Africanisation' of Hausaland (Miles 2003: 65–69).[38]

In urban centres like Kano, with its big Christian diaspora, Shari'a has led not to assimilation but to a hardening of ethno-religious boundaries. Christian Igbo and Yoruba from the south have preserved strong links with their home communities, so are less likely to convert and embrace the dominant culture. Yet in an environment placed under Islamic rules, they are made to feel like second-class citizens who are largely excluded from participation in public affairs. Locked in their role as permanent guests, they are expected to accept the conditions set by others without protest. In the words of Dr Datti Ahmed, president of the Supreme Council for Shari'a: 'If any individual feels too uncomfortable with any set-up established by the majority in any state, he has the right to choose another state.'[39]

Since Shari'a reformers have rejected the secular principles of the constitution, it has become more difficult for Muslims and Christians to arrive at an agreement that would secure the rights of religious minorities. In cases of conflict they cannot refer to common rules which would determine how faith-based communities should relate to each other. Instead of a consensus they will reach, at best, partial and unstable arrangements which are not rooted in common convictions. Such compromises that stipulate the extent to which Christians have to submit to Islamic hegemony depend on local constellations of power, so they change over time and vary from region to region. Where Christians form a small minority, as in Zamfara or Kano states, they have had to accept that public life has been thoroughly Islamised, at least in the beginning of the Shari'a period. In states like Kaduna or Gombe, however, the Christian minorities have been strong enough to risk violent confrontation. After clashes over the Shari'a issue in February and May 2000 left thousands of people dead, Islamic laws could be implemented only in a very limited form.

The limits of Islamic law

Islamic law as a basis for vigilante activity offers advantages for both vigilante members and those they claim to protect. Such law is in parts clearly formulated, so provides more legal security than the informal justice of OPC 'warriors' who hold their trials in secret or pronounce their sentences on the spot. The classical books of Islamic jurisprudence lay down rules for division of labour between 'judges', who hold public trials, and 'vigilantes', who play a subservient role. A Hisba that worked strictly within the framework of Shari'a norms could be integrated with other state institutions and could contribute to the reconstruction of a functional state. Moreover, Islamic law might bridge the divide between rich and poor, binding all of the faithful to a common set of divine rules which no individual may alter to suit his or her personal interests. As Shari'a is clearly derived from holy scriptures, it is in its essentials not disputed among legal and theological authorities. With its aura of divine righteousness and impartiality, it appears ideally suited to provide Islamic vigilantes with a clear mandate and a robust legitimacy.

There is, however, a major problem. Shari'a is meant to regulate in minute detail all aspects of human behaviour: 'Our way of life, that is, from the day you were born to the day you enter the grave is governed by

Shari'a. How you eat, walk, talk ... everything.'[40] In a modern large-scale society, such a tight system of legal prohibitions, ritual prescriptions and purity taboos cannot be implemented properly, and its partial and episodic enforcement leads to arbitrary punishments, double standards and hypocrisy. In Nigeria's Shari'a states a number of teenage women were flogged for pre-marital sex, but when the son of an emir was sentenced to caning for drinking alcohol, the emir ordered that the Hisba group be dissolved (Fwatshak 2003: 19).[41] Members of the elite, who are able to conduct their entertainments away from public view in clubs and guest-houses, can typically get away with breaching the law (Casey 2007: 104).[42] Under the new religious regime they have cultivated neither a sense of decency nor one of social justice. From Zamfara, the heartland of Shari'a, it was reported that the 'forceful acquisition of land and other properties of the less-privileged by those in authority, particularly village and district heads, [has] reached alarming proportion [sic]' (Paden 2005: 166).[43]

The political elites which introduced the divine law do not always find they are in a position to control the way in which it is implemented. In cases where governors were reluctant to enforce the new legislation, independent Hisba groups emerged that were linked to radical preachers and imams. This religious vanguard was not inclined to honour agreements which exempted Christians from most Shari'a prohibitions. Some even felt authorised to turn against the ruling circles that had enacted the law of God but paid only lip-service to its commands. For the Hausa–Fulani elite the Shari'a campaign had been, above all, a means to put pressure on President Obasanjo and other Christian politicians who had risen under Obasanjo's rule. Northerners had dominated Nigerian politics for decades, but the transition to democracy in 1999 had involved a shift in power. On assuming office Obasanjo had retired dozens of Hausa and Fulani army officers, so the northern elites had reason to fear that they would be marginalised and lose access to the oil revenues distributed by the Nigerian state. Without control of the army the northern elite had few means available by which they could force the new rulers to compromise. The Shari'a campaign probably constituted their most efficient 'bargaining chip' because it threatened the minority groups of Christian Igbo, Ijo and Yoruba living in the north (Mazrui 2001: 2; Harnischfeger 2008a: 119–54). As a means of political blackmail the campaign was successful, but the religious enthusiasm it fomented eventually got out of control. Islamic governors who insist – in opposition to the federal government – that God's commands supersede Nigeria's constitution and any other man-made law, have set a political paradigm that has the effect of eroding the legitimacy of state authorities and empowering religious counter-elites. Radical Muslims, by invoking the supreme authority of the word of God, reject state-controlled Shari'a with its half-hearted compromises and call for a 'pure' Islamic order that can only be established by toppling the corrupt ruling class.

Governors have tried to integrate independent Shari'a vigilantes into state-controlled Hisba groups. In Kano, both organisations existed side by side until a new governor, elected on a pro-Shari'a ticket, put the more radical elements on the state's payroll. Some 9,000 volunteers were trained and given a wide mandate to prosecute 'anti-Islamic behaviour'. They have been authorised to arrest thieves, suppress traditional music and magic, counsel women on marriage issues, and stop usury, speculation and lending money at interest (Olaniyi 2005: 60–63).[44] Their activities are supervised, at state and local government levels, by Shari'a Implementation Committees which are manned by Islamic scholars, imams and political office holders. Among them are also representatives of the police.

Despite the official recognition of Islamic vigilantes, relations between the vigilantes and the police have been tense from the beginning. Police officers have been accused of sabotaging Shari'a by converting police stations into beer parlours and providing armed guards for trucks bringing beer into Kano (Peters 2003: 29; Gwarzo 2003: 307). In return, police officers and others have accused Hisba groups of colluding with criminals. Among the volunteers who have joined the Shari'a guards are members of 'yan daba – street gangs that have played a prominent role in clashes with Christians. Overlapping membership and informal contacts between both types of groups have facilitated complicity and a division of labour: 'Hisba preached to unmarried women, arranging for marriages for them, while silently encouraging *and* openly condemning 'yan daba attacks and rapes of Muslim women, married and unmarried, who ventured out of their homes unaccompanied' (Casey 2007: 104).

President Obasanjo had ensured that police commissioners posted to crisis areas were opposed to Shari'a, and indeed the police often acted as a check against Hisba excesses. In Kano in early 2006, two Hisba leaders were arrested. However, this step was only taken after the Shari'a monitors had lost public support: they had provoked violent resistance after trying to stop women riding on motorcycle taxis. Women's and human-rights groups had protested only feebly and unsuccessfully against this restriction of personal liberties. The people who risked confrontation with the Shari'a authorities were the motorcycle drivers, who saw their commercial interests at risk. After Hisba members confiscated more than 2,000 motorcycles, the drivers attacked them and destroyed dozens of official Hisba vehicles in return (Adamu 2008: 149).

In general, the federal government has been reluctant to interfere in Hisba activities because the Shari'a controversy threatens to aggravate religious divisions within the police and the army. Some police and army officers participated actively in the Islamisation drive, without regard to orders from above. In Zamfara state, for instance, a Christian woman was detained for several days after a policeman, a soldier and an administrative officer entered her house and found a carton of beer in her bedroom.[45] With a plurality of conflicting secular and religious laws, the behaviour of state agents becomes unpredictable, as they may decide individually, according to their personal conviction, which law to apply.

Although Hisba members are supposed to hand over suspects to the police, in fact the vigilantes have often punished suspects on the spot. Flogging is a common means of dealing with alleged offences, but I did not come across any reports to the effect that they had executed criminals. Compared with OPC vigilantes, Hisba groups acted with much restraint – but with little success in curbing violent crime. More militant forms of crime-fighting are sometimes practised by informal vigilantes. A Fulani leader in Gombe state, with good contacts with the political establishment, instructed his followers to chop off the hands of armed robbers.[46] In his court he conducted 'trial by ordeal after reading verses from the Holy Quran'.[47] A more comprehensive form of Islamic justice has been pursued by Islamic rebels, mostly students and graduates, who have been referred to as 'Taliban' by the media. They have attacked some rural police stations and local government buildings, raised flags inscribed with 'Afghanistan' and begun to impose on local peasants a fundamentalist interpretation of Islamic life. The army, in order to dislodge them from their lairs on the border with Cameroon and Niger, deployed heavy artillery.[48]

In search of common rules

Nigeria's academics and human-rights activists are divided when assessing the consequences of ethnic nationalism and religious self-determination. Some want to 'minimize the political importance of ethnicity and other sectional or particularistic identities' (Aka 2005: 61), arguing that it is better 'to replace cultural rights with civic rights' (Opata 2004: 52) and pushing for nation-building as the only way to create bonds of trust and reciprocity that will overcome ethnic and religious animosities. They agree to some extent with Western critics of discourses on autochthony who see the discrimination against outsiders as 'shameful' and 'perverse' (Human Rights Watch 2004: 3, 60). A Human Rights Watch (HRW) report has urged that in order to prevent communal conflicts over citizenship rights, Nigeria's government should delete from the constitution all references to 'indigenes' and 'non-indigenes' (*ibid.*: 62–64).

Yet it is unlikely that, in actuality, Nigerians will grant each other equal rights. There is, as HRW acknowledges, an 'increasingly widespread notion that only indigenes of any given place have the right to hold political power' (*ibid.*: 58). This revaluation of indigeneity and communal rights is a rational response to state failure. When the police and the judiciary cannot guarantee that citizens enjoy the same civil rights all over the country, then there is no point in claiming these rights. Constitutional safeguards are becoming fictitious. As the central government does not protect people, they seek refuge in ethnic and religious solidarity (Young 2007: 251–2), and this leads to a fragmentation of policing: when protection is provided by one's community, it is only natural that community members discuss security arrangements among themselves, to the exclusion of others.

Among Muslims in northern Nigeria, there is a wide consensus that public and private life should be policed according to religious precepts. The idea of Shari'a is still popular, though most of the faithful are disappointed about the arbitrary way in which governors have implemented it. As one Muslim 'activist' put it: 'People want Shari'a but are not satisfied with what they're getting' (quoted in Human Rights Watch 2004: 90). Ideas about divine justice differ widely, yet the faithful do not object to religious legislation as such, and even intellectuals are cautious *not* to reject the political claims of Islam. In southern Nigeria, people debate more openly which legal arrangements are best suited for a country with 500 ethnolinguistic groups. Intellectuals speaking in support of ethnic militias present them as civil-society organisations which fight, in concert with 'other progressive social forces', for the liberation of all oppressed peoples: here, 'ethnic militancy is a contribution to democracy and diversity' (Douglas & Ola 2003: 47, 42). Not all observers in southern Nigeria are so enthusiastic about ethnic autonomy, but most of them would agree that Western notions of citizenship and individual human rights do not provide a suitable way to resolve the country's crisis.

The shift from individual to communal rights looks inevitable. However, the fragmentation of the system of laws and of law-enforcement agencies makes it difficult to reach agreement on how to regulate the use of violence. In the concluding part of this chapter I will sum up the main areas of disagreement, looking first at internal controversies *within* communities, and second, at debates on how to contain armed conflicts *between* them.

Internal divisions

The cases of the OPC and Hisba provide little support for the idea that community-based policing in Nigeria will strengthen democracy and establish popular control over security agents. Both vigilante groups invoke the right of self-determination, and their ideals of law and order are indeed more sensitive to local culture than the law that guides the federal police. State law that has been derived from Europe ignores local customs and does not concern itself with enforcing observances of moral values, religious rites or rules of purity that bind specific communities together. Adultery is not treated as a felony, and citizens are not forced to dress 'properly' or to (re)establish male authority over women. Instead, it is left to individual citizens to decide which way of life they choose. From the perspective of Western constitutionalism, it is a major function of state law to set up a social space wherein individuals may act as they wish, without having to justify their behaviour. For most Nigerians, however, this emphasis on individual liberties is problematic. A legal system that encourages the pursuit of one's personal interest seems to nurture recklessness, lack of responsibility and social corrosion. Shari'a supporters would even argue that it is the Western ideal of personal autonomy that is at the root of Nigeria's crisis. They argue that returning to the strict rules of divine justice will have the effect of limiting the 'excessive freedom' which benefits, above all, the rich and unscrupulous (Last 2000: 152). Since moral laxity and decay have permeated the whole fabric of social relations, it seems legitimate to them that Shari'a enforcers intrude into all spheres of life. According to orthodox Muslims, the project of social renewal can only succeed if all members of the community are forced to participate. The faithful have to rid themselves of un-Islamic behaviour and avoid being 'contaminated' by the deviant thoughts and practices of infidels (Casey 2007: 116). This leads to a holistic concept of policing which defines security in physical as well as in spiritual terms, and which is driven, at times, by a millenarian sense of urgency and rigour (Last 2008: 41–42, 49, 58, 61).[49]

Since the enthusiasm for state-enforced Shari'a law has abated somewhat, just two or three years after its introduction, Muslims now tend to evade the control of Hisba guards. By tacittly ignoring the instructions of religious authorities, they have regained much of their freedom. This does not mean, however, that their basic human rights are institutionally guaranteed. A holy law that is enforced sporadically and arbitrarily creates insecurity

> because people can no longer take the law as a reliable guide to permissible and impermissible conduct. To maintain a law without intending to enforce it is dangerous because it leaves too much discretion in the hands of those charged with enforcing the law, enabling them to select cases for enforcement based on selfish and other corrupt purposes (An-Na'im 1990: 88).

What is permissible or forbidden in any given situation depends on shifting power structures – on the influence of local politicians and emirs, Hisba groups and militant preachers. The only way to create legal security would be for the parliaments of the Shari'a states to dispense with a significant proportion of the divine laws and regulations. But this would be tantamount to declaring the will of parliamentarians superior to the will of God. Moreover, there is no consensus about precisely which elements of Shari'a should be abandoned, and the alternatives to a theocratic order are not clear. Politicians and 'traditional' authorities such as emirs, who resent a tight religious regime, are not necessarily in favour of Western notions of human rights.

In the south of Nigeria, debates about self-determination are not encumbered by considerations of religious restrictions. Christians and Muslims (insofar as they reject Shari'a) have no blueprint for a just society, and there is deep insecurity in which direction they should turn. Some Yoruba intellectuals have suggested that people should once again listen to the wisdom of the *orisa*, the ancient deities. The idea of cultural revival is also propagated in the OPC 'national' hymn: 'Time to go back home, Oduduwa sons/If we can't see the way forward/Ought we not to go back home?' (quoted in Olukotun 2003: 67). However, the message of the ancient deities is vague and contested. OPC faction leader Dr Fasehun strongly identifies with modernity and enlightenment, defining his people as part of Nigeria's 'westernised progressive South' whose culture is 'irreconcilable' with the 'traditionalist, conservative North' (Faseun [Fasehun] 2002: 2; see also Adebanwi 2005: 348, Nolte 2007: 221, 224.). For him, as for many other Yoruba nationalists, African traditions have a very limited function. They are not a guide for the future but a 'resource for political engineering' used to construct some sense of belonging (Adebanwi 2005: 341).

Power-sharing between armed communities

The plurality of laws and law of enforcers, with ill-defined powers and overlapping spheres of operation, makes it difficult to settle violent conflicts. How can communities that keep armed gangs to patrol 'their' territory avoid clashes with other such communities? Nigeria's Western-style constitution is ill-suited to solving this problem. With its catalogue of human rights, it defines the relationship between individual citizens and the state, but it does *not* regulate the relationship between ethnic or religious groups which claim a high degree of autonomy.

A number of intellectuals and human-rights activists in southern Nigeria have suggested that Nigerians, instead of sticking to 'foreign models' which are not 'suited to the needs and circumstances of African states', should look for 'autochthonous constitutions' (Osaghae 2005: 103; see also Jinadu 2004: 16). These could be based on the idea that 'citizenship in pre-colonial African societies' was rooted in 'principles of collectivism, communalism and cooperation' which were 'negated' when Nigerians adopted 'Western attributes of citizenship' (Dibua 2005: 7). Advocates of ethnic self-determination argue that the country can no longer afford a constitution derived from 'neo-liberal individualistic assumptions' (Jinadu 2004: 14.). According to them, Nigerians should come to terms with their ethnic realities: 'What is vital is to recognise our social pluralism, to recognise that from now, Nigeria is a federation of ethnicities and nationalities, nothing else.'[50] They advocate organising a 'National Conference' with delegates from all ethnic groups, in order to negotiate the legal framework for 'true federalism'. A restructured federation, as ethnic nationalists understand it, would no longer be based on geographical units such as the present 36 states, but would take autonomous ethnic groups as its 'building blocks'.[51] According to this view, Nigeria's nationalities become the crucial rights-bearing entities: they have a will, they take decisions, and they enter into contractual relationships with each other.

Representatives of ethnic groups attending the National Conference could agree on a new constitution which would dissolve the federal police and greatly reduce other functions of central government. With little power left at the federal level, competition for such power would no longer be a do-or-die affair and central power could be shared through a rotating-presidency system. However, such a devolution of power would not solve the most urgent problems: what is the legal status of 'settlers'? Who will protect ethnic diasporas? Who is the owner of the oil resources, and how should the oil revenues be shared? Without a strong central state acting as a third-party enforcer to uphold agreements, it would be left to rival ethnic (and religious) communities to sort out their conflicts themselves. But on which legal basis? African traditions of 'communalism' do not provide any political models for how autonomous ethnic groups can associate equitably. The only pre-colonial systems which covered large territories with a multitude of peoples were empires or kingdoms like Oyo, Benin or Kwararafa. Some of these were merely loose associations of ethnic groups, each of which preserved much of its autonomy because the function served by the king and his court were mainly ritual ones. Such alliances, reinforced by ritual cooperation of their elites, could create enough stability to build up extensive trade networks. But they also established ethnic hierarchies, with dominant groups that tried to exclude others from royal office and accumulate power so as to be able to impose tributes or monopolise trade.[52]

The likelihood of reaching agreement on a new Nigerian constitution decreases further when some actors define self-determination in religious terms. Shari'a activists who declare that God's law is supreme are not obliged to follow any man-made law which is not in line with their divine rules. They may sign treaties with non-Muslims, but legal and constitutional concessions to infidels will bind them at best temporarily; consequently, agreements negotiated with such activists cannot be trusted by the other party in the agreement. Moreover, Shari'a activists renounce those 'pagan' African traditions which they used to practise in common with their fellow citizens. This further erodes trust. Nigerians are losing the feeling that they share moral and legal convictions on which a common polity can be built.

Most Muslims in the north of Nigeria do not look for 'autochthonous' solutions to the Nigerian crisis. Inspired by Islamic reformers in Saudi Arabia and Iran, they demand submission to a universal religious law that tends to eclipse ethnic differences. The attempt to spread a unifying culture and promote assimilation with the help of religious policing is not only motivated by piety; it also reflects the hegemonic ambitions of the dominant group in the north, the Hausa–Fulani elite. While the leaders of the Yoruba and Igbo, the two biggest ethnolinguistic groups in the south, have strong autonomist tendencies, their counterparts in the north reject the right of ethnic self-determination 'because the Hausa-speaking emirate leaders have transregional aims and interests based on both precolonial history and religious culture' (Sklar 2004: 43). Through Shari'a, the Muslim majority tries to constitute itself as a political community with control over a vast territory where it can 're-establish' a *dar al-Islam* ('abode of Islam'; Last 2008: 58–60). Like Usman dan Fodio's caliphate of the nineteenth century, such a community would include at its margins many non-Hausa minorities, among them predominantly Christian groups with strongly autonomist tendencies, like the Tangale in Gombe state or the Sayawe in Bauchi state. The Muslim governors of the latter states, though they passed Shari'a laws, did not risk sending Hisba guards to police areas populated by Christian minorities. However, they would not accept that the Tangale and Sayawe, claiming ethnic autonomy, place 'their' territory under the control of their own vigilantes.

Although religious and political authorities in the Muslim north have rejected essential elements of the present constitution, they have little interest in negotiating a new one. When self-determination groups in the south made a first attempt to organise a national conference in April 2006, only a few northerners attended, and they made it clear that they would rather defend the *status quo* than risk a radical restructuring.[53] For northerners, the current practice of simply ignoring undesirable constitutional restraints seems preferable to a legal compromise with Christians which would set limits for the implementation of sacred law. Thus it is unlikely that future Hisba guards will operate under a clearly defined constitutional mandate. The way they interfere in people's lives and what 'crimes' they prosecute will not be determined by generally recognised laws. As in the past, the rigour of Islamist vigilantes will vary from place to place depending on how much resistance is put up by Christian minorities and other opponents of Shari'a.

In recent years the rift between 'indigenes' and 'non-indigenes' has widened in all parts of Nigeria, yet there are forces which work against an escalation of communal violence. Politicians in Yoruba-, Igbo- and Hausaland (though not in the Niger Delta) have now lost interest in ethnic and religious mobilisation. Thanks to the high prices for crude oil they are profiting from Nigeria's oil rents like never before. The opportunity to embezzle billions of dollars each year has generated a strong interest in stabilising the federation. Under military rule, large sections of the elites felt excluded from the wealth of the nation, whereas today no major region or ethnic elite is left out. The government of President Obasanjo distributed the state resources more or less evenly and sought to balance ethno-religious interests. Obasanjo's successor, Umaru Yar'Adua, who was hand-picked by Obasanjo, continued this policy of de-escalation. However, it is far from clear that future presidents will show the same degree of restraint. Without the security of legal institutions that bind all relevant actors, it is difficult to share power between armed communities. Compromises can only emerge through informal, personal arrangements which are unstable as they have to be renegotiated at a time when the balance of power is shifting.

Notes

1 Press release by the government of Zamfara state, in *Hotline* (Kaduna), 3 June 2000: 24.

2 According to Guichaoua (2006: 8) who studied OPC vigilantism in Oyo state, these figures are exaggerated.

3 Yoruba academic historians have accepted the historicity of Oduduwa (or Oodua): he is seen as the first Yoruba king who ruled about a thousand years ago and whose sons became kings of other Yoruba kingdoms (Falola 2006: 34).

4 Cf. Kirsch & Grätz, this volume.

5 For a detailed comparison of militias and vigilantes in Nigeria, including groups in Igboland and the Niger Delta, see Harnischfeger (2008b).

6 Guidelines for Hisba in Zamfara state, cited in Adamu (2008: 143).

7 The Shari'a penal code of Zamfara state, which was adopted with minor modifications in most other states that have adopted Shari'a, rules: 'Whoever ... takes part in the worship or invocation of any juju ... shall be punished with death' (Zamfara State of Nigeria 2000: Section 406). The term *juju* is given a broad definition that in fact covers all sorts of African religious practices: '"juju" includes the worship or invocation of any object or being other than Allah" (*ibid.*: Section 405).

8 Nigeria's constitution of 1999 gives official recognition to the popular distinction between 'indigenes' and 'non-indigenes'. Members of ethnic groups that 'belong' to a certain state or local government area enjoy prerogatives in their home area. Such groups are entitled to pass laws which discriminate against 'non-indigenes' when filling administrative positions, granting scholarships and providing free schooling, or allocating housing and agricultural land (cf. Bach 1997: 337–42).

9 *Newswatch* (Lagos), 30 November 1998: 11.

10 *Africa Today* (London), February 2000: 25.

11 *Tell* (Lagos), 31 January 2000: 19.

12 *Tell* (Lagos), 13 December 1999: 19.

13 *Tell* (Lagos), 13 December 1999: 15; see also Human Rights Watch (2003: 14–16).

14 *The Source* (Lagos), 30 October 2000: 11.

15 *Newswatch* (Lagos), 30 October 2000: 22; Human Rights Watch (2003: 16–18).

16 *The News* (Lagos), 31 January 2000: 19.

17 *Vanguard* (Lagos), 31 March 2002: 21; *Financial Times* (London), 23–24 June 2001; see also Human Rights Watch (2003: 49).

18 *Newswatch* (Lagos), 6 November 2000: 23.

19 *Tell* (Lagos), 31 January 2000: 16, 17, 19; *Newswatch* (Lagos), 6 November 2000: 21, 23; cf. Guichaoua (2007: 100).

20 *The News* (Lagos), 13 November 2000: 23.

21 *Tell* (Lagos), 7 August 2000: 33; *Newswatch* (Lagos), 6 November 2000: 23. According to Dr Fasehun, Soyinka was a member of the OPC's 'intellectual vanguard' (Adekson 2004: 112).

22 *The News* (Lagos), 4 December 2000: 15.

23 *The News* (Lagos), 15 May 2000: 18, 20.

24 At the height of its war on criminals the OPC claimed to be keeping 2,000 suspects in detention (*The News* [Lagos], 13 November 2000: 23). According to Adebanwi (2005: 360), 'extra-judicial killings of suspected armed robbers became the rule'. A photograph in *The News* (10 September 2001: 38, 41) showed OPC activists nailing a suspected robber to a cross. A detailed description of OPC methods is contained in Human Rights Watch (2003: 10–35).

25 *Nigerian Tribune* (Ibadan), 9 August 2001.

26 *Guardian* (Lagos), 1 January 2006: 37.

27 *The Punch* (Lagos), 4 November 2005: 16.
28 Another explanation was provided by an OPC activist interviewed by Guichaoua (2006: 12): when the military killed about 300 OPC members in Mushin, a suburb of Lagos, 'we went back to recruit all sorts of people, area boys (street boys) and any kind of person that was interested'.
29 *Nigerian Tribune* (Ibadan), 1 December 2005.
30 Islamic and Christian pieties have become such important elements of daily life that they cannot be eclipsed by a revival of African roots, but must be integrated into Yoruba nationalism. The OPC has founded units of Christian and Islamic 'Prayer Warriors' with the sole aim of praying for Yoruba self-determination. A lot of social engineering is employed to neutralise the religious divide. Adams, a practising Muslim, has also a Christian prayer-room in his home where he and his family observe night vigils (Adebanwi 2005: 352–4).
31 Governor Bola Tinubu, cited in *Tell* (Lagos), 23 September 2002: 46.
32 *Tell* (Lagos), 17 April 2000: 48.
    Hotline (Kaduna), 9 April 2000: 37.
33 *Hotline* (Kaduna), 16 April 2000: 30.
34 In Lagos, where an equal number of Muslims and Christians coexist, clashes over Shari'a could end up being far more destructive than in the cities of northern Nigeria: 'I can see the blood flowing in southern and northern Sudan being chickenfeed, compared to what will happen in this country' (Brigadier Benjamin Adekunle, in *Tell* [Lagos], 27 March 2000: 17).
35 Among Muslims in the north, the extent to which their states shall be Islamised is a matter of dispute. However, there is little argument among them regarding the status of settlers from the south. Even Shehu Sani, leader of the Civil Rights Congress in Kaduna, told me: 'Igbo have no right to meddle into politics. They are here as traders'.
36 Ahmed Sani, governor of Zamfara state, cited in *Tell* (Lagos), 8 September 2003: 39; see also Mazrui (2001: 2, 4, 8).
37 In the words of Last: 'La culture domestique "traditionelle" que j'ai connue il y a trente ans n'existe plus' (2000: 148).
38 *Tell* (Lagos), 10 April 2000: 25.
39 Emir of Gwandu, *The News*, 24 April 2000: 18. The Sharia Penal Code of Zamfara state, on the basis of which state-controlled Hisba operate, explicitly criminalises any behaviour that is interdicted in the holy texts of Islam: 'Any act or omission which is not specifically mentioned in this Sharia Penal Code but is otherwise declared to be an offence under the Qur'an, Sunnah and Ijtihad of the Maliki school ... shall be punishable: a) With imprisonment for a term which may extend to 5 years, or b) With caning, or c) With fine which may extend to N 5,000.00' (Zamfara State of Nigeria 2000: Section 92).
40 See also *Tell* (Lagos), 16 February 2004: 24.
41 Murray Last was told that 'anti-*hisba* gangs are available for hire' (Last 2008: 152).
42 The Hisba in Zamfara was expected to enforce a 'ban on gossiping, deceit, and distrust' (Maier 2000: 190).
43 *Tell* (Lagos), 27 December 1999: 10.
44 At least 60 thieves were sentenced to amputation, but in only three cases was this sentence known to have been carried out (Human Rights Watch 2004: 36–37). Without brutal punishments Shari'a did not serve as an effective deterrent against violent crime. Governor Ahmed Sani of Zamfara had to admit that his state was plagued by a 'crime wave', although he blamed 'some bad elements from outside the state' for it (*Tell* [Lagos], 16 September 2002: 68).
45 *Tell* (Lagos), 30 May 2005: 66–67.
46 *Tell* (Lagos), 26 April 2004: 22–26; *Newswatch* (Lagos), 11 October 2004: 22–25.
47 The tendency to try to police morality and everyday life is most pronounced in

religious forms of policing, but it is not absent in the case of ethnic vigilantes. An OPC public relations officer in Oyo state announced: 'By January, there will be a code of dressing for Yoruba people whether they agree or not' (*Nigerian Tribune* (Ibadan), 1 December 2005: 44).

48 Claude Ake, in *The News* (Lagos), 25 November 1996, quoted in Douglas & Ola (2003: 41).
49 Campaign for Democracy, 1998, in Ibrahim (2002: 203); see also Adekson (2004: 66), Ejobowah (2000: 31).
50 *Tell* (Lagos), 17 April 2006: 35.

References

Abrahams, Ray 2007 'Some thoughts in the comparative study of vigilantism' in Pratten & Sen 2007: 407–30

Abrahamsen, Rita & Williams, Michael C. 2007 'Introduction: The privatisation and globalisation of security in Africa' *International Relations* 21, 2, 131–41

Adamu, Fatima L. 2008 'Gender, Hisba and the enforcement of morality in northern Nigeria' *Africa* 78, 1, 136–52

Adebanwi, Wale 2005 'The carpenter's revolt: Youth, violence and the reinvention of culture in Nigeria' *Journal of Modern African Studies* 43, 3, 339–65

Adekson, Adedayo Oluwakayode 2004 *The 'Civil Society' Problematique: Deconstructing Civility and Southern Nigeria's Ethnic Radicalization* (New York/London: Routledge)

Ado-Kurawa, Ibrahim 2000 *Shari'ah and the Press in Nigeria: Islam versus Western Christian Civilization* (Kano: Kurawa Holdings)

Agbu, Osita 2004 *Ethnic Militias and the Threat to Democracy in Post-Transition Nigeria* (Uppsala: Nordiska Afrikainstitutet)

Aka, Philip C. 2005 'The need for an effective policy of ethnic reconciliation' in Udogu, E. Ike (ed.) 2005 *Nigeria in the Twenty-First Century: Strategies for Political Stability and Peaceful Coexistence* (Trenton NJ/Asmara: Africa World Press): 41–67

Akinyele, R. T. 2001 'Ethnic militancy and national stability in Nigeria: A case study of the Oodua People's Congress' *African Affairs* 100: 623–40

Albert, Isaac Olawale 2001 [1999] 'Ethnic and religious conflicts in Kano' in Otite, Onigu & Albert, Isaac Olawale (eds) 2001 [1999] *Community Conflicts in Nigeria: Management, Resolution and Transformation* (Ibadan: Spectrum Books): 274–309

Alli, Warisu O. 2005 'Commentary [to Abdulkader Tayob, *The Demand for Shari'ah in African Democratisation Processes*]' in Ostien, Philip *et al.* (eds) 2005 *Comparative Perspectives on Shari'ah in Nigeria* (Ibadan: Spectrum): 57–66

An-Na'im, Abdullahi Ahmed 1990 *Toward an Islamic Reformation: Civil Liberties, Human Rights, and International Law* (New York: Syracuse University Press)

Babawale, Tunde (ed.) 2003 *Urban Violence, Ethnic Militias and the Challenge of Democratic Consolidation in Nigeria* (Lagos: Malthouse)

Bach, Daniel 1997 'Indigeneity, ethnicity, and federalism' in Diamond, Larry; Kirk-Greene, Anthony & Oyediran, Oyeleye (eds) 1997 *Transition without End: Nigerian Politics and Civil Society under Babangida* (Boulder CO/London: Lynne Rienner): 333–49

Baker, Bruce 2008 *Multi-Choice Policing in Africa* (Uppsala: Nordiska Afrikainstitutet)

Casey, Conerly 2007 '"Policing" through violence: Fear, vigilantism, and the politics of Islam in northern Nigeria' in Pratten & Sen 2007: 90–121

Dibua, J. I. 2005 'Citizenship and resource control in Nigeria: The case of minority communities in the Niger Delta' *Afrika Spectrum* 39, 1, 5–28

Douglas, Oronto & Ola, Doifie 2003 'Nourishing democracy, nurturing diversity: Ethnic militancy as resistance politics in Nigeria' in Babawale 2003: 41–47

Economist Intelligence Unit 2005 *Country Profile 2005: Nigeria* (London: EIU)

Ejobowah, John Boye 2000 'Who owns the oil? The politics of ethnicity in the Niger Delta of Nigeria' *Africa Today* 47, 1, 29–47

Falola, Toyin 2006 'The Yoruba nation' in Falola, Toyin & Genova, Ann (eds) 2006 *Yoruba Identity and Power Politics* (Rochester NY: University of Rochester Press): 29–48

Faseun, Fredrick [Fasehun, Frederick] 2002 *National Conference: Need to Make Nigeria a Political Reality* (Lagos: Sovereign National Conference). Available online at: <www.ngex.com/snc/editorials/ fasheun020602.htm> (last accessed 31 August 2008)

Fourchard, Laurent 2008 'A new name for an old practice: Vigilantes in south-western Nigeria' *Africa* 78, 1, 16–40

Fwatshak, Sati U. 2003 'Shari'a enforcement in northern Nigeria: The *Hisba* and the publics'. Paper presented at conference: The Sharia Debate and the Shaping of Muslim and Christian Identities in Northern Nigeria, University of Bayreuth, Germany, 11–12 July

Gombe State 2000 'Report of the Committee to Consider the Implications of the Introduction of Sharia Legal Code on Christians and Other Non-Muslims in Gombe State. Vol. 1: Findings, observations and recommendations' Unpublished document, Gombe State

Guichaoua, Yvan 2006 *The Making of an Ethnic Militia: The Oodua People's Congress in Nigeria* (*CRISE Working Papers* 26). Available online at: <www.crise.ox.ac.uk/pubs/working paper26.pdf> (last accessed 8 March 2008)

—— 2007 'Les mutations d'une milice ethnique sous le régime civil d'Olusegun Obasanjo' *Politique africaine* 106: 92–109

Gwarzo, Tahir Haliru 2003 'Activities of Islamic civic associations in the northwest of Nigeria: With particular reference to Kano State' *Afrika Spectrum* 38, 3, 289–318

Hansen, Thomas Blom & Stepputat, Finn 2005 'Introduction' in Hansen, Thomas Blom & Stepputat, Finn (eds) 2005 *Sovereign Bodies: Citizens, Migrants, and States in the Postcolonial World* (Princeton NJ/Oxford: Princeton University Press): 1–36

Harnischfeger, Johannes 2004 'Sharia and control over territory: Conflicts between "settlers" and "indigenes" in Nigeria' *African Affairs* 103, 431–52

—— 2008a *Democratisation and Islamic Law: The Sharia Conflict in Nigeria* (Frankfurt: Campus)

—— 2008b '"Balance of terror": Rival militias and vigilantes in Nigeria' *Afrikanistik Online* 1756. Available online at: <www.afrikanistik-online.de/archiv/2008/1756/> (last accessed 31 August 2010)

Higazi, Adam 2008 'Social mobilization and collective violence: Vigilantes and militias in the lowlands of Plateau State, central Nigeria' *Africa* 78, 1, 107–35

Hills, Alice 2000 *Policing Africa: Internal Security and the Limits of Liberalization* (Boulder CO/London: Lynne Rienner)

Human Rights Watch 2003 *The O'odua People's Congress: Fighting Violence with Violence* (New York: Human Rights Watch). Available online at: <www.hrw.org/reports/2003/ nigeria0203/ Nigeria0203.pdf> (last accessed 12 October 2005)

—— 2004 'Political *Shari'a?' Human Rights and Islamic Law in Northern Nigeria* 16, 9 (A), September. Available online at: <www.hrw.org/english/docs/2004/09/21/nigeri 9364_txt.htm> (last accessed 18 May 2005)

Ibrahim, Jibrin 2002 'The National Conference and the challenge of developing democratic federalism in Nigeria' in Igbuzor, Otive & Bamidele, Ololade (eds) 2002 *Contentious Issues in the Review of the 1999 Constitution* (Lagos: Citizens' Forum for Constitution Reform): 159–222

Ikelegbe, Austine 2005 'State, ethnic militias, and conflict in Nigeria' *Canadian Journal of African Studies* 39, 3, 490–516

Jinadu, L. Adele 2004 'Explaining and managing ethnic conflict in Africa: Towards a cultural theory of democracy' *African Journal of Political Science* 9, 1, 1–26

Kukah, Matthew 2002 *Democracy and Civil Society in Nigeria* (Ibadan: Spectrum)

Last, Murray 2000 'La charia dans le nord-Nigeria' *Politique Africaine* 79: 141–52

—— 2008 'The search for security in Muslim northern Nigeria' *Africa* 78, 1, 41–63

Maier, Karl 2000 *This House Has Fallen: Midnight in Nigeria* (New York: Public Affairs)

Mazrui, Ali A. 2001 'Shariacracy and federal models in the era of globalization: Nigeria in comparative perspective'. Paper presented at conference: Restoration of Shariah in Nigeria: Challenges and Benefits, sponsored by Nigeria Muslim Forum, London, 14 April. Available online at: <www.shariah2001.nmnonline.net/mazrui paper.htm> (last accessed 30 April 2004)

Meek, C. K. 1931 *A Sudanese Kingdom: An Ethnographical Study of the Jukun-Speaking Peoples of Nigeria* (London: Kegan Paul)

Miles, William F. S. 2003 'Shari'a as de-Africanization: Evidence from Hausaland' *Africa Today* 50, 1, 51–75

Nolte, Insa 2004 'Identity and violence: The politics of youth in Ijebu-Remo, Nigeria' *Journal of Modern African Studies* 42, 1, 61–89

—— 2007 'Ethnic vigilantes and the state: The Oodua People's Congress in south-western Nigeria' *International Relations* 21, 2, 217–35

—— 2008 '"Without women, nothing can succeed": Yoruba women in the Oodua People's Congress (OPC), Nigeria' *Africa* 78, 1, 84–106

Olaniyi, Rasheed 2005 *Community Vigilantes in Metropolitan Kano, 1985–2005* (Ibadan: IFRA)

Olukotun, Ayo 2003 'Ethnic militias and a democracy: A media perspective' in Babawale 2003: 58–70

Opata, Damian U. 2004 'Ethnics, homelands, and different types of national narrative' in Onuoha, Jonah I. & Okpoko, Pat Uche (eds) 2004 *Ethnic Nationalism and Democratic Consolidation: Perspectives from Nigeria and the United States of America* (Nsukka: Great AP Express Publishers): 47–57

Osaghae, Eghosa E. 2005 'State, constitutionalism, and the management of ethnicity in Africa; *African and Asian Studies* 4, 1–2, 83–105

Paden, John N. 2005 *Muslim Civic Cultures and Conflict Resolution: The Challenge of Democratic Federalism in Nigeria* (Washington DC: Brookings Institution Press)

Peel, J. D. Y. 2000 *Religious Encounter and the Making of the Yoruba* (Bloomington IN/ Indianapolis IN: Indiana University Press)

Peters, Ruud 2003 *Islamic Criminal Law in Nigeria* (Ibadan: Spectrum)

Pratten, David 2008 'The politics of protection: Perspectives on vigilantism in Nigeria' *Africa* 78, 1, 1–15

Pratten, David & Sen, Atreyee (eds) 2007 *Global Vigilantes: Perspectives on Justice and Violence* (London: Hurst & Co.)

Reno, William 2003 'Gier gegen Groll: Nigeria' in Ruf, Werner (ed.) 2003 *Politische Ökonomie der Gewalt: Staatszerfall und die Privatisierung von Gewalt und Krieg* (Opladen: Leske & Budrich): 291–8

Reynolds, Jonathan T. 1997 'The politics of history: The legacy of the Sokoto caliphate in Nigeria' in Lovejoy, Paul E. & Williams, Pat Ama Tokunbo (eds) 1997 *Displacement and the Politics of Violence in Nigeria* (Leiden/New York/Cologne: Brill): 50–65

Sklar, Richard L. 2004 'Unity or regionalism: The nationalities question' in Rotberg, Robert I. (ed.) 2004 *Crafting the New Nigeria: Confronting the Challenges* (Boulder CO/ London: Lynne Rienner): 39–59

Sulaiman, Ibraheem 1986 'Islam and secularism in Nigeria: An encounter of two civilisations' *Impact International* 24 Oct–13 Nov: 11–12

Tabiu, Muhammed 2001 'Sharia, federalism and Nigerian Constitution'. Paper presented at conference: 'Restoration of Shariah in Nigeria: Challenges and Benefits', sponsored by Nigeria Muslim Forum, London, April 14. Available online at: <www.shariah 2001.nmnonline.net/tabiu paper.htm> (last accessed 30 April 2004)

Ukiwo, Ukoha 2003 'Politics, ethno-religious conflicts and democratic consolidation in Nigeria' *Journal of Modern African Studies* 41, 1, 115–38

Yoruba Agenda, The 2005 Produced by Ad-hoc Planning Committee [no place]

Young, Crawford 2007 'Nation, ethnicity, and citizenship: Dilemmas of democracy and civil order in Africa' in Dorman, Sara; Hammett, Daniel & Nugent, Paul (eds) 2007 *Making Nations, Creating Strangers: States and Citizenship in Africa* (Leiden/Boston: Brill): 241–64

Zamfara State of Nigeria 2000 *Gazette. No. 1, 15 June, 2000. Vol. 3: Law No. 10. Shariah Penal Code Law* (Gusau: Ministry of Justice, Zamfara State)

3

Dévi & his Men
The Rise & Fall of a Vigilante Movement in Benin

TILO GRÄTZ

Introduction

Upon arriving at the small village of Loko-Atoui, not far from the town of Dogba in southern Benin, the visitor notices a large statue erected by the villagers in the middle of the settlement, representing a combatant, complete with cartridge belts, depicted partly as a kind of Rambo, partly as an African hunter. The monument depicts 'Colonel Dévi', a once-famous vigilante leader and still a local hero. When asked about him, villagers are usually eager to talk at length about his deeds and compete with each other in praising him. The man himself actually lives opposite the statue, in the only two-storey building in the village, which is large enough to house himself and various wives and children; several of his cars are parked at the entrance. In person, Dévi appears quite self-confident and relaxed; it is difficult to imagine that he was once notorious throughout southern Benin. He still justifies his former activities, even though officially he has permanently renounced his vigilante career. He seems a proud but angry old man who points out that crime rates in the region are once again rising, and that decisive action of some kind is needed to combat them.

The following account follows up on the suggestion that vigilantism should be studied empirically as a form of practice (Pratten & Sen 2007).[1] It explores the activities of a vigilante group in southern Benin founded in 1999 by Dévi Zinsou Ehoun. Born on 11 June 1956, Dévi was a former peasant and carpenter who occasionally worked at the nearby textile enterprise in Dogba. He would come to call himself 'Colonel Civil Dévi'. Groups like this have arisen in sub-Saharan Africa at various times, but have recently gained renewed attention within the field of African studies (Buur & Jensen 2004; Pratten 2008) and beyond (Pratten & Sen 2007). Whether or not the number of such groups has actually grown, many public commentators attribute their emergence to a general 'failure of the central state' and its weakness in terms of ability to guarantee order and

1   *Statue of Colonel Dévi, Loko-Atoui village, Bénin* (courtesy of Jascha Derr)

security, so that vigilante groups 'fill a gap'. However, from the ensuing scholarly debate a broad consensus has emerged that the rise of vigilantes, whatever their scope of action and shape, can to a certain degree be seen as an *additional* mode of policing – a not-unusual constituent of African political landscapes today, with their fragmented, multi-centred figurations of power and modes of political action from below (Bayart 1991; Bayart *et al.* 1992; Chabal & Daloz 1998; Von Trotha 2000; Mbembe 2001). As is argued in the introduction to this volume, in predominantly diffuse conditions of statehood, local powers such as those discussed in the present volume have always been able to pursue their own agendas, with different degrees of integration into the colonial and postcolonial state. This indicates that most vigilante groups do not always act in opposition to the state or local polities but are, in terms of actors and strategies, entangled with the latter at various levels.

My case study from southern Benin supports the above arguments and, like the contributions to this volume by Johannes Harnischfeger and by Sten Hagberg and Syna Ouattara, enhances the study of vigilante groups by using a *processual* approach. I argue that, even though Dévi's group started by adopting a position manifestly in opposition to official legal institutions, at least regionally, many of the group's strategies and modes of actions were in part 'borrowed' from various official institutions and combined with local inventories of political culture and organisation. Thus, to understand how this group was actually able to establish an effective crime-fighting regime, we have to take into consideration local history and political culture, as well as follow the changing modes of organisation of the group and the discursive strategies it used to gain wider acceptance.

The group led by Colonel Dévi originated between 1999 and 2001 and came to an end (at least for the moment) in January 2002, with the arrest of its leader by the military. In the following discussion I will first describe the growth of the group as a local movement and its social basis and main strategies. I will then discuss the conditions underlying the group's success and later failure, as well as its significance in the context of political changes within the country. As I will explain below, the group emerged as a response to a situation of insecurity and public concern about rising crime rates in the region, and it acquired its legitimacy mainly from an expressed wish on the part of the population to end this situation. I argue that the success and later failure of the group depended not only on the group's effective modes of organisation, but also – and in fact mainly – on the changing relationship between it and the institutions of the central state. Thus, in this respect, the story is not a simple one of a movement replacing the state or working against its institutions; rather, the movement only became a problem for the central state authorities at a particular point in time, namely at the time when the group markedly changed its modes of action and organisational forms, which had the effect of threatening government sovereignty and presenting the group as a danger to public life and local development.

The rise of Dévi's group

In 1999 Dévi formed a group of vigilantes in a region of south-western Benin located between the localities of Lokossa, Dogba and Aplahoué (that is, within the administrative departments of Mono and Couffo). The vigilantes proclaimed a struggle against the growing insecurity and criminality in that region.

According to various reports and witnesses, in 1998 and 1999 two large, armed criminal gangs, plus several smaller ones, were operating throughout the region. They were said to proceed with extraordinary brutality – robbing, raping women and killing people in cruel ways. The criminals began their activities with night attacks on long-distance motorcycle taxis – generally called *zémidjan* – using road blocks set up at localities some way distant from settlements. The drivers of local taxis were among those most badly affected by growing insecurity. Drivers were often ambushed while travelling to and fro between villages; their vehicles would be stolen and many of them were killed so that there would be no witnesses. Such activities caused *zémidjan* and drivers of small lorries to terminate their services at sundown, so market days would have to finish earlier than usual. The raiders then began operating during the day as well – attacking market traders and other individuals, especially those using motor taxis to travel to the markets; they also attacked trading posts in neighbouring Togo. Next they started to intrude into private homesteads, appropriating any object of value. There are various reports about the gangs' cruelty and lack of scruples:

> The robbers came at any time, stealing cars, motorcycles and all kinds of goods, even in front of the *gendarmerie* outpost. The victims were traders, drivers, but also anyone thought to possess something valuable. Often they simply shot their victims dead or abused them seriously. They even went as far as announcing their arrival by fixing a brief notice to your door, saying that they would arrive at night and that you had to put all your belongings at their disposal and leave, otherwise they would kill you. Repeatedly they broke into a house, and as well as robbing they abused the women in the presence of their husbands, who were often castrated if not beaten to death (Antoine, Lokossa, February 2007; this and all other translations by the author).

Local *gendarmerie* and police were not able to counter these criminal activities and were accused of being ineffective, fearful and having no real counter-strategies.[2] Bandits would even attack policemen, especially any who tried to arrest them. The result of all this was general panic in the region, with economic and social life being very much affected. Market activities decreased and public life deteriorated, especially after sundown. Local authorities, village heads, elders, and wealthy traders like

Dévi Zinsou Ehoun started to think about how they might deal with the situation.

At a certain point in time Dévi started to organise a group of youths (they were always referred to as 'Dévi's men'; the group never had any formal title) who were entrusted with the role of watchmen to protect people in Dévi's home village of Loko-Atoui from robberies at night.[3] In 1999 Dévi's group was estimated to number 500 to 1000 individuals (Matchoudo 1999: 3), most being young peasants or craftsmen from the Adja (Aja) ethnic group. The group had an effective internal organisation, with decentralised subunits and a network of informers. It resembled a mixture of para-military group and assembly of local, self-organised watchmen. The group was organised along the lines of sectarian or secret societies, with members being recruited less on the basis of territory than according to their personal capacities. Thus, while local units saw themselves as part of a larger regional movement, the movement featured elements of an (imagined) 'community' in times of crisis – a process of group integration that takes criminality as its starting point (Paulenz 2002: 2).

Soon afterwards, similar groups emerged in neighbouring villages close to the town of Dogba; at the time of writing many of these groups are still operating. Involvement in the groups is theoretically voluntary, but in practice every young man over the age of 16 years is expected to become a member. Over time, these groups grew into a veritable movement. Dévi, often also referred to as *commandant*, employed a kind of private secretary and installed so-called *cellules* in each village and urban quarter as standing watch groups. He established his headquarters in Atoui-Ehounhoué, near Djakotomey. The members of these subunits had to report all activities of suspected bandits to Dévi and, if possible, arrest the latter whenever they were caught in the act. Over time Dévi found himself able to rely more and more on a growing network of informers and collaborators because his group increasingly gained support from the wider population, as well as from village heads and especially the wealthier traders, who largely financed provision of transport facilities and equipment (including arms) for the group.

Dévi's men succeeded in punishing some of the thieves. After engaging in real fighting in the process of tracking thieves to their shelters in the bush, the vigilantes effectively pushed the gangs out of the region. It was said that Dévi was invincible – having sought the assistance of local healers and Vodun priests, and therefore using occult powers – so he was thought to be able to capture suspects without himself being injured or even touched. Dévi's notoriety was also partly a product of the media, especially the press, which benefited from considerable freedom during that period.

In mid-1999 Dévi's group organised a series of rallies throughout the region: huge public meetings at which Dévi would proclaim his 'campaign against crime'.[4] The rallies provided probably the most obvious means for Dévi to express his determination, serving as a show of force to intimidate his rivals and increase his reputation. The rallies were a blend of various kinds of public performance: a typical *tournée* by government agents, ministers or other politicians who would visit a region once a year, staged as a series of celebrations; through its *caractère triomphale*, a staging typical of election campaigns, with candidates crossing the region with a caravan of supporters and helpers; and finally, a kind of crusade typical of that of the Pentecostal evangelists (especially from Ghana and Nigeria) who cross West Africa from time to time. People throughout the region remember these events today and talk about the enthusiasm Dévi was able to generate among the masses – the brilliance of his words 'touching the hearts of the locals'. An important element of his discourse was an appeal for them to rely on local forces of their own, not only in the sense of actions, but also spiritually.

One such rally was covered by various Beninese newspapers which ran photographs and positive statements from a range of local inhabitants and was followed by a heated public debate.[5] The tone of newspaper articles oscillated between consternation, condemnation and thrilling, sensation-seeking accounts.[6] Polemical discussions during a call-in show were also triggered by Cotonou private radio station Golfe FM, on 10 October 1999 (Gandaho 1999b), as well as by photographs in the media showing *les fétiches* – that is, the divinities, shrines and altars for sacrifice which Dévi was said to be able to command in order to detect criminals and make himself invulnerable. *Le Matinal* (1999b: 5) pictured Dévi being enthusiastically welcomed and receiving donations from various people on a visit to a popular market in Dogba – a burgeoning town located at a trading crossroads that was often hit by burglars and other thieves. The most controversial yet impressive media contribution came in October 1999 after two journalists, Aubin Towanou and Anicet Oké (1999), visited Dévi's headquarters at his invitation and interviewed him.[7]

The group's major strategies

Dévi's group had been initially set up as a self-defence organisation, but later it and its subunits began to take the initiative in imposing extralegal justice, using self-made small arms in action against criminals and passing judgements on them throughout the region. The vigilantes organised regular patrols and raids, set up watches, established road blocks, encouraged local people to report any suspicious movements and organised punitive assemblies.

Many suspects were brought to Dévi's homestead in Loko-Atoui, or he himself was driven to the scene of crime together with close associates; he would then pass judgment on the alleged bandits. If the suspects were found guilty of robbery or rape, they were usually tortured and put to death.[8] In other cases, such as minor disputes, they were made to pay fines and then ostracised. In other instances suspected thieves were not tried at all but simply pinned down and immediately killed by Dévi's local followers, in most cases with the help of other youths in the locality. The 'habitual' manner of summary public execution 'in the name of Dévi' was usually to burn the suspects alive by 'necklacing' (throwing a tyre over the victim's neck, pouring petrol or other fuel over him or her and setting him or her alight). Such killings would be carried out by furious mobs (*vifs-brûleurs*) in public, usually accompanied by the acclamation of crowds of spectators.

It is estimated that Dévi's men killed about 100 people in this way (Matchoudo 1999: 3). With regard to these *ad hoc* killings of suspects, the activities of Dévi's group in southern Benin, like those of the Bakassi Boys in Nigeria (Baker 2002) or the Young Lions in South Africa (Buur 2006), differed considerably from those cases where supposed criminals are finally handed over to the official authorities (for example, as by the Annang vigilantes in south-eastern Nigeria; see Pratten, this volume). Broadly speaking, Dévi's activities exhibited many of the typical elements of vigilante police and even militia activity, but also of contemporary mob justice. However, in other respects the group (at least performatively) borrowed practices from official institutions. For example, according to my informants tribunals usually began just as 'normal' courtroom trials do, by calling on everyone present to stand when the judges enter, calling on the accused to give his or her name, and so on.

The reaction of the central state and the group's formal dissolution in 2002

Initially, Colonel Dévi and his men operated on the margins of the attention of the central state. All the same, off the record Dévi's actions were welcomed by many policemen and gendarmes because this meant that he was doing the state's 'dirty work' for them.

By the end of 2001 the status of Dévi and his men gradually changed as they began to exclude the police from the region and to establish a kind of territorial supremacy. This process was accompanied by increasing arbitrariness in Dévi's actions. Even minor infractions were now being addressed. Furthermore, many people throughout the region started to act 'in the name of Dévi' – that is, to capture and torture alleged thieves, apparently without his express approval. Matters got more and more out of control, including perpetration of punishment on people who were plainly innocent, without any serious inquiry. People began to fear being falsely accused of misdemeanours by envious neighbours or of being penalised for minor offences such as transgressions of the highway code. In various places youths at road blocks started to demand 'contributions', just as some members of the local *cellules* did for their 'services'.

These developments appear to indicate that the group had transformed itself into a mafia-like organisation that refused to collaborate in any way with local representatives of the state security forces. From this moment on the vigilantes were challenging the central state authorities with regard not only to the state's monopoly on violence, but also its endeavour to control public services, official and unofficial 'taxation', and roads.

The incident that ultimately changed the *de facto* attitude of *laissez-faire* on the part of the Ministry of Interior was an accusation of witchcraft. According to media reports, Dévi's men brought two women alleged to be 'sorcerers' to his home, where they were tortured and later died. The event caused resentment throughout the population; it apparently constituted a major transgression of a tacit accord *not* to interfere in cases of alleged witchcraft. After this event Dévi's reputation was weakened, and the parents of the dead women filed a murder charge against him. He formally denied the allegations; however, he also made sure that when a government commission came to investigate, the officials were chased out of the region by his men.

In January 2002 government forces, including soldiers and police, moved into the area in a joint action and arrested many of the group, including Dévi. These individuals were taken to a remote prison to avoid popular unrest. Dévi was released from jail on bail in August 2003, although still subject to a lawsuit pending before the high court. Officially he promised not to start such activities again, as did the members of the core group. Nevertheless, today Dévi is still respected, and for many is a hero, at least at the local level.

Dévi's case in the wider Beninese context

To understand the rise of Dévi and his men more fully, one must take into consideration the political culture in Benin at national level that prevailed at the time. At the time, debates on the decentralisation of administration were very much at the forefront of the public agenda. Such policies were officially conceptualised as heralding the completion of the so-called democratic renewal (*renouveau démocratique*) of the country after 1990, which was also promoted by foreign aid donors (Raynal 1991; Allen 1992; Ahanhanzo-Glélé 1993; Dossou 1993; Nwajiaku 1994; Bierschenk *et al.* 2003). A national conference had set the conditions for the implementation of a new constitution, the transition to a multi-party system, free elections on all levels and the establishment of formal democratic institutions including a constitutional court. In addition, the country had seen a shift towards greater freedom of expression and the liberalisation of the economy.

However, many of the new democratic institutions proved to be nothing more than a façade (Kohnert 1996; Mayrargue 1999). The state's services did work, somehow, but were often inaccessible to many ordinary citizens. Especially at the local level of public administration, basic problems of governance and of corruption on the part of state agents were clearly evident (Bako-Arifari 1995; Bierschenk 2000; Bierschenk & Olivier de Sardan 2003, Bierschenk *et al.* 1998; Grätz 2006; Banégas 1998; Sommer 2001). Confidence in state agencies such as the police and *gendarmerie* is generally low (Alber & Sommer 1999, Alber 2001). In this regard, the recent establishment of partly autonomous municipalities at regional level has changed the relationship between the administration and the administered only to some extent. However, enhanced political and economic openness within the country also led to an influx of weapons, the proliferation of armed gangs and a general rise in criminality; the government was for long periods ill-prepared to take effective action against this.

The topic of insecurity had been dominating public debates and the press since the late 1990s. All this surely contributed to creating the climate conducive to the emergence of Dévi. State institutions in various sectors generally performed badly, but it was the legal sector that most lacked credibility (cf. Pognon 1996; Bierschenk 2004). Since the arrival of President Boni Yayi in 2006 (Mayrargue 2006; Stroh & Never 2006), the state has been trying to regain more effective control of the public realm, though with limited success so far. Yet, recent developments such as those in Djougou[9] reveal continued popular distrust with the state and its agents, pointing to the still-persistent inadequacies of the official legal system. Thus a future resurgence of groups similar to that mounted by Dévi cannot be ruled out.[10]

In this context, Dévi's success can be understood as a particular discursive as well as pragmatic reaction to these debates on decentralisation and devolution of central government in Benin. At the time of Dévi's rise, the government's implementation of these policies was still patchy, despite being a much-discussed issue in public life. All the changes were (and are) planned to be implemented after rounds of negotiations within the political class, and mainly imposed from above. It can therefore be argued that local actors interpreted the discourse of decentralisation according to their own agendas, against the background of perceived local needs – in this case, security. This became part of a rhetoric of self-empowerment – a kind of popular appropriation of political discourses from below (see also Blundo & Mongbo 1999). As Dévi's various public statements demonstrate, he saw himself as a regionally legitimate leader, anticipating in his own way the devolution of policing competencies as well. From his own perspective the movement could even have been recognised by the state and its activities integrated into official policies. Thus, the discourse of decentralisation gave Dévi self-legitimising strategies.

Variants of legitimacy

Broadly speaking, there were three crucial dimensions to the local discourse that gave a certain legitimacy to Dévi's group: first, the narratives referring to actions by criminals in conjunction with accounts of the failures of state agents; second, political predictability; and third, references to local and/or ethnic traditions, Dévi's personality, and religion. In the following I will deal mainly with the third dimension, though prefacing this with a few remarks on the other dimensions.

With regard to the first dimension, today people still continually refer to the atrocities committed by gangs and the horror they caused. Such violence perpetrated by criminals seemed to justify enacting a similar degree of violence upon the perpetrators once they had been caught, as well as providing a general justification for killings and tortures.

Regarding the second dimension, it should be noted that a pivotal aspect of Dévi's popular legitimacy is predictability. In Benin, official policies have been and still are often followed inconsistently. Sometimes the state attempts to overlook local initiatives, and it does not always control informal economic networks. At other times, however, government agencies conceive of the same local initiatives as problematic and start campaigning to change the situation, either by initiating dialogues with those concerned or simply by recourse to violent action.[11] Unlike most accounts of the relationship between central states and local communities (for example, Le Roy 1996; Villalón 1998; Boone 1998; Huxtable 1998; Englebert 2000; Comaroff & Comaroff 2006), the alternating engagement or non-engagement by the state in Benin can be conceived of as a sort of pendulum swinging between phases of attention to regional issues, attempts to integrate or control, and periods of indifference with regard to the periphery (for a similar account of the political history of Burkina Faso see Otayek 1989, Otayek *et al.* 1996). This not only questions generalised ideas about statehood in Africa, but also raises issues about the predictability of governance, for example, as a central concern for local producers and businessmen alike. Against such a background, a power regime that develops locally may gain acceptance, even if this proves disadvantageous for some actors, so long as it is perceived as being predictable to such a degree that people can adapt to it. As soon as it loses this predictability, it may also lose its legitimacy.

In the case at issue, Dévi's regional regime was widely accepted temporarily, in contrast to the local agencies of the state already mentioned which performed variably. Market traders would collect money to pay for the protection offered by Dévi's men only as long as the group's activities were predictably in support of the traders; the latter turned away from Dévi later, after this predictability could no longer be relied upon. Local support for the group weakened when Dévi's men started to kill almost anyone who was presumed to be a thief, and violence became arbitrary. In creating an atmosphere of fear instead of peace and security, Dévi made it easier for the central state to put an end to his activities.

Concerning the third dimension of legitimacy, namely references to local traditions, it should be noted that in southern Benin today a wide variety of non-official security actors are to be found, ranging from private security guards to Vodun temple watches and village brigades. In this respect Dévi's group does not represent anything unique or new. The novelty of his group rather consisted in the *combination* of various discursive elements to produce legitimacy, referring to specific modes of action known from previous periods in the country and also from other regions in West Africa, in which older local vigilante institutions were combined with contemporary political references in a particular way. Dévi could not claim a direct link between his group and any older institution, but did refer to the famous example of the traditional *zangbéto* night-watches. These anonymous custodians and helpers of Vodun spirits are charged with guarding local residents through the night and with driving out both bad spirits and thieves; they would usually appear in large straw costumes, which are still popular in the region. Another, more recent reference of which the local subunits remind one are the *Comités de la Défense de la Révolution* of Benin's Marxist-Leninist period (1972–89) and of the early revolutionary period of the 1970s; the latter consisted of youngsters.

As regards the role of 'ethnic traditions' in sustaining the legitimacy of Dévi's men, many informants told me that before the group emerged, the visibility and collective consciousness of the 'Adja people' were denigrated, even though this ethnic group – which constituted the majority population in the region – was said to have once been more powerful than neighbouring ethnic groups.[12] With the arrival on the scene of Dévi's men, self-pride and self-empowerment were said to have returned. Dwelling on local culture as a discursive resource Dévi referred to a prevalent identity-related regional narrative involving the proud and 'pure Adja' – a once-important but later 'deprived' ethnic group – as well as to elements of autochthony, self-protection and self-empowerment, and to the task of 'doing something for the people of the region'.[13]

The particular way in which Dévi 'did something for the people' added to his legitimacy. Few people in Benin were in principle against the killing of thieves who, as mentioned above, were in fact often despatched by large crowds and in public. This kind of lynching was not something new to the region and still occurs very frequently in Benin, having spread from various other parts of West Africa (Paulenz 1999a).[14] Dévi found it easy to play on this established register of violence against criminals which, in this public staging of rage, retributive satisfaction and horror, represents an impressive performance of the influence, power and popular support he enjoyed.

Of course, all this made sense to people only when viewed against the backdrop of the moral panic and fears of social decay shared by many citizens of Benin into the early 21st century (Paulenz 2002). Paulenz interprets vigilante activities in Benin as a kind of popular action developing in a situation whereby neo-liberal reforms are under way, accompanied by growing economic insecurity, with all this giving rise to spontaneous forms of political action. Paulenz thus joins those scholars who interpret such initiatives as part of a process aiming to privatise public services (Elwert 1997; Pérouse de Montclos 1998; Mehler 2004).

To a certain extent, structural descriptions like Paulenz's – pointing, for example, to a crisis of governance brought about by problems of market integration, or contradictions between modernised legal systems and revitalised yet futile 'traditional' forms of sanctioning (Paulenz 1999b)[15] – are helpful in providing a background against which we may interpret the plausibility of popular discourses that accompany the rise of vigilante action. However, such descriptions fail to explain why a particular group like Dévi's should emerge at a *particular* locality and not elsewhere within the same country, and why such a group should experience considerable success, at least for a time. The success of Dévi's men was rather contingent upon their meaningful *interpretation* of the situation, the legitimacy attributed to them by local communities, the creation of apt regimes of control and their striving for a vertical form of encompassment, analogous to the structuring role of state agencies, that is typical of many such movements (Ferguson & Gupta 2002).

Another dimension of Dévi's legitimacy concerns his life story and his relation to religion: Dévi is said to have started his activities after his twin brother was killed by gangsters, and it is reported that starting his campaign made him feel personally blessed. All this served to 'personalise' his stance and the determination of his actions as a sort of vendetta.[16] What is more, the success of Dévi's actions was seen as being based on his ability to make use of religious blessings and 'good magical powers'.[17] Against this background Dévi himself became a mythical figure. In this regard his group resembles other leader-centred vigilante groups, such as *Mapogo a Mathamaga* in South Africa (Oomen 2004). In these two cases the leader's strength and charismatic virtues, the narratives of his capacities and the typical invocation of his transcendent qualities seemed to create a favourable environment that drew more and more people into the movement.[18] However, this focus on his person also made it easier for copycats to fight criminality 'in his name'. Thus, following Dévi's detention the association of the movement with the strength of his person became a point of weakness because his men now lacked a suitable successor.

Taking all these factors together, Dévi was able to draw upon a polysemic and multi-layered form of legitimacy: beyond the conventional claim to be replacing the ineffective official security forces, his movement referred, for example, to the 'necessity of local initiative', the 'strength of traditional local values' and 'the values of the Adja people'.

Comparative aspects and Dévi's changing relationship with the state

The case of Dévi's group offers some valuable points of comparison with other vigilante groups in Africa. Like Dévi's men, many of these groups often modify their scope of action, mode of organisation and strategies. For example, they may start out as local defence committees and become a regional militia. Some vigilante groups attempt to exert control over strangers to the area, such as migrants and new settlers. Many such groups, including Dévi's, seek to establish local hegemony by referring to discourses of autochthony; these prevail especially in West Africa. However, in the case discussed in this chapter the rise of the vigilante group was not a reaction to increasing incidences of interethnic clashes, as was the case in other parts of the continent, but of a perceived need to fight generalised criminality.

Regarding the general explanation for the rise of vigilante groups in Africa, my analysis follows the interpretation that this is only in part a reaction to the growing illegitimacy of the state. Undoubtedly, local actors such as vigilante groups, village councils and committees are gaining in political heft, and the deficiencies of many state authorities at the local level may well lead to 'institutional insecurity', as Le Meur (1999) puts it, which leads to new demands to re-create public order (Baker 2004), especially in terms of the viability of arbitrating and sanctioning powers. Groups such as Dévi's men are successful in seizing such opportunities to take up these needs for protection and retribution.

On taking a closer look, however, it becomes clear that these groups gain more success the more they are able to play simultaneously on both registers: on local modes of communal adjudication as well as on modes usually offered by the state. In other words, the groups must respect local ideas of justice (Benda-Beckmann & Pirie 2007: 8) without ignoring those offered by the state, and be able to maintain their position between both realms without trying to substitute one for the other. Dévi's group, like vigilante groups elsewhere, was not established completely beyond the state, but rather in a conflictual relationship with it.

Dévi's case is also instructive with respect to the observation that a situation of flux, conflict or disorder may create an arena of new micro-politics, offering the potential for new groups to appropriate legislative powers. Local actors may develop their own power regimes which, from the point of view of the population, may work, at least for a certain period of time (see also Von Trotha 2000). Compared with vigilante groups in other parts of Africa, Dévi's men shared a stance of 'defending a particular home territory', drawing on local ritual culture and symbolism as important strategies of re-traditionalisation and empowerment, but also implementing various typical modes of action such as road blocks, patrols and public executions. In so doing, at least until the events of early 2002, they produced a nimbus of invincibility.[19]

Conclusion

In this chapter I have discussed the role of a vigilante group in southern Benin that was successful for a certain period due to its popular legitimacy and support, to government inactivity, and to its effective internal structure and ability to adapt and transform its *modus operandi*. Vigilantes such as those organised by Dévi do not always constitute a kind of private indirect government (Mbembe 2001: 67). However, they obviously find their niche in an enabling political environment and in periods of partial (and cyclical) neglect by the central state, as was the case in 1999 with Kérékou's (second) government and its partial *laisser-faire* policy with regard to local powers (Bierschenk & Olivier de Sardan 2003, Bierschenk *et al.* 2003, Bierschenk 2009).

However, as I have tried to demonstrate, this is not sufficient to explain the rise of such a group at a particular locality and point in time. We also have to take into account regional configurations of power and legitimacy, as I have argued by pointing out the particular combination of various effective strategies, broad popular support – including links to religious authorities and entrepreneurs – and a multifaceted discourse of legitimacy and self-empowerment. Nonetheless, adopting this focus does not mean portraying cases of extralegal justice as a simple return to traditional, pre-colonial practices, since in the meantime societies have undergone various political and economic changes that make this impossible. References to 'tradition' should rather be interpreted as a contemporary response to present-day issues, and not only, as has been argued, on the fringes of the state (Abrahams 1998: 24).

Analysing the example of Dévi in detail, it also became clear that one needs to go further than depicting non-official legal contexts as resulting from legal insecurity and violence alone (cf. Paulenz 1999b: 13).[20] Many forms of excessive violence exercised by Dévi's group are undeniably seen as indefensible. However, Dévi and his men simultaneously employed a larger range of policing and adjudicating strategies, at least for a particular period of time. This also means that although the group drew its legitimacy from a discourse in which it replaced state institutions, it did not represent a complete legal alternative or innovation. Instead, the group also employed typical police tactics, partly also tribunal standards and other modes of local-level jurisdiction in a creative manner – a fact which, in the end, increasingly brought it into conflict with state agencies and contributed to its being declared illegal.

Notes

1 The study is based on a variety of sources, above all interviews in the Mono and Couffo regions of Benin conducted in 2004 and 2007, including with members of the group, plus discussions with various witnesses and experts, journalists, anthropologists, human rights activists and policemen, as well as reports and newspaper articles. Interviews with Dévi himself were conducted in March 2006 and February 2007 (by the author) and in March 2008 (by Jascha Derr). I particularly thank Simon Paulenz for discussions of earlier versions of this chapter. Aubin Towanou of Cotonou and Jascha Derr provided further information and photographs.

2 Policemen were said to be involved in the organisation of robberies, lending the bandits arms and even uniforms. In addition, there was a popular theory that, because most gendarmes and policemen did not originate from the regions in which they served, they had no particular interest in defending 'their people', unlike Dévi's men.

3 Indirectly legitimising support for Dévi, the village head of Loko-Atoui published, 'in the name of the local people', a letter to the government authorities denouncing the early release of criminals and demanding their deportation from the region (*Le Matinal* 8.10.1999: 7).

4 The most crucial event was a giant meeting in the Lokossa stadium on 3 October 1999, with more then 20,000 people attending. His speech was published almost in its entirety in *Le Matinal* (1999a).

5 In this debate, the then President Kérékou (Djiguy 1999b: 3), as well as his predecessor Soglo and the Benin chapter of the Human Rights League (Togbadja 1999), condemned Dévi's actions, while Ministers Tawema of the Interior (Towanou 1999: 3), Gnacadja of the Environment and Osho of Defence (*Le Matin* 15.10.1999: 3) announced actions against Dévi, with whom they reject all collaboration, and the re-establishment of government authority in the region. On the other hand, the opposition MP Dê Sodji, like university Professor Mahougnon Kakpo (Kakpo 1999: 12), criticized the government and showed understanding of popular reactions to insecurity (Gandaho 1999a: 2).

6 Some journalists who criticized Dévi were threatened by telephone (Djiguy 1999a: 2).

7 In this interview with the journalists from *Le Matinal*, who were apparently enchanted by his personality ('voyou sympathique'), he demanded the official legalisation of his group and offered cooperation with the police while benefiting from the great autonomy of actions in his home region. He proudly claimed that he was able to mobilise a force of more than 20,000 for his support, denying, however, that this was any kind of militia. He argued that he only tried to pursue 'the big criminals', and that actions against small thieves were regretfully being carried out in his name but without his approval. Dévi also denied inflicting the death penalty. He claimed that for a certain period he had had a kind of re-education camp. It was this interview in particular that created wider public attention nationwide (Towanou and Oké 1999). Both journalists managed to reach his camp under dangerous circumstances and despite obstructions by government envoys (Aubin Towanou, interview with the author in Cotonou, March 2008).

8 Not all witnesses had positive feelings about these events: 'I still have nightmares because I once saw a man who was set on fire, crying bitterly before passing away, while the crowd was shouting continuously' (Bernard, Lokossa, 11 February 2007).

9 In February 2007, there were clashes in Djougou between the gendarmerie and the local population, who were demanding the delivery to them of suspected murders, causing two deaths and several injured.

10 In many cases, the gendarmerie asks the victims of crimes who make complaints to pay the costs of the arrest (personal information, S. Paulenz). People often complain

that, even when they have been arrested, criminals are treated leniently by the legal system. The latter are said to leave prison after a short while, either because their crimes were considered unimportant, or on bail, or through corruption. Tribunals do not act quickly because of their heavy workloads. Prisons, people say, make inmates even harder, more determined to pursue a criminal career, and – morally repudiated and already detached from their home regions – further drawn into criminal networks. Prisons are generally overcrowded and evidently do not represent the starting point of any attempts at re-socialisation.

11 A telling example of the inconsistency of state policies is the illicit trade in fuel, imported along clandestine routes from Nigeria and sold illegally on the streets and in markets. Pointing to the negative economic, health and environmental effects, the government from time to time takes measures against this traffic – usually after the appointment of a new minister for environmental affairs –, but shifts from information campaigns to rounds of negotiation to the simple destruction of the market stalls selling the fuel, all without much lasting success.

12 Historically, the (proto) Adja group, with its erstwhile mythical place of origin at Tado (today in Togo), is considered as involving the origins of today's ethnic groups in the region, being later sub-dividing into the Fon, Kota-Fon, and others. This reference is still very much present in the collective memory of most Adja people.

13 See Pratten (this volume) for similar discursive elements employed by leaders of the Annang vigilantes in Nigeria.

14 In his account on mob-lynching in Benin, Paulenz (2002) tries to reconcile 'rationalist' and 'socio-psychological' approaches to the phenomenon. He argues that mob-lynching, as a spontaneous form of self-justice, represents a hybrid form of non-state violence. On the one hand, participants in these acts should be seen as members of rationally acting temporal interest groups, aiming at a restoration of economic life that has been threatened by criminals. On the other hand, participants are emotionally driven by fears to loose their livelihoods, which entails a moment of both hubris and tacit solidarity with fellow participants (Paulenz 1999b: 12).

15 In a general popular discourse in southern Benin, people are arguing that hitherto implemented forms of corporal punishment and rituals of shaming and ostracising malefactors are no longer effective, for robbers are often strangers and continue their careers after prison. This gives rise to more 'radical' solutions, including lynching.

16 On the importance of founding myths for vigilante groups, see Buur (this volume), Oomen (2004).

17 Malevolent rumours accusing him to use human skulls for rituals were, however, never affirmed (*Le Matinal* 2002).

18 This differs, however, from the case of the Bakassi Boys (Baker 2002; Smith 2004; Tertsakian 2002), where each individual member was said to have his own mythical forces.

19 Unlike other cases of vigilante groups (Pratten in this volume), Dévi and most of the leaders of the local committees did not manage to become politically more influential in local society, thus transforming power into official positions etc.

20 Features of violence and arbitrariness may apply to actors on the 'official' side of jurisdiction as well.

References

Abrahams, Ray 1987 'Sungusungu: Village vigilante groups in Tanzania' *African Affairs* 86, 343, 179–96

—— 1998 *Vigilant Citizens* (Oxford: Polity Press)

Adjovi, Apol Emerico & Boton, Babylas 1999 'Dévi change de discours' *Le Matinal* 20 October 1999: 4

Ahanhanzo-Glélé, Maurice 1993 'Le Benin' in Gonac 1993: 173–7

Alber, Erdmute 2001 'Hexerei, Selbstjustiz und Rechtspluralismus in Benin' *Afrika-Spektrum* 36, 2, 145–65

Alber, Erdmute & Sommer Jörn 1999 'Grenzen der Implementierung staatlichen Rechts im dörflichen Kontext: Eine Analyse der Rechtswirklichkeit in einem Baatombu-Dorf in Benin' *Afrika-Spektrum* 34, 1, 85–111

Allen, Chris 1992 'Restructuring an authoritarian state: "Democratic renewal" in Benin' *Review of African Political Economy* 19, 54, 42–58

Anderson, David M. 2002 'Vigilantes, violence and the politics of public order in Kenya' *African Affairs* 101, 405, 531–55

Baker, Bruce 2002 'When the Bakassi Boys came: Eastern Nigeria confronts vigilantism' *Journal of Contemporary African Studies* 20, 2, 1–22

—— 2004 'Protection from crime: What is on offer for Africans?' *Journal of Contemporary African Studies* 22, 2, 165–88

Bako-Arifari, Nassirou 1995 'Démocratie et logiques du terroir au Benin' *Politique Africaine* 59, 7–24

Banégas, Richard 1998 '"Bouffer l'argent": Politique du ventre, démocratie et clientélisme au Benin' in Bricquet, I. L. & Sawicki, F. (eds) 1998 *La politique clientélaire* (Paris: Presses Universitaires Français): 75–110

Bangstad, Sindre 2005 'Hydra's heads: PAGAD and responses to the PAGAD phenomenon in a Cape Muslim community' *Journal of Southern African Studies* 31, 1, 187–208

Bayart, Jean-François 1991 *L'État en Afrique: La politique du ventre* (Paris: Fayard)

Bayart, Jean-François; M'Bembe, Achille & Toulabor, Comi 1992 *Le politique par le bas en Afrique noire: Contributions à une problématique de la démocratie* (Paris: Karthala)

Bierschenk, Thomas 2000 'Herrschaft, Verhandlung und Gewalt im modernen Afrika: Zur politischen Soziologie einer afrikanischen Mittelstadt (Parakou, Benin)' *Afrika-Spektrum* 34, 3, 321–48

—— 2004 'Die Informalisierung und Privatisierung von Konfliktregelung in der Beniner Justiz' in Eckert, Julia (ed.) 2004 *Anthropologie der Konflikte: Georg Elwerts konflikttheoretische Thesen in der Diskussion* (Bielefeld: Transkript): 186–216

—— 2009 *Democratization without Development: Benin 1989–2009* (Institut für Ethnologie und Afrikastudien Working Papers 100) (Mainz: Johannes Gutenberg-Universität)

Bierschenk, Thomas & Olivier de Sardan, Jean-Pierre 2003 'Powers in the village: Rural Benin between democratisation and decentralisation' *Africa* 73, 2, 145–73

Bierschenk, Thomas; Floquet, Anne & Le Meur, P. Y. 1998 'L'État est-il soluble dans la société civile? Le Benin rural avant la décentralisation' *Bulletin de l'APAD* 16: 19–40

Bierschenk, Thomas; Thioleron, Elisabeth & Bako-Arifari, Nassirou 2003 'Benin' *Development Policy Review* 21, 161–78

Blundo, Giorgio & Mongbo, Roch (eds.) 1999 *Décentralisation, pouvoirs sociaux et réseaux sociaux (Decentralization, local-level politics, and social networks)* (APAD Bulletin 16) (Münster: Lit-Verlag)

Boone, Catherine 1998 '"Empirical statehood" and reconfigurations of political order' in Villalon, Leonardo A. & Huxtable, Phillip A. (eds) 1998 *The African State at a Critical Juncture* (Boulder CO: Lynne Rienner): 129–42

Buur, Lars 2006 'Reordering society: Vigilantism and expressions of sovereignty in Port Elizabeth's townships' *Development and Change* 37, 4, 735–57

Buur, Lars & Jensen, Steffen 2004 'Introduction: Vigilantism and the policing of everyday life in South Africa' *African Studies* 63, 2, 139–52

Chabal, Patrick & Daloz, Jean-Pascal 1999 *Africa Works: Disorder as Political Instrument* (Oxford: James Currey)

Comaroff, Jean & Comaroff, John L. 2006 *Law and Disorder in the Postcolony* (Chicago: University of Chicago Press)

Djiguy, Laurent 1999a 'Déjà des menaces de mort' *Le Matin* 12 October: 2

—— 1999b 'Dévi au menu du conseil des ministres' *Le Matin* 16 November: 3

Dossou, Robert 1993 'Le Benin: du monolithisme à la démocratie pluraliste' in Gonac 1993: 179–97

Elwert, Georg 1997 'Gewaltmärkte: Beobachtungen zur Zweckrationalität von Gewalt' *Kölner Zeitschrift für Soziologie und Sozialpsychologie (Sonderheft* 37): 86–101

Englebert, Pierre 2000 *State Legitimacy and Development in Africa* (Boulder CO: Lynne Rienner)

Ferguson, James & Gupta, Akhil 2002 'Spatializing states: Toward an ethnography of neoliberal governmentality' *American Ethnologist* 29, 4, 981–1002

Fleisher, Michael L. 2000 '*Sungusungu*: State-sponsored village vigilante groups among the Kuria of Tanzania' *Africa* 70, 2, 209–28

Gandaho, Euloge 1999a 'Dê Sodji accuse Soglo' *Le Matin* 18 October: 2

—— 1999b 'Les risques d'une récupération politique' *Le Matin* 11 October: 2

Gonac, Gérard (ed.) 1993 *L'Afrique en transition vers le pluralisme politique* (Paris: Economica)

Gore, Charles & Pratten, David 2003 'The politics of plunder: The rhetorics of order and disorder in southern Nigeria' *African Affairs* 102, 407, 211–40

Grätz, Tilo 2006 *Tanguiéta: Facettes d'histoire politique et de la vie quotidienne d'une commune Beninoise à la veille de la decentralisation* (Cotonou: Éditions du Flamboyant)

Harnischfeger, Johannes 2001 'Die Bakassi-Boys in Nigeria: Vom Aufstieg der Milizen und dem Niedergang des Staates' *Konrad-Adenauer-Stiftung-Auslandsinformation* 12, 1, 13–46

Huxtable, Phillip A. 1998 'The African state toward the twenty-first century: Legacies of the critical juncture' in Villalon, Leonardo A. & Huxtable, Philip A. (eds) 1998 *The African State at a Critical Juncture* (Boulder CO: Lynne Rienner): 279–93

Kakpo, Mahougnon 1999 'Lettre ouverte à Kérékou et ses ministres' *Le Matinal* 21 October: 12

Kohnert, Dirk 1996 'On the divide between constitutional legislation and constitutional reality in the democratization process in Benin Republic' *Nord-Süd aktuell* 10, 1, 73–84

Le Matin 1999a 'Sastre: Je suis en relation avec Dévi' *Le Matin* 18 October: 2

—— 1999b 'Soglo condamne Dévi et rend hommage á Kérékou' *Le Matin* 15 October: 3

Le Matinal 1999a 'Discours du "commandant Dévi"' *Le Matinal* 6 October: 3

—— 1999b 'Le reportage en images: Dans l'intimité de Dévi, le brûleur d'hommes' *Le Matinal* 8 October: 5

—— 2002 'Perquisition chez Dévi après son arrestation' *Le Matinal* 15 January: 3

Le Meur, Pierre-Yves 1999 'Coping with institutional uncertainty: Contested local public spaces and power in rural Benin' *Afrika-Spektrum* 34, 2, 187–211

Le Roux, Cornelius J. B. 1997 'People Against Gangsterism and Drugs: PAGAD' *Journal for Contemporary History* 22, 1, 51–80

Le Roy, Etienne 1996 'Gouvernance et décentralisation ou le dilemme de la légitimité dans la réforme de l'État africain de la fin du XXème siècle' *Cahier du GEMDEV (l'État en afrique: indigénisations et modernités)* 24: 101

Matchoudo, Pierre 1999 'Plus de 100 personnes tuées' *Le Matin* 6 October: 3

Mayrargue, Cédric 1999 'Le Benin depuis le retour de M. Kérékou: Démocratie apaisée ou paralyse politique?' in CEAN (ed.) 1999 *L'Afrique politique* (Paris: Karthala): 107–24

—— 2006 'Yayi Boni, un président inattendu? Construction de la figure du candidat et dynamiques électorales au Benin' *Politique africaine* 102, juin: 155–72

Mbembe, Achille 2000 'At the edge of the world: Boundaries, territoriality, and sovereignty in Africa' *Public Culture* 12, 1, 259–84

—— 2001 *On the Postcolony* (Berkeley CA: University of California Press)

Mehler, Andreas 2004 'Oligopolies of violence in Africa south of the Sahara' *Nord-Süd aktuell* 18, 3, 539–48

Nwajiaku, Kathryn 1994 'The National Conferences in Benin and Togo revisited' *Journal of Modern African Studies* 32, 3, 429–47

Oomen, Barbara 1999 'Vigilante justice in perspective: The case of *Mapogo a Mathamaga*' *Acta Criminologica* 12, 3, 45–53

—— 2004 'Vigilantism and the policing of everyday life in South Africa' *African Studies* 63, 2, 153–71

Otayek, René 1989 'Burkina Faso: Between feeble state and total state, the swing continues' in Cruise O'Brien, Donal (ed.) 1989 *Contemporary West African States* (Cambridge: Cambridge University Press): 13–30

Otayek, René; Sawadogo, Filiga Michel & Guingane, Jean-Pierre 1996 *Le Burkina Faso entre révolution et démocratie (1983–1993)* (Paris: Karthala)

Paulenz, Simon 1999a 'Selbstjustiz in Benin' *Afrika-Spektrum* 34, 1, 59–83

—— 1999b 'Alte Strafen für neue Delikte: Über die Ideologie des "traditionellen afrikanischen Rechts"' *Blätter des iz3w* 238: 11–13. Available online at: <www.archiv3.org/volltext_131166. htm> (last accessed 20 August 2007)

—— 2002 'Rechtsexport in schlechte Verhältnisse: Die Entwicklung der Sanktionspraxis in Benin und die Krise des rechtsstaatlichen Universalismus' *Forum Recht, Linksnet.* Available online at: <www.linksnet.de/artikel.php?id=796> (last accessed 21 August 2007)

Pérouse de Montclos, Marc-Antoine 1998 'La privatisation de la sécurité en Afrique subsaharienne: Le phénomène milicien dans le sud du Soudan' *Politique Africaine* 72, 203–11

Pognon, A. 1996 'Le dysfonctionnement de la justice au Benin' in (ed.) *Etats généraux de la justice: Colloque tenu à Cotonou du 4 au 7 novembre 1996* (Cotonou: Ministère de la Justice de la Legislation et des Droits de l'Homme): 66–72

Pratten, David & Sen, Atreyee (eds) 2007 *Global Vigilantes: Perspectives on Justice and Violence* (London: Hurst & Co.)

Pratten, David 2006 'The politics of vigilance in south-eastern Nigeria' *Development and Change* 37, 1, 707–34

—— 2008 'The politics of protection: Perspectives on vigilantism in Nigeria' *Africa* 78, 1, 1–15

Raynal, Jean-Jacques 1991 'Le renouveau démocratique Beninois: Modèle ou mirage?' *Afrique contemporaine* 160, 4, 3–26

Smith, Daniel J. 2004 'The Bakassi Boys: Vigilantism, violence, and political imagination in Nigeria' *Cultural Anthropology* 19, 3, 429–55

Sommer, Jörn 2001 *Unterschlagen und Verteilen: Zur Beziehung von Korruption und sozialer Kontrolle im ländlichen Benin* (Frankfurt-am-Main: Campus)

Stroh, Alexander & Never, Babette 2006 *Kaurimuschel statt Chamäleon: Dritter demokratischer Präsidentenwechsel in Benin* (*GIGA Focus* 8) (Hamburg: German Institute of Global and Area Studies)

Tertsakian, Carina 2002 *State-Sponsored Terrorism: The Bakassi Boys. The Legitimization of Murder and Torture* (New York: Human Rights Watch) (85659, 2002)

Togbadja, Julien 1999 'La ligue des droits de l'homme réagit' *Le Matinal* 12 October: 2

Towanou, Aubin 1999 'Le gouvernement prépare une action d'envergure' *Le Matinal* 06 October: 3

Towanou, Aubin & Oké, Anicet 1999 'Entretien avec Ehoun Zinsou, alias "colonel civil"' *Le Matinal* 8 October: 6–7

Villalón, Leonardo A. (ed.) 1998 *The African State at a Critical Juncture: Between Disintegration and Reconfiguration* (Boulder CO: Lynne Rienner)

Von Benda-Beckmann, Keebet & Pirie, Fernanda 2007 'Introduction' in Von Benda-Beckmann, Keebet & Pirie, Fernanda (eds) 2007 *Order and Disorder: Anthropological Perspectives* (New York: Berghahn Books): 1–15

Von Trotha, Trutz 2000 'Die Zukunft liegt in Afrika: Vom Zerfall des Staates, von der Vorherrschaft der konzentrischen Ordnung und vom Aufstieg der Parastaatlichkeit' *Leviathan* 28, 2, 253–29

4

Vigilantes in War
Boundary Crossing of Hunters in Burkina Faso & Côte d'Ivoire

STEN HAGBERG
& SYNA OUATTARA

Introduction

Throughout the 1990s hunters' movements emerged in several West African countries – notably Burkina Faso, Côte d'Ivoire, Guinea, Mali and Sierra Leone. These movements combine the traditional basis of hunting (*dozoya*), involving the hunting of game and secret knowledge and initiation into the cult of hunters, with the confrontation of present-day sociopolitical problems, such as insecurity, theft and war.

In the two countries covered in this chapter (Burkina Faso and Côte d'Ivoire), these sociopolitical challenges and the responses of hunters' movements to them differ. On the one hand, in Côte d'Ivoire in the 1980s, gangsters, *coupeurs de route* and other criminals controlled rural areas and roads to such an extent that gendarmes and police officers appeared powerless. In reaction to this situation, hunters' associations in villages in northern Côte d'Ivoire grew in importance and formed vigilante groups to protect the inhabitants of the district from criminal activity. In Burkina Faso, on the other hand, the hunters' association *Benkadi* emerged as an anti-Fulbe association. This association protected villagers against theft and insecurity, but in doing so it simultaneously promoted a supra-ethnic identity of farmers that transcended certain ethnic and territorial boundaries in opposition to so-called 'outsiders' or 'strangers' like Fulbe and Mossi (Hagberg 2000, 2004b). Nonetheless, despite the sociopolitical differences between the hunters' organisations in the two countries, it was generally held in both countries that hunters were much more efficacious in securing rural areas than the gendarmerie and police.

Hunters' movements in West Africa challenge the monopoly of legitimate violence by the state. They are perceived by many as efficient protectors of people and wealth in local communities, but in this role they often take the law into their own hands and support local farming communities against different categories of 'stranger'. At the same time, it is important to note that hunters not only serve the community by

98

using the institution of *dozoya* for security and protection and in political contests, but they also make a living by it: first, hunters are hired as guards and security operatives (Hagberg 2006; Ouattara 2006, 2008); second, they are enrolled as combatants in wars, as in the case of the Kamajors in Sierra Leone (Leach 2000; Muana 1997); third, they provide environmental protection services as part of development programmes (Bassett & Zuéli 2000; Hagberg 1998, 2006; Leach 2000); and fourth, they trade their secret knowledge of magical protection methods (Hagberg 2006; Traoré 2000). In other words, hunters in present-day West Africa are located at the crossroads of culture, politics and economy. In addition, and what is of particular relevance for the study of vigilantism in Africa, the hunters' movements analysed in this chapter provide an interesting example of organisational shape-shifting, in which a traditional hunters' association was transmogrified first into a vigilante movement that initiated activities in securing, patrolling and policing, and then into a rebel force and army unit directly involved in the Ivorian civil war.

This chapter focuses on the activities of hunters operating on both sides of the international border between Burkina Faso and Côte d'Ivoire, and particularly on the question of how hunters from both countries have come to occupy a new politico-economic space in the midst of the civil war in Côte d'Ivoire.[1] Hunters' movements have in recent years been examined in several scholarly works; some of these have stressed trans-national dimensions (Hagberg 2004b; Hellweg 2001; Leach 2000, 2004). However, the nature of the specific cultural, political and economic bonds between hunters on both sides of the international border between Burkina Faso and Côte d'Ivoire has not yet been fully understood. This has become even more true since the outbreak of the Ivorian civil war, in which hunters came to play a major role and which led to the current situation in Côte d'Ivoire whereby the north of the country remains under rebel control.[2]

We have organised the chapter as follows. First, we describe the colonial and postcolonial history of the ties between Burkina Faso and Côte d'Ivoire, which will allow us to contextualise recent ethno-national-istic politics that rely on the concept of '*ivoirité*' ('Côte d'Ivoire for the Ivorians'). Second, we deal with hunters' movements in the wider West African context and discuss how these have been analysed by scholars. Third, we examine how hunters' movements in Côte d'Ivoire were articulated with national politics in the 1990s. Finally, we present two ethnographic case studies of how hunters operate across the border between Burkina Faso and Côte d'Ivoire; both studies concern hunters' involvement in the Ivorian civil war that started in 2002.

These case studies highlight the opportunities for hunters provided by the new politico-economic space in the context of this war, but also the challenges that non-state, transnational armed forces (such as hunters' movements) pose to the state. Moreover, they shed light on how vigilantes

are shifting shapes, corroborating Abrahams' observation that 'vigilantism ... is not always what it seems or claims to be' (1998: 7). In the
conclusion we will argue that the political economy of the Ivorian war
has transformed the way hunters operate across the international border.
Thus, while the civil war has certainly led to violence and immense
suffering, significant sociopolitical actors, such as the hunters described in
this chapter, are skilfully clearing new grounds.

Contexts of the crisis

Hunters' cross-border operations during the Ivorian crisis – acting as
'vigilantes in war' – are related to three different contexts of political and
economic relations between Burkina Faso and Côte d'Ivoire.

The first context concerns *political* relations between the two states. The
political links between Burkina Faso and Côte d'Ivoire have considerable
historical depth because the two countries were for long time part of the
same French colony (Blion 1996; Kambou-Ferrand 1993; McFarland &
Rupley 1998). Although the colony of Haute-Volta (since 1984 Burkina
Faso) was separated from Haut-Senegal-Niger in 1919, it was partitioned
in 1932 when most of the territory of Haute-Volta became part of Côte
d'Ivoire.[3] Only in 1947 did Haute-Volta once again became a separate
territory (McFarland & Rupley 1998). From the 1940s onwards, political
alliances were defined in relation to political parties more than with
regard to territorial divisions; for example, Félix Houphouët-Boigny's
party *Rassemblement Démocratique Africain* (RDA) covered several French
West African territories. After independence in 1960, Côte d'Ivoire and
Haute-Volta continued to maintain a close relationship, despite instances
when diplomatic relations were disturbed (Balima 1996: 300–1; Hagberg
& Tengan 2000: 9–10). In the 1980s official relations between the
countries were strained when the Burkinabe president Thomas Sankara
repeatedly criticised his Ivorian counterpart, Houphouët-Boigny (Andriamirado 1989). The coming to power of Blaise Compaoré in Burkina Faso
in 1987 improved diplomatic relations for a period. However, after the
death of Houphouët-Boigny in December 1993, relations between the two
countries again became tense; this was linked with emergent ethno-
nationalist discourse in Côte d'Ivoire and the identification of former
Ivorian Prime Minister Alassane Dramane Ouattara as 'the Burkinabe in
Ivorian politics' (Marshall-Fratani 2006).

The second context of relations between the two countries concerns
people's *livelihoods*. At the time of writing up to three million people of
Burkinabe origin live and work in Côte d'Ivoire, with many having
Ivorian passports. This means that the bonds linking the two countries
are not only political but also economic and cultural. In Burkina Faso it
is often held that the wealth of Côte d'Ivoire was built on the labour of
'strangers' (*étrangers* in French, *dunaw* in Dyula) – notably people

originating from Burkina Faso and Mali. Due to these economic ties, problems in Côte d'Ivoire tend to have immediate repercussions in Burkina Faso. This is partly because Burkina Faso is economically dependent on its southern neighbour so that, for example, price changes in Côte d'Ivoire always have an impact on the Burkinabe economy. This economic interdependence has also fostered cultural ties: in farming communities in Burkina Faso, migration to Côte d'Ivoire has for generations been seen as a way to become an adult and to acquire a new status in society (Hagberg & Tengan 2000; Hahn 2007; Thorsen 2007).

The third context of relations between Burkina Faso and Côte d'Ivoire is associated with *change in Ivorian political discourse* between the 1980s and 1990s. Following Houphouët-Boigny's death in 1993, in Côte d'Ivoire the national ideology of *ivoirité* gained prominence. Among other things, this involved the idea that 'strangers' should 'return home'. As a result, when economic crisis hit Côte d'Ivoire, labourers from other countries increasingly became scapegoats in Ivorian nationalist discourse.

The politics of *ivoirité* have been examined not only in the mass media, but also in academic writings, such as in thematic issues of the journals *Politique Africaine* (2000, 2003) and the *African Sociological Review* (2003). The latter social-scientific work has demonstrated that a main difference between the national political projects of Félix Houphouët-Boigny (president 1960–93) and of his successor Henri Konan Bédié (president 1993–9) was the way these politicians attempted to deal with the structural economic crisis caused by falling cocoa and coffee prices. Whereas in 1988–9 Houphouët-Boigny invoked speculation on the international market to explain the Ivorian crisis, from 1995 onwards Konan Bédié reacted to it by mobilising the *ivoirité* concept together with an ethno-nationalist vision (Losch 2000: 13–14). As part of this explanatory strategy, Bédié's supporters accused his main political opponent at that time – former Prime Minister Alassane Dramane Ouattara – of being a non-Ivorian and therefore, according to the constitution of Côte d'Ivoire, ineligible to stand as president of the republic. In practice, this political strategy transformed Ouattara into 'the Burkinabe' *par excellence* (Akindes 2004; Banégas & Otayek 2003; Hagberg & Bjarnesen in press) and created two different types of Ivorian citizen: those of 'pure' Ivorian origin, and those of 'mixed heritage' (Marshall-Fratani 2006: 23).

In December 1999, when Bédié was overthrown in the *coup d'état* that brought Robert Guéï to power, people expected a shift away from the politics of *ivoirité* because Guéï declared that he would soon organise elections for all Ivorian citizens, after which, he said, he himself would withdraw from politics. However, in March 2000 Guéï seemingly changed his mind and declared that he would run for president in the elections. Then, in October 2000, when Guéï lost the election and President Laurent Gbagbo came to power, discourse about *ivoirité* was again revived because Gbagbo had been one of its main proponents since the 1980s. Henceforth, foreigners and 'Northerners' – that is, people from northern Côte d'Ivoire

– became targets for harassment, violence and killings that were at least tacitly tolerated by the Ivorian government, if not officially sanctioned by it. In September 2002, army units consisting of soldiers and – most important for our analysis in this chapter – hunters originating from northern Côte d'Ivoire tried to seize power and overthrow President Gbagbo, but the attempted *coup d'état* failed. Nonetheless, rebels (referred to as *Forces Nouvelles*) soon occupied the northern and western parts of Côte d'Ivoire, representing two-thirds of the national territory.

The discussion above makes it clear that, despite longstanding links between Burkina Faso and Côte d'Ivoire, the discourse over *ivoirité* created political tensions when it became an 'official' part of the Ivorian politics of the 1990s. In this process, the basis for Ivorian citizenship became a contested issue. As a consequence, non-Ivorian citizens, people from the northern parts of Côte d'Ivoire, Ivorian citizens of Burkinabe and Malian origin, and sometimes even 'Muslims' were lumped together as 'strangers' and made the target of different kinds of charges and resentments. People of Burkinabe origin were particularly targeted by these new discourses of autochthony (Akindes 2004; see also Geschiere & Nyamnjoh 2000) and, as we will show below, it is precisely in this context that the involvement of hunters' movements in the Ivorian civil war must be understood.

Hunters in West Africa

Present-day hunters' movements draw on traditions that have evolved over more than 1,000 years. Hunters' associations are a well-known feature throughout West Africa; since the tenth century hunters in the role of kings and powerful diviners have dominated all those regions that, starting with the 13th century, formed the heart of the Mali Empire (Thoyer 1995: 11). To become a 'hunter' requires initiation into the cult and worship of the 'spirits of the hunters' (Cissé 1964; Hellweg 2001, 2006; Ouattara 2006). After initiation, hunters dress in a characteristic way: they wear a cap, a yellow-brown garment painted with black geometric patterns and amulets, and they carry a fly-whisk and a whistle. But the initiation signifies not merely that a hunter is someone who kills game, but also someone who has secret knowledge and ritual competences, and who is obliged to follow a number of morally meaningful prescriptions.[4] Accordingly, certain hunters are believed to have expertise in herbal medicine and divination, while others may be suspected of sorcery.

Generally speaking, the internal organisation of a hunters' association is based on the relationship between the 'master hunter' and his disciples. Master hunters of different associations meet at funerals and festivals, which helps them maintain personal networks. However, master hunters are also said to be able to communicate with one other spiritually, regardless of geographical distance.

Scholarly publications on hunters have pursued three different avenues. First, they have examined hunters' epics, poems and songs in terms of oral-literature traditions (Belcher 1999; Cissé 1964, 1994; Thoyer 1997; Traoré 2000). At major gatherings, hunters' bards play the *kora* (long-necked harp lute) and celebrate the deeds of 'great hunters'. In academic writings of this kind, hunters are mostly seen as the guardians of tradition. Second, several scholars have focused on 'hunters' as 'vigilantes' and their role in self-defence organisations and local conflicts. In these studies, hunters are depicted as social actors who have increasingly become aware of their political importance, whether in the context of war and violence (Bassett 2003, 2004; Hagberg 2006; Leach 2000; Muana 1997; Ouattara 2006; Richards 1996), or in the context of environmentalist and development projects (Bassett & Zuéli 2000; Hagberg 1998, 2004a, 2004b, 2006; Leach 2000, 2004). Third, some social scientists have focused on the experiential and phenomenological aspects of becoming a *dozo* hunter. In these works, the social construction of identity and masculinity is the core analytical focus (Hellweg 2001, 2006; Ouattara 2006, 2008).

Finally, in previous publications Hagberg (2004a, 2004b) has argued for the need to integrate *political* and *cultural-cum-experiential* analyses of present-day hunters' movements. In this chapter we follow this approach, expanding it innovatively so as to explore hunters' *political* involvement in the Ivorian civil war, and demonstrating that their secret knowledge and *cultural experiences* were critical in this involvement, as was the fact that warfare was important for the *economic* subsistence of master hunters and their disciples. Taken together, therefore, the political, cultural and economic dimensions can be shown to be mutually constitutive of present-day *dozoya*.

When comparing hunters' movements in Burkina Faso and Côte d'Ivoire, it is important to keep in mind that different hunters' movements are related to one another, first through personal networks of master hunters and their disciples, and second through formal organisational links. However, while the connections between hunters' movements in different West African countries were explored in a special issue of the journal *Africa Today* (2004) with regard to Mande hunters, in this chapter we do not aim at a general comparison but instead on a more focused comparison of how hunters' crossings of the border between Burkina Faso and Côte d'Ivoire have been articulated during the Ivorian crisis from September 2002 onwards.

Before embarking on this comparison, it should also be noted that the border separating the two countries is a colonial and postcolonial construct. However, since the outbreak of the Ivorian civil war in 2002, the most pertinent border for hunters has *not* been that between the territories of the two states, but the boundary between government-controlled Ivorian territory on the one hand and the territory controlled by the *Forces Nouvelles* rebels on the other. The boundary between these territories is a

2   Hunters' celebration, Korhogo, Côte d'Ivoire (© Syna Ouattara)

buffer zone controlled by the French *Licorne* force which, in turn, has been deployed to back up a UN force and prevent a further escalation of the conflict. In other words, while the international boundary between the two states remains important, a new type of boundary has come to play an increasingly prominent role for the hunters.

Hunters' movements in Côte d'Ivoire

To understand present-day hunters' movements in Côte d'Ivoire one has to take account of the fact that during the 1980s, insecurity increased in the country. The failure of the state's fight against crime and violence prompted the government to regularise a system of 'security agents' in parallel with the regular gendarmerie and police force. These agents were to provide security for the inhabitants of the country's cities.

However, by the end the 1980s, groups of young people calling themselves *loubards* also made their appearance in Abidjan. A typical *loubard* distinguished himself from ordinary citizens by dressing in expensive imported clothing and attempting to display an impressive bodily physique. Broadly speaking, *loubards* were combatants who at times also acted as vigilantes, working as paid bodyguards or providing protection at specific events such as baptisms or festivals. In most cases 'employers' closed their eyes to the disturbing and often violent side of the *loubards'* activities. The *loubards* were composed of various gangs – given names such as 'Black Power', 'Siciliens', 'Scorpio' or 'Turbo' – and established their territories in urban areas which the police force did not enter and where the laws of the nation-state did not reach (Ouattara 2006: 124–6).

In the 1990s, the crime rate in Côte d'Ivoire rose to a frightening level. Rural areas and roads in the countryside were now under the control of gangsters, *coupeurs de route* and other criminals, and gendarmes and police officers proved to be powerless and all too often corrupt. To counter this situation, residents in several districts of northern Côte d'Ivoire organised their own protection in the form of hired security guards. As part of this development, hunters' associations also grew in importance. These associations themselves formed vigilante groups and demanded fees for protection services of 300–1,000F CFA a month.[5] In addition, on the initiative of Fanny Inza, one of the leaders of the National Association of Hunters of Côte d'Ivoire, a nongovernmental organisation (NGO) called *Afrique Environmentale* was established to offer security as well as environmental protection services, and it employed hunters to carry out its various tasks (Bassett & Zuéli 2000; Hellweg 2004; Konaté 2001).

People's recourse to private security agents as a way of complementing the regular police force coincided with the beginning of the democratic process launched by President Houphouët-Boigny in 1990 (Marshall-Fratani 2006; Ouattara 2006). Under the popular pressure of the 'street' and demands from the international community, a multi-party political system was installed in May 1990. Fourteen political parties took part in presidential elections in October 1990. Houphouët-Boigny was opposed for the first time by another candidate – Laurent Gbagbo, who represented the party *Front Populaire Ivorien* (FPI) – but the former was re-elected president with 82 per cent of the vote. Alassane Dramane Ouattara became Prime Minister.

In this context, at the beginning of the 1990s, hunters formed a major presence in security operations in most parts of Côte d'Ivoire (Ouattara 2008). And their importance was in no way diminished when, after Houphouët-Boigny died in 1993, the president of the National Assembly, Henri Konan Bédié, became president of the country. After the elections a first-rank member of the National Association of Hunters of Côte d'Ivoire, Balla Keïta, was designated a 'presidential special advisor'. In addition, Bédié was in power only for a one-year transition period, so needed to establish his power-base prior to elections in 1995; consequently, Bédié began to tour the entire country.[6] During these tours, *dozo* hunters often participated in welcoming ceremonies. For example, Keïta mobilised the Hunters' Association of the North 'to parade through the streets of Korhogo to show their support for the Bédié campaign' (Bassett 2003: 11). This means that at that time the president legitimised the hunters' movement (Konaté 2001), and the movement reciprocated by legitimising President Bédié.

However, in April 1998 the Bédié government decided that the security of the people should solely be the concern of the national police, and it issued a statement restricting hunters' activities to their 'original geographic and cultural region' (Bassett 2003: 15–16; Hellweg 2004: 9). The then Minister of the Interior, Emile Constant Bombet, defined this region as the northern half of the country. In addition, any modern firearms in the hands of hunters from southern Côte d'Ivoire would be confiscated; hunters from the north could continue their patrols using flintlock muskets. Hellweg notes that this 'restored the primacy of state police in the south while leaving open the possibility that *dozos* continue their security patrols in the north. This "bifurcated" logic provided an expedient solution to the problem at hand' (Hellweg 2004: 9). As a result of this decision, all activities of hunters from neighbouring countries, such as Burkina Faso, Guinea and Mali, were prohibited (Bassett 2003, 2004; Hellweg 2004; Ouattara 2008). Moreover, people became reluctant to hire hunters as guards when the law forbade them to work as security agents (Bassett 2003: 44; Ouattara 2006: 132). The government's decisions therefore also had economic consequences for hunters. Balla Keïta opposed the decision of the government to forbid hunters' activities in the security sector, but shortly thereafter was dismissed as a special advisor, so his suggestions were ignored.

It was only after the *coup d'état* of December 1999 which brought Robert Guéï to power that hunters were rehabilitated. Keïta was once again designated a special advisor, this time to President Guéï. Hunters resumed working as security agents and cooperated with the regular executive forces (the police, gendarmerie and army). However, the new government too soon started to oppose the collaboration between hunters and regular forces, once again questioning the former's activities as security agents. For instance, during the 2000 presidential campaign Adama Coulibaly, mayor of the northern city of Korhogo, argued when welcoming President Guéï to the city that hunters should be retained as security agents. However, Guéï rejected the suggestion, insisting that it was unthinkable to tolerate hunters because they had regularly abused power (*Soir Info*, 22 June 2000).

In October 2000, when Guéï lost the presidential elections and Gbagbo came to power, many regular-army soldiers and hunters left the country. Keïta was among those who sought exile. However, on 1 August 2002 he was found stabbed to death in his residence in Ouagadougou, Burkina Faso. Although the circumstances of Keïta's death were never completely clarified, accusations were made against the Gbagbo government. Then, less than two months later, on 19 September 2002, armed units comprising former soldiers of the Ivorian army and hunters attacked in a bid to overthrow the Gbagbo regime. Below, we will discuss the hunters' involvement in this attempt in greater detail.

Hunters' cross-border operations

The effects of the politics of *ivoirité*, mentioned above, can productively be examined by looking at how hunters have been treated by the Ivorian government. Basically, the international border between Burkina Faso and Côte d'Ivoire has never proved a barrier to hunters. They have 'relatives' on both sides of the border and have moved freely across it during hunting activities. This capacity to 'trespass' over the political boundary has often been seen as an advantage in surveillance activities, not the least for state services. For example, the wildlife conservation programme GEPRENAF used hunters to protect game reserves from poachers on both sides of the border (Hagberg 1998: 227–9, 2006), since it would have been much more complicated for state agencies to do so. However, when the Ivorian state attempted to restrict hunters' operations to the north of the country, as discussed above, the hunters' crossings of boundaries acquired a new political meaning.

Hunters' involvement in the Ivorian civil war
In an interview that Ouattara conducted with a spokesman of the National Association of Hunters of Côte d'Ivoire in Korhogo in November 1999, the hunters' leader asserted: 'If the government intends to forbid *dozoya* [hunting], we will enter into conflict with it and we will see [what will happen].'

Less than three years after this interview the Ivorian civil war broke out, with hunters deeply involved. As mentioned above, in September 2002 former soldiers of the Ivorian army and hunters tried to overthrow the regime of President Gbagbo. They launched attacks in three of the country's most important cities: Abidjan in the south, Bouaké in the centre and Korhogo in the north. Government forces secured Abidjan, but in the course of this conflict the entire northern half of the country fell to the rebels (Bassett 2003, 2004; Hellweg 2004; Ouattara 2006). The national and international press reported that several hundred hunters had joined the rebellion in Bouaké (AFP 2002; Banégas & Losch 2002; Bassett 2004). Some prominent leaders of the rebellion – such as Zakaria Koné and Chérif Ousmane – even claimed to be *dozo* hunters themselves (Bassett 2003: 45–6; Ouattara 2006: 143). In November 2002 hunters organised a demonstration outside Bouaké to show their support for the rebel forces. In May 2003 the security of Bouaké was entrusted to the hunters (Ouattara 2006: 141–6), and a camp of *dozo* combatants (referred to as *Compagnie des Guerriers de la Lumière*) was established (Ouattara 2006: 43–6).

When Ouattara interviewed the head of the *Compagnie* in Korhogo in September 2003, his interlocutor insisted it was the hunters who had initiated the rebellion. This man, whom we shall refer to by the pseudonym 'Guerrier', explained that at least since the time of President Guéï (1999–2000), the Ivorian government had organised a 'manhunt' (*chasse à l'homme*) to target soldiers from northern Côte d'Ivoire, as well as hunters. He claimed he himself had been attacked by government forces well *before* the outbreak of the war. 'On 15 January 2001,' Guerrier said, 'Gbagbo sent soldiers to exterminate me in my home in Tolakouadiokro [a village within Bouaké municipality]'. He said the army unit's failure was partly because it arrived in Guerrier's village at a time when he and his fellow hunters were at a site of worship.

Reporting on the antecedents of this incident, an article in the Ivorian daily *Fraternité Matin* stated that the 'armed forces lost two agents on Monday, 15 January 2001, during a shooting between *dozos* and themselves'. It all started, according to the newspaper, when agents of the armed forces stopped a *dozo*. On being interrogated, the hunter declared that he was on his way to the site of a ritual ceremony that was to take place some 2km from Tolakouadiokro. The soldiers then told the hunter: 'You should show us the site and you should tell us exactly what you do there'. The newspaper report continued:

> A group of five soldiers, one gendarme and one police agent, all of whom were under the command of Adjutant Fanny Dioulatié, went into the bush in the company of the *dozo*. This small group finds [*sic*] itself in an area occupied by some 50 *dozos*. Being almost encircled by them, Adjutant Fanny and his men are said to have attempted to reassure the *dozos*, telling them that they had *not* come to declare war on them. They were only interested in getting to know their leader. The situation rapidly deteriorated. It came to a shootout, with Adjutant Fanny and Sergeant Tanoh Allou dying from the bullets of the *dozos*. The other agents saved themselves by fleeing. Alerted by this incident, the armed forces under the command of Col Jean-Baptiste Kobon-Monney, commander of 3rd Military Region, arrived at the site. After a thorough search of the area, nine *dozos* were arrested and imprisoned in the Gendarmerie Brigade in order that the case could be investigated. (*Fraternité Matin*, 17 January 2001; authors' translation)

In the interview with Ouattara, Guerrier said that some time later, the soldiers also came to his home, from where his family had fled after the first attack. When the soldiers arrived, Guerrier had just returned from the hospital with one of his fellow hunters, who had been wounded during the fight in the morning:

> They arrived around eight o'clock with a group of soldiers, heavily armed, and positioned themselves around my house while I was taking a shower [and] ... they started shooting around and inside my house. [...] I saw, in front of the gate, a convoy of soldiers carrying Kalashnikovs. [...] While I was making my way right out between two soldiers who were standing in the centre of the door, I moved forward and reached my car which was parked near their cargo liner. I got into my car and when I started it, they all fled. A little further along the street there was a large tree in which other soldiers were posted;

they fell from the front shaft before I could reach them. They stood up and ran away, leaving their weapons behind. I collected their weapons and arranged them before leaving for my errands. In reality, there was no battle because we did not have any real confrontation at all.

After this incident, Guerrier and some of his fellow hunters exiled themselves to Burkina Faso for six months. On their return a series of activities were initiated to prepare for the 'the liberation of our people'.

Describing how the rebels' attack on President Gbagbo's government was organised, Guerrier recounts: 'Overall, there were 85 men – 78 *dozos* and seven soldiers – when we launched the attack. We devised a strategy in dividing up our troop into groups, each of which comprised one soldier and ten *dozos*. I was monitoring the operations between the various positions using my own car.' Then, after the attacks of 19 September 2002, hunters began to occupy an empty maternity centre in the Yankadi neighbourhood of Bouaké. This centre was later transformed into the hunters' camp. In Guerrier's words:

> We installed electric power, telephone and water. I joined forces with the Brotherhood, and we started by requisitioning offices and distributing responsibilities between master hunters. We placed calls to all *dozos* for the union and empowerment of the camp. This is how *La Compagnie des Guerriers de la Lumière* was born.

Despite the somewhat idealised self-presentation by Guerrier during the interview with Ouattara – caution is probably needed in interpreting the above statements – four salient features emerge from this conversation. First, while crossing the border was a way to escape persecution, the return to Côte d'Ivoire represented an attempt to seize political power. Second, the hunters' participation in the rebellion fuelled President Gbagbo's accusations of Burkinabe involvement: hunters' networks were trespassing over the international border, and hunters were perceived to be 'traditional combatants' from Burkina Faso who were fighting against Côte d'Ivoire's regular army. Third, hunters were, at least according to Guerrier, the dominant force within the rebellion, and they outnumbered soldiers. Fourth, hunters not only came to occupy a politically important position, they also benefited economically from being enrolled in the civil war, especially through the foundation of *La Compagnie*.

A more general observation is that hunters became politically powerful in Côte d'Ivoire at the very time they were being marginalised and treated with suspicion there. Still, crossing the border in the context of the Ivorian civil war was not just an issue for the small number of hunters who actually joined the rebellion, because the rebellion soon also involved many other people on both sides of the Burkinabe–Ivorian border. In other words, while Guerrier's story describes the high-level political involvement of vigilantes in the war, the case study below deals with hunters' involvement as *seasonal combatants* for the Ivorian *Forces Nouvelles*.

Hunters' participation in the war as seasonal combatants

The social organisation of *dozo* hunters in Burkina Faso bears witness to the ambiguity with which both governments and public opinion in that country regard them. For a long time the hunters' association *Benkadi*, founded by master hunter Tiéfing Coulibaly in 1995, was the main structure dedicated to defending hunters' interests, especially in opposition to Fulbe pastoralists (Hagberg 1998, 2001a, 2006, 2007). Not only did the late Tiéfing's have status as a master hunter, but it was also he who was said to have 'brought' the association from Côte d'Ivoire to Burkina Faso – a claim he repeatedly stressed when Hagberg interviewed him in 1996 and 1999 (Hagberg 1998, 2004b). Yet *Benkadi* was never officially recognised by the Burkinabe state, despite many years of lobbying and political activism. This was probably because the government feared that recognising this organisation could eventually turn it into an armed militia. These reservations were never publicly admitted, and the government always reacted with silence to *Benkadi*'s requests for recognition (Hagberg 2004a). In January 2004, however, *Benkadi* was transformed into an organisation called *Faso Dosso* ('Hunter of the Father's House', also meaning 'fatherland') in Comoé Province, the capital of which is Banfora. In this process, supported by the late Mamadou Koné – at that time the 'big man' in Banfora – hunters organised themselves within a new institutional structure that was eventually recognised by the state (Hagberg 2006). It seems that when the hunters' organisation changed its name and began voicing its demands at provincial level, the time had come for it to be officially recognised by the state.

In Comoé Province, *Faso Dosso* was led by a renowned master hunter who lived in a village some 15km from Banfora. He was a traditional hunter in a double sense: first, he was considered to be a master hunter of great knowledge and expertise, and second, he had, unlike many other hunters, a tradition of hunting in his family. In brief, he was a respected, feared and almost legendary master hunter. He died in late 2007, in very old age.

The son of this master hunter, whom we shall call 'Dow', is the main protagonist in the following case study because he has been crossing the international border between Burkina Faso and Côte d'Ivoire as *seasonal combatant* since the outbreak of the Ivorian war in 2002.

Over the years, Hagberg has encountered Dow at several gatherings of hunters. Hagberg first met him in 1999, when he interviewed Dow's father about the hunters' association. Then, in May 2005, Hagberg again came across Dow when visiting the master hunter's homestead. While talking to Dow's father, Hagberg asked about the present-day relations of Burkinabe hunters with hunters in Côte d'Ivoire. Since Burkinabe–Ivorian contacts had been quite intense in the past (Hagberg 2004a, 2004b), Hagberg was interested in assessing the impact of the war on these relations. In the conversation that followed Dow asserted that he had been to Côte d'Ivoire as part of a military deployment for the *Forces Nouvelles*. Then, in July 2006, Hagberg again met Dow, who indicated that he had been part of a further deployment in Côte d'Ivoire.

Taken together, it seems that Dow was practising a new kind of seasonal migration. Instead of moving to Côte d'Ivoire as a labourer or to undertake farming, as previous generations of migrants from Burkina Faso had done, Dow and his peers travelled intermittently to Côte d'Ivoire to take part as combatants in the civil war. Since 2002 Dow has been recruited for the Ivorian *Forces Nouvelles* every year, with each deployment lasting from three to five months. During this time he supported the rebels in combat against the regular military forces of President Gbagbo.

In this southwestern region of Burkina Faso, seasonal migration to Côte d'Ivoire has a long history. For generations, young men have been travelling to Côte d'Ivoire in order 'to search for money' (*chercher de l'argent* in French, or *ka wari nyini* in Dyula), and thus to improve their livelihoods. In addition, the journey southwards to coastal countries by men from rural areas is an integral part of local cosmologies concerning what it means to become a male adult (Dessein 2000; Fiéloux 1980; Hagberg 2001b). There is, in other words, a long history of seasonal migration from western and southern Burkina Faso to Côte d'Ivoire which was temporarily halted and then modified by the Ivorian war.

After the outbreak of the war, people said that 'Côte d'Ivoire is spoiled' (*Kotowar tiena* in Dyula) because Burkinabe nationals and their descendants in Côte d'Ivoire were increasingly exposed to all sorts of harassment perpetrated with what they saw as the at least tacit recognition of the Ivorian state authorities. Nevertheless, while the border between the two countries was closed for a year in 2002–3, people continued to cross it, and as the situation stabilised many people from Burkina Faso returned to Côte d'Ivoire, thus giving rise to new patterns of seasonal migration.

As discussed above, it is common knowledge that hunters participated in the civil war on the rebel side; this was covered extensively in international news reporting (see, for example, AFP 2002; Pawson 2004, Baxter 2002; News24 2002). However, the specific character of Burkinabe hunters' participation in the Ivorian war has not been thoroughly described. Some hunters, like Dow, did indeed go to Côte d'Ivoire with the explicit aim of being enrolled in the *Forces Nouvelles* and taking part in combat. Meanwhile, most hunters who travelled to Côte d'Ivoire were farmers who, prior to the war, had fields there. These people had been chased away (or feared being chased away) under the pretext that they were 'strangers to Côte d'Ivoire', following which they moved to Burkina Faso and waited for the situation to calm down. In Burkina Faso, many of them tried to obtain 'medicine' from master hunters in order to protect themselves and their fields from invaders. They wanted not so much the skills of handling guns, but to acquire 'anti-bullet medicine' and also 'secret knowledge' related to *dozoya*. In this situation, master hunters like Dow's father became important providers of know-ledge and protection for these farmers-turned-hunters. Once back in Côte d'Ivoire, several of these farmers/hunters seem to have joined the *Forces Nouvelles*. In other words, they were 'farmers' who became involved in the Ivorian conflict as 'hunters'. This conforms to the ways in which farmer/hunters have been involved in violent conflicts with Fulbe herders in Burkina Faso (Hagberg 1998, 2007).

However, Dow had a slightly different story. He had gone to Côte d'Ivoire with the explicit aim of fighting for the *Forces Nouvelles*. Even though he was not paid a regular salary, he received food and occa-sionally money while serving with the rebels. In addition, the provision of anti-bullet medicine to others soon became an economic activity for him. Dow was regularly asked to prepare the medicine for so many hunters that it probably became a lucrative business. For instance, when Hagberg met with him in March 2007, Dow was about to provide 30 hunters going to Côte d'Ivoire with anti-bullet medicine the following day.

The salient point of this case is that while Dow gave political support to the rebels, at the same time he earned a substantial living from seasonal migration and from providing medicine to other hunters going to Côte d'Ivoire. Dow's deployments were regulated by official documentation; for example, one travel document (*ordre de mission*) that Hagberg was shown was issued by the 'République de la Côte d'Ivoire, Forces Nouvelles', indicating that the rebels claimed to represent the legitimate structure of the Ivorian state. In this document Dow's profession was specified as '*dozo*', thereby confirming the perception that he was a 'hunter' enrolled to fight for the *Forces Nouvelles*. This example shows that the relationship between the *Forces Nouvelles* and the hunters had at this stage attained a quasi-legal character and that the *Forces Nouvelles*' use of the hunters followed a certain bureaucratic logic.

It is very important to emphasise the economic dimension of crossing borders in this context. Hunters make money from being enrolled in the *Forces Nouvelles*, either through payment given to them as soldiers or through the trading of amulets, talismans and medicines. Hunters may acquire secret knowledge for money, but that is usually not enough to be protected in war. In fact, many people have themselves initiated in a hunters' association in order to protect themselves, and not because they wanted to have more knowledge about *dozoya*. But initiation into the cult of hunters is not enough for protection. Dow made this clear to Hagberg when he asserted that he had never seen the corpse of a real *dozo* during the Ivorian war. He emphasised his point that those hunters who had been killed were *not* 'real hunters', but merely people who dressed like hunters. According to him, the latter tried to instil respect and fear, though they did not, as 'real hunters' do, possess a solid know-ledge of *dozoya*.[7]

The case of a young hunter who had been killed in Côte d'Ivoire was recounted to Hagberg by a hunters' leader in Banfora. This hunter had been initiated by a master hunter, who is known to have earned quite a lot of money and influence from massive initiations. But the young hunter had only the secret knowledge he had acquired during the two months of preparation for his initiation.[8] Some time later the man's corpse was returned home after he had been killed in the Ivorian war. Commenting on this story, the hunters' leader said: 'You do not prepare someone for war in just two months!'

Thus, broadly speaking, hunters are feared because of their reputations as bearers of secret knowledge and as brave warriors. Yet, it is not enough, at least in the master hunters' logic, to have a superficial initiation, put on hunting dress and then go to war. Instead, according to their understanding, years of preparation – traditionally not fewer than seven – are needed to become a 'real *dozo*'. However, as we have seen, the new politico-economic space of hunters in the context of the Ivorian war draws a lot of people to *dozoya*, even when their initiation is brief.

Discussion

In this chapter we have considered how a traditional hunters' association turned into a vigilante movement by taking on patrolling and policing activities. Then, in the context of the civil war in Côte d'Ivoire, many of these 'hunter-vigilantes' became rebels and warriors organised into military units, such as the *Compagnie des Guerriers de la Lumière*. In addition to political goals, their involvement in the Ivorian war improved their economic livelihoods. A market for secret knowledge developed, which made it possible for master hunters to trade in magical protection. However, it must also be noted that this shape-shifting by hunters' organisations is not a completely new phenomenon, but represents the hunters' latest adaptations to and manipulations of changing political and economic circumstances.

The different case studies of hunters' border crossings, discussed above, show that they have come to occupy a new politico-economic space in the region. Occupying this space, hunters are identified by labels such as 'northerners', 'strangers' and 'rebels'. These labels are ascribed to them by other political actors, and they do not conform to how hunters view themselves. This is because one result of the shifting political landscape outlined above, in which hunters are sometimes included in and sometimes excluded from Ivorian citizenship, consists in their reinforced transnational self-identification as hunters. It can therefore be argued that hunters are crossing the border neither as Burkinabe citizens nor as Ivorian citizens, but as hunters with a supra-ethnic and transnational identity.

In the case of Guerrier and his fellow hunters, they needed to flee Côte d'Ivoire to survive and to allow them to plan future attacks. When things became too dangerous for them in Côte d'Ivoire, crossing the border was vital. However, politics is not enough to account for these crossings, because it does not merely concern the (altruistic) question of coming to the help of 'brothers' in a neighbouring country. Instead, hunters also benefit from the war by selling their services, products and knowledge – that is, by making economic use of *dozoya*.

In line with previous work on hunters, the ethnographic examples presented in this chapter demonstrate that hunters are not bound by territorial demarcations or ethnic classifications. By regularly crossing the international border, and even being enrolled in the Ivorian *Forces Nouvelles*, hunters are ingeniously coping with and, to some extent, avoiding the containment of the state (Bassett 2004; see also Hagberg 2004b). While one could certainly claim that these actors are supporting the rebellion against the Ivorian central government, it could equally be argued that they are (re)asserting their agency as hunters.

Thus, taken together, the political economy of rebellion and war has transformed hunters' crossings of the international border, as well as increased supra-ethnic and transnational political opportunities for master hunters. Although it should be acknowledged that the war has led to suffering and violence even for hunters, as new socio-political actors they are skilfully clearing new grounds. They emerge as actors who are benefiting from the current state of 'no peace, no war' (Richards 2005) in this area, because in a well-organised, peaceful Ivorian state it would be hard to see how *dozo* hunters could have been enlisted into the army.

The Burkinabe government's long silence in a bid to prevent legal recognition of *Benkadi* supports this point. Hunters do present serious challenges to the state's monopoly on legitimate violence. Therefore, in line with Pratten's (2008) argument in the *Africa* special issue on vigilantism in Nigeria, vigilantism by hunters should be explored as practices related to cultural logics and social imperatives. It is not only the failed state, but also the skilful political and economic use of *dozoya* that explains the involvement of hunters in the Ivorian war. There are lucrative economic opportunities to be exploited by political actors in contexts of crisis, where there is not yet peace on the ground, but not a full-scale war either.

Notes

1 We are grateful, for insightful and valuable comments, to the editors, Tilo Grätz and Thomas Kirsch, as well as to Jan Ovesen, Charlotta Widmark, Oscar Jansson, Hugh Beach and other participants in the research seminar in cultural anthropology at Uppsala University.

2 Methodologically, the authors of the current article are relying on their respective long-term anthropological fieldwork in Burkina Faso (Hagberg) and Côte d'Ivoire (Ouattara). Hagberg's perspective is based on fieldwork on hunters in Burkina Faso in contexts of violence and local politics, Ouattara's on fieldwork on initiation into the cult of *dozoya*, as well as on hunters' organisations in Mali and Côte d'Ivoire. In

addition to our respective fieldwork activities, the analysis is informed by news media reports on the Ivorian civil war.

3 Except for the regions of Ouahigouya and Dédougou, which were annexed to French Sudan (present-day Mali), and the regions of Dori and Fada, which were added to Niger, the remaining parts of the colony were attached to Côte d'Ivoire (McFarland & Rupley 1998).

4 In this chapter, we use variously the Bambara/Dyula terms *dozo* (pl. *dozow*) and the English term 'hunters'. Different published works may use variant spellings or realisations of the Bambara/Dyula word, such as *dozo* in Côte d'Ivoire and sometimes Burkina Faso; *donso* or *dosso* in Burkina Faso; *dozobele* among Senufo-speakers in Mali, Côte d'Ivoire and Burkina Faso; and *donzo* in Côte d'Ivoire. The version we have selected is *dozo*, since this is the one most commonly used in Ivorian public discourse.

5 Referring to CFA francs. At time of writing, one Euro was equivalent to 656F CFA.

6 The 1995 elections were nevertheless eventually boycotted by opposition parties, in protest at restrictions imposed on their candidates.

7 For a discussion of 'real hunters' and 'new hunters', see Hagberg (1998: 229–30).

8 For a comparative case of shortened initiation rituals among hunters from seven years to one day, see Hagberg (2004b).

References

Abrahams, R. 1998 *Vigilante Citizens: Vigilantism and the State* (Cambridge: Polity Press)

Akindes, F. 2004 *The Roots of the Military-Political Crises in Côte d'Ivoire* (Uppsala: Nordic Africa Institute)

Andriamirado, S. 1989 *Il s'appelait Sankara: Chronique d'une mort violente* (Paris: Jeune Afrique Livres)

Balima, S.-A. 1996 *Légendes et histoire des peuples du Burkina Faso* (Paris: L'Harmattan)

Banégas, R. & Losch, B. 2002 'La Côte d'Ivoire au bord de l'implosion' *Politique africaine* 87, 139–62

Banégas, R. & Otayek, R. 2003 'Le Burkina Faso dans la crise ivoirienne: Effets d'aubaine et incertitudes politiques' *Politique Africaine* 89, 71–87

Bassett, T. J. 2003 'Dangerous pursuits: Hunter associations (*donzo ton*) and national politics in Côte d'Ivoire' *Africa* 73, 1–30

—— 2004 'Containing the *donzow*: The politics of scale in Côte d'Ivoire' *Africa Today* 50, 31–49

Bassett, T. J. & Zuéli, K. B. 2000 'Environmental discourses and the Ivorian savanna' *Annals of the Association of American Geographers* 90, 67–95

Belcher, S. 1999 *Epic Traditions of Africa* (Bloomington/Indianapolis IN: Indiana University Press)

Blion, R. 1996 'Migrants internationaux et de retour au Burkina Faso: Acteurs et témoins d'une circulation migratoire multiforme' in Otayek, R.; Sawadogo, F. M. & Guingané, J.-P. (eds) 1996 *Le Burkina entre révolution et démocratie (1983–1993)* (Paris: Karthala): 133–55

Cissé, Y. T. 1964 'Notes sur les sociétés de chasseurs malinké' *Journal de la Société des Africanistes* 19, 175–226

—— 1994 *La confrérie des chasseurs malinké et bambara: Mythes, rites et récits intiatiques* (Ivry/Paris: Editions Nouvelles du Sud/Association ARSAN)

Dessein, J. 2000 'Drawing or bridging boundaries? Agricultural extension in the Upper West Region of Ghana' in Hagberg & Tengan 2000: 181–97

Fiéloux, M. 1980 *Les Sentiers de la nuit: Les migrations rurales lobi de la Haute-Volta vers la Côte d'Ivoire* (Paris: ORSTOM)

Geschiere, P. & Nyamnjoh, F. 2000 'Capitalism and autochthony: The seesaw of mobility and belonging' *Public Culture* 12, 423–52

Hagberg, S. 1998 *Between Peace and Justice: Dispute Settlement between Karaboro Agricultural-ists and Fulbe Agro-Pastoralists in Burkina Faso* (*Acta Universitatis Upsaliensis: Uppsala Studies in Cultural Anthropology* 25) (Uppsala: Uppsala Universitet)

—— 2000 'Strangers, citizens, friends: Fulbe agro-pastoralists in western Burkina Faso' in Hagberg & Tengan 2000: 159–79

—— 2001a 'À l'ombre du conflit violent: Règlement et gestion des conflits entre agriculteurs karaboro et agro-pasteurs peul au Burkina Faso' *Cahiers d'Etudes africaines* XLI-1, 161, 45–72

—— 2001b *Poverty in Burkina Faso: Representations and Realities* (*Uppsala-Leuven Research in Cultural Anthropology* 1) (Uppsala: Department of Cultural Anthropology and Ethnology, Uppsala University)

—— 2004a 'La chasse aux voleurs! Une association des chasseurs et l'administration de l'état dans l'ouest du Burkina Faso' in Latouche, S.; Laurent, P.–J.; Servais, O. & Singleton, M. (eds) 2004 *Les raisons de la ruse: Une perspective anthropologique et psychanalytique* (*Révue du MAUSS*) (Paris: La Découverte): 199–219

—— 2004b 'Political decentralization and traditional leadership in the Benkadi Hunters' Association of western Burkina Faso' *Africa Today* 50, 51–70

—— 2006 '"It was Satan that took the people": The making of public authority in Burkina Faso' *Development and Change* 37, 779–97

—— 2007 '"Each bird is sitting in its own tree": The authority and violence of a hunters' association in Burkina Faso' in Derman, B.; Odgaard, R. & Sjaastad, E. (eds) 2007 *Conflicts over Land and Water in Africa* (Oxford: James Currey): 187–201

Hagberg, S. & Bjarnesen, J. In press *'Good Guys' and 'Bad Guys': The Burkinabe Public Debate on the Ivoirian Crisis*

Hagberg, S. & Tengan, A. B. (eds) 2000 *Bonds and Boundaries in Northern Ghana and Southern Burkina Faso* (*Acta Universitatis Upsaliensis: Uppsala Studies in Cultural Anthropology* 30) (Uppsala: Uppsala University)

Hahn, H. P. 2007 'Migration as discursive space: Negotiations of leaving and returning in the Kasena homeland (Burkina Faso)' in Hahn & Klute 2007: 149–73

Hahn, H. P. & Klute, G. (eds) 2007 *Cultures of Migration: African Perspectives* (Münster: LIT Verlag)

Hellweg, J. R. 2001 'The Mande hunters' movement of Côte d'Ivoire: Ritual, ethics, and performance in the transformation of civil society, 1990–1997' PhD thesis, University of Virginia

—— 2004 'Encompassing the state: Sacrifice and security in the hunters' movement of Côte d'Ivoire' *Africa Today* 50, 3–28

—— 2006 'Manimory and the aesthetics of mimesis: Forest, Islam and state in Ivoirian *dozoya*' *Africa* 76, 461–84

Kambou-Ferrand, J.-M. 1993 *Peuples voltaïques et conquête coloniale 1885–1914: Burkina Faso* (Paris: L'Harmattan)

Konaté, Y. 2001 '*Dozoya* et Ivoirité: Qui a peur des *Dozos?*' Paper presented at La chasse traditionnelle en Afrique de l'Ouest d'hier à aujourd'hui: Actes du colloque international de Bamako, Bamako, 2001

Leach, M. 2000 'New shapes to shift: War, parks and the hunting person in modern West Africa' *Journal of the Royal Anthropological Institute* 6, 577–95

—— 2004 'Introduction to Special Issue. Security, socioecology, polity: Mande hunters, civil society, and nation-states in contemporary West Africa' *Africa Today* 50, vii–xvi

Losch, B. 2000 'La Côte d'Ivoire en quête d'un nouveau projet national' *Politique africaine* 78, 5–25

Mali 2001 'La chasse traditionnelle en Afrique de l'Ouest, d'hier à aujourd'hui' in *Actes du Colloque International de Bamako, 26–28 January 2001* (Bamako: Ministère de la Culture du Mali)

Marshall-Fratani, R. 2006 'The war of "who is who": Autochthony, nationalism, and citizenship in the Ivoirian crisis' *African Studies Review* 49, 9–43

McFarland, D. M. & Rupley, L. A. 1998 *Historical Dictionary of Burkina Faso* (Lanham

MD/London: Scarecrow Press)

Muana, P. K. 1997 'The Kamajoi militia: Civil war, internal displacement and the politics of counter-insurgency' *Africa Development* 22, 77–100

Ouattara, S. 2006 'Deux sociétés secrètes dans l'espace public: L'association des *Dozobele* (chasseurs) et des *Tcholobele* (Poro) en milieu Sénoufo en Côte d'Ivoire et au Mali' PhD thesis, University of Gothenburg

—— 2008 *Deux sociétés secrètes dans des espaces publics: Bois sacrés, initiations et rites de passage chez les Sénoufo de la Côte d'Ivoire et du Mali* (*Acta Universitatis Gothoburgensis: Gothenburg Studies in Social Anthropology* 20) (Gothenburg: School of Global Studies, University of Gothenburg)

Pratten, D. 2008 'Introduction. The politics of protection: Perspectives on vigilantism in Nigeria' *Africa* 78, 1–15

Richards, P. 1996 *Fighting for the Rain Forest: War, Youth and Resources in Sierra Leone* (London/Oxford: International African Institute/James Currey)

—— (ed.) 2005 *No Peace, No War: An Anthropology of Contemporary Armed Conflicts* (London/Athens: James Currey/Ohio University Press)

Thorsen, D. 2007 'Junior–senior linkages: Youngsters' perceptions of migration in rural Burkina Faso' in Hahn & Klute 2007: 175–99

Thoyer, A. 1995 *Récits épiques des chasseurs bamanan du Mali.* (Paris: L'Harmattan)

Traoré, K. 2000 *Le jeu et le sérieux: Essai d'anthropologie littéraire sur la poésie épique des chasseurs du Mande (Afrique de l'Ouest)* (Köln: Rüdiger Köppe)

News media sources

AFP 2002 = Agence-France Presse 2002 'Les chasseurs "dozos" déclenchent la "guerre mystique"', 7 November

Baxter, Joan 2002 'Eyewitness: Ivorian rebels defiant' *BBC News* [London], 29 October. Available online at: <http://news.bbc.co.uk/2/hi/africa/2373377.stm> (last visited 31 Aug 2010)

Fraternité Matin 2001 'Des Dozos tirent sur les forces de l'ordre: Deux militaires abattus' *Fraternité Matin* 17 January, 10859 (daily newspaper, Abidjan). Available online at: <www.fratmat.info>

Konaté, M. 2005 'Festival: Les chasseurs d'Afrique de l'Ouest sont à Bamako' *L'Essor* (daily newspaper, Bamako), 27 May. Available online at: <www.malikounda.com/nouvelle_ voir. php?idNouvelle=3708> (last visited 31 Aug 2010)

News24 2002 'Ivory Coast's demons are back' *News24 SA* (South Africa) 4 October

Pawson, Lara 2004 'Crossing Ivory Coast's checkpoints' *BBC News* [London], 20 April. Available online at: <http://news.bbc.co.uk/2/hi/africa/3640027.stm> (last visited 31 Aug 2010)

Soir Info 2000 'Adama Coulibaly plaide pour les dozos', 22 June. *Soir Info* (daily newspaper, Abidjan). Available online at: <http://www.soirinfo.com>

5

Bodies of Power
Narratives of Selfhood & Security in Nigeria

DAVID PRATTEN

Introduction

It is often asserted that crime and disorder are related to transitions within political systems – from authoritarianism to democracy, from military to civilian rule, from communist regime to market economy, or from civil war to peace (Shaw 2000). Also, in tracing the emergence of contemporary vigilantism in Nigeria it is tempting to point to watershed moments that link vigilantism to transition and rupture within the nation's political fabric. The Nigerian Civil War (1967–70) is often cited as such a watershed, not least because of the subsequent availability of arms for criminal use. The impact of structural adjustment and neoliberal reforms from the 1980s onwards, which heralded the demise of the powerful petro-state, might equally represent a significant turning point. Recent trends towards devolved and privatised security, including moves on the part of the federal government to embrace policies of 'community policing',[1] along with the massive growth of the private security sector,[2] have similarly led to official tolerance and, at times, promotion of vigilante groups, especially during the well-publicised 'crime waves' of the 1990s. And most proximately, the return to democracy in 1999 has introduced a fundamental decentralising impetus within the nation-state in which vigilantism has come to express re-ignited religious tension, ethnic cultural nationalism and the strategic ambitions of increasingly well-resourced state governors.[3]

How contemporary vigilantism articulates to these various watershed moments and dynamics is a necessary and problematic question. Several points should be noted. First, as several commentators on Nigerian vigilantism have noted, while these watershed moments have brought major incentives to vigilantism, there are also significant continuities in vigilante practice that should be traced across pre-colonial, colonial and post-colonial histories (Nolte 2004; Pratten 2007b; Fourchard 2008; Last 2008). Second, there is no easy logic that inflects national or global trends to local practices, and no simple model of state–society relations captures the ambiguous nature of vigilantism. There is a risk of misunderstanding vigilantism, I think, if our analysis is coloured by the limited lenses of the discourses on rights, law, popular mobilisation and civil society. It should be clear that vigilantism 'cannot be reduced to either expressions of the mob or to mere antidotes to formal law' (Buur & Jensen 2004: 140). And third, vigilantism's own tenacity needs to be related to its own cultural logics, social motivations, historical discourses and embodied practices. Thus, following Sally Falk Moore's example, the ethnography presented here examines the ways in which local social action 'has its own imperatives, and its own designs' (Moore 1996: 602).

The focus of this chapter is on the further development of aspects of an ethnography which concerns the historical narrative and cultural registers of violence in which vigilantism operates among the Annang of Akwa Ibom state in south-eastern Nigeria.[4] In the literature on African vigilantes we frequently confront an impersonalised, often faceless, voiceless and undifferentiated category of vigilante. If we are to fully incorporate an 'inside story' of Nigerian vigilantes as others purport (Meagher 2007), then it is surely necessary to provide an analysis of the emic understandings by which vigilantism is legitimated and made meaningful, and to listen to what vigilantes say about themselves, their practices and the violence in which they are engaged. As scholars have argued in other contexts of conflict and violence in Africa, the evidence that combatants, vigilantes and others provide about their own understandings of power and purpose, identity and intent provides a necessary corrective to conventional accounts which speak *for* and not through them (Peters & Richards 1998; Eriksson Baaz & Stern 2008).

On the basis of testimonies from Annang vigilantes, this chapter examines aspects of an 'inside' story of Nigerian vigilantism. The first dimension is to demonstrate the significance and persistence of ontological frameworks in explaining the repertoires of violence, the improvised procedures of justice, and the oppositional categories that are embedded in vigilante practice. Of particular salience are the historical and metaphysical oppositions which form categorical distinctions between vigilantes and thieves, and between community benevolence and external malevolence. These distinctions are inscribed in punishment on the bodies of thieves as a primary site of violent closure defining insider and outsider. Hence violence itself serves as a powerful and productive signifier, and in this context vigilantes perform exemplary acts of violence in order to make and mark community boundaries.

It is necessary therefore to provide localised and historicised evidence in evaluating Arjun Appadurai's (1998) claim that where lived experience becomes unstable, indeterminate and socially volatile violent action can become one means of satisfying a sense of the categorical self. Indeed, the second related aspect is that vigilantism not only defines exclusion but is also constitutive of inclusive boundary mechanisms and of community subjectivity, of masculine identity and moral ethnicity. Of particular note in this regard are the ways in which masculinity is embedded in routine practices and ritual observances which are both sources of protection and of subject formation. Patrols, oaths and the rehabilitation of local offenders also reinforce the definition of a moral community, and hence of indigeneity.

And third, the intermediary role of vigilantes who navigate a multiplicity of constituencies is also politically productive of new forms of authority and of delegitimising discourses. Hence, in addition to selfhood and otherness, vigilantism is also productive of a political space in which careers can be made (and lost). These are micro-political processes by which people 'make' post-colonial modes of governance and 'make do' in the face of disorder. Individuals and collective groupings therefore engage with a diverse and heterogeneous set of institutions of the Nigerian nation-state, and in this context the instability of the state's norms, laws and institutions make it a privileged site for negotiation, bargaining and brokerage (Olivier de Sardan 1999).

In the following discussion I will outline the careers and personalities of a small selection of vigilantes and extend the above-mentioned three areas of discussion: the bodily inscription of difference through punishment, practices of self-identification and subject formation, and the precarious but productive role that vigilantes occupy as intermediaries.

Vigilante voices

A brief description of local historical context is necessary to orient the following accounts. In the pre-colonial era, surveillance (*ukpeme idung*, 'to watch village') was organised by Annang lineage or village heads, who would pick small groups of young men to monitor paths and plots from hides built of palm leaves (*ufok usung*, 'road house'). Protecting agricultural produce was of paramount importance; night-guarding was therefore an important seasonal practice since the theft of seed yams and cassava stems – essential for the following year's harvest and for food security – was considered an act of deviance tantamount to a physical life-threatening assault (Austen 1986).[5] The night-guards would parade any thieves they had caught around the village and the market (in a process called *etak ino*, 'to parade thief'). During the colonial period such modes of vigilance were undermined by efforts to criminalise those judicial fora such as night guards which operated covertly beyond the colonial native-court system. Successive local demands for re-instatement of *ufok usung*, however, point to the persistence and popularity of the practice. Indeed, evidence from the 1940s and 1950s indicates that 'watch committees' of traditional *ufok usung* guards were licensed in limited respects to work alongside rural police patrols.[6]

This pre-existing model of village surveillance has served as a familiar template for subsequent mobilisation and vigilante practices which were adapted in response to a heightened fear of crime waves in Akwa Ibom state during the 1980s and 1990s. In 1988 a youth association called *Mboho Ade Uforo Ikot Akpa Nkuk* (MUKAN), or 'Unity for Progress', in the Annang village of Ikot Akpa Nkuk formed security patrols called 'vanguards' in a bid to counter an upsurge in armed robbery. The formation of vigilante groups all over Nigeria was endorsed at various political levels during this period. In August 1996, for instance, the paramount ruler of Ukanafun Local Government Area, in which this village is located, proposed a resolution at the Traditional Rulers' Council that each village should be responsible for forming a vigilante committee.[7] And Akwa Ibom state's police commissioner, while criticising local-government funding for the police, called on communities to mount vigilante patrols in the face of renewed 'underworld activity' (*Post Express* [Lagos], 3 November 1998).

The MUKAN vigilantes imposed an all-night curfew, mobilised a group of hand-picked 'strong' guards, and mounted checkpoints on the paths and roads leading to the village. By 1997, MUKAN had recorded 23 cases of apprehending and parading thieves, and 18 cases in which suspects apprehended by the vigilante group were later convicted in the local magistrates' court.

By 2000 MUKAN had been superseded by another group called simply the 'Youth/Vigilante Committee', which was also backed by the village's council of elders. In most respects the new group's efforts towards nocturnal vigilance followed a familiar pattern, though this group, rather than selecting individual men who were well equipped (physically and spiritually) for patrol work as MUKAN had done, called on *all* young men in the village to mount patrols on a rota basis of one night of guard duty per person each week. The implications of this inclusive mode of membership are discussed further below, but in effect at a time of heightened fear of armed robbery and of an expanding population of 'outsiders' in the village it was felt necessary to define male citizenship and integrity through vigilante patrolling. Despite an incident in 2004 in which leading vigilante-group members were arrested for possession of illegal firearms, the committee's success in combating crime heralded an expansion in its range of activities beyond night patrols. MUKAN had long sponsored attempts by poverty-stricken young men to find employment, just as the group had disciplined 'stubborn' or truant young children. From 2000, however, the vigilante committee also constituted itself as an evening court for the settling of disputes and assumed responsibilities for debt collection, screening of political candidates, catching stray goats, and securing payment and employment opportunities from outside contractors (Pratten 2007b). In short, the basis of the vigilante group's legitimacy and power expanded quickly, especially in relation to and often in competition with the chieftaincy, the local government and the police.

The accounts here, reproduced from field notes and interviews mostly recorded in 2003 and 2004, are from vigilante members who were recruited into MUKAN at its inception and who became senior patrol leaders of the Youth/Vigilante Committee after 2000.

'Fifty'[8]

Fifty formerly worked as a storeman in Port Harcourt. An amateur boxer, he is the village's football coach, but has no regular employment other than being vice-chairman of the vigilante committee.

> One of our brothers, Friday Udo Ubom, was killed by armed robbers at the boundary between Ikot Eka Uyo and Ikot Akpa Nkuk. That is when all the boys, whoever you are, were called up at the village council. When we got there the youth chairman asked: 'What shall we do now that the robbers have come to kill one of our important brothers in the village?' We gathered up our senses and decided that we should guide this village. The vigilante group then was known as MUKAN. Later on we got control of the situation in the village. When we held criminals we showed that we were not hiding them – once you hold a thief you have to expose them and let the village know that they are a bad person. That is why when we capture somebody we taken him round, and beat drums for him to dance ... When the village is dangerous you cannot even sleep. Robbers steal 'front and back'. Formerly we didn't sleep in the house. Before 7pm you must find a church to go and lay down. That is why we are suffering every night now, so that the village can be in peace. I used to sleep outside but now, when I know that my boys are patrolling, I can sleep in the house. There are many strangers living with us now, buying land, building houses. They wouldn't want to invest here if the village was too dangerous ... From MUKAN we learnt how to organise the vigilante patrols. I was a general patrol leader then, but I did not patrol when Jonny Ephraim was chairman of the vigilantes because he was the one who gave a boy an oath to swear – individually – when the right to do that is held by the village council. We have no power without the village council promoting us. Through that mistake [giving an oath without village-council endorsement] so many souls in this village could have died [from counter-oaths]. So he was suspended from the office. The current committee is the only administration that has lasted more than a year – now it has lasted a year and seven months. Due to our performance we are still 'on seat'. People have been lodging petitions against us about embezzlement of the funds used for battery and torches. They didn't know we were keeping a record. They called us to the village council but we had made an accurate account ... Among the boys we have bad boys, and we have good boys. But among the bad boys we know the way to get them to submit. Some of the boys who are walking with us have sometimes been corrupted by stealing. There is a way that you can hold a criminal these days to change that person [by parading]. But if it is natural blood – inside natural blood – it is not possible to change. But for bad boys who are now among the vigilantes it was because of hardship which made their eyes climb over things [covet property]. So we put them in order, gave them the law and the rules and they are now keeping cool. They were the people who worried the village. Some of the villagers doubt that we can control all these hard, hard boys without making problems for ourselves. But if you feed them regularly ... we know the way of handling all those boys – that is why we still have the vigilante group up to today.

'Fineboy'

As a younger man Fineboy used to perform with the *ekong* (warrior) and *ekpo* (ancestral) masquerades.[9] He is now married with four children and attends the Full Gospel Church. Fineboy has been the taskforce chairman of the National Cyclists' Union for 18 years and enforces the various by-laws and taxes that the union regulates. He is routinely to be seen on patrol or detaining riders for such things as failure to contribute to dues or to a burial. Fineboy is an imposing figure, broader, almost, than he is tall. He is a patrol leader and when we spoke he had been up four nights in a row guarding a lane that leads from the main expressway to the secondary school. He includes the following incident among an expanding list of single-handed feats that he recalls with pride.

> Two nights ago my patrol saw a white vehicle which we had been seen three times before. This time I saw the people getting out of the car – they seemed to be looking for a compound to enter. I fired shots from one of my guns [one is a locally made pistol given to him by the village, the other is his personal, foreign-made weapon]. I fired into the air and the ground, not directly at them (if you fire horizontally at night it is very dangerous – you could shoot any innocent person accidentally). I dodged around and fired again to make it seem that I was not alone. I saw them off on my own! As they ran to their car and retreated I could hear them shout 'MOPOL away!' ['MOPOL' is a covername for a notorious local armed-robbery gang, derived from the acronym for the paramilitary Nigerian Mobile Police].[10]

Fineboy joined the village vigilante group when MUKAN was founded. At that time he learned a few of the tricks of how to guard – 'how to hang' [act inconspicuously] when one sees a suspicious car; sending only one person to check the vehicle while others hide; flashing a torch and then dodging away from that spot so as to give the impression that there are more vigilantes present than there actually are; not smoking on patrol; and using the small *owolom* wooden drum as a way to call for back-up. Fineboy was keen to explain how he had managed to survive on the front line as a vigilante for so long, with the help of embodied forms of medicine:

> I do not 'go empty body' – none of us do. Each of the vigilantes is individually protected. If I follow the laws of my protection [referring to *ato afiono* 'bullet-proof medicine'], bullets will pass around my body, and my bullets, if I have them blessed, will hit their target. One of the important rules is that I should not sleep with a woman before a patrol – if you refrain from sleeping with a woman the bullet will not enter your body. Also, I have survived this long because I dress for safety. You would not recognise me at night: I wear a kaftan and a long beard. If everyone knows your face at night, then they will know the people patrolling at particular places. Some vigilantes wear women's cloth for the same reason, so that people will not know them – it is a vigilante's individual choice, their 'personal style'. So long as the colour of their cloth is black.

'Udom'

Udom is married with two children and is a member of the Qua Iboe church. He is a bicycle repairman and a skilled herbalist. He is constantly on the lookout for fresh roots and has become a popular source of advice and treatment for illnesses. Udom is old enough to remember the *akuku* (village head) calling out the night-guards who built small hides (*ufok usung*) from which to monitor road junctions and village boundaries. Udom started going out for guard duty at the time MUKAN was founded:

> There were only a few guards then and those few original guards were *okpochong owo* ['powerful men'].[11] Strong vigilantes have their own protection. It is not possible for someone to patrol all night without protection for so many years; *ato afiono* must be used. Individual vigilantes obtain their power from different, secret sources. Now, because of the operation of armed robbers, there are many of us who patrol in the night. But right now there are no thieves again, all of the young people who liked to steal are now inside the guard [members of the vigilante group]. Now everybody's property can stay outside overnight without any problem ... The guards decorate thieves with charcoal and paint so that they can be easily identified as a thief among the large group of people that will gather. To paint a thief with charcoal represents shame. We use firewood charcoal, from any wood but not from the palm tree branch, and this is mixed with palm oil so that the colour will stick to the skin – sometimes we will pour *alan eyop* ['palm oil'] all over the thief. It is the same as when they rub their bodies [in oil and charcoal] in the *ekpo* masquerade so that the black colour will not wash off. The property the thief stole will be carried on their head, or tied around the neck. The thief is handed over to the police or to the family, and everyone will shout 'the thief is eating shame'.

'Regard'

Regard is short and lean. He has been a guard since 1989, when he was a schoolboy at the local Lutheran high school. There were only a few guards during MUKAN's period of operation and he was soon recognised as a staunch member. Regard was a member of the *ekpo* masquerade performed regularly in Ikot Akpa Nkuk. He now sells motor oil from the front of his house, which faces onto the main federal highway. People consider Regard to be an *okpochong owo*, a powerful man. Each of the successive youth chairmen has kept him very close to them:

> The reason [for this] is that I was chosen by the former youth chairman to be initiated at a shrine in Abiakpan, Cross River state, with supernatural anti-criminal powers. The person who controls the power of the spirit should be a young person; it cannot be a married, family man. When I want to marry, another person will be chosen to take over this position. The initiation at the shrine took three days. I was baptised on the first day, and my eyes were 'opened'.[12] After that I did one day of dry fasting (with no water, no bath and no food), and then a day of blessing. The laws of the Okomura spirit are that on any day I move with its power I cannot meet [sleep with] a woman, I

cannot eat anything that fire burns [cooked food], and I cannot greet a woman who cannot born *pikin* again [a post-menopausal woman] because there is something like witch in their soul. If you break any of these laws the power of the spirit will be reduced.

Many have witnessed Regard's power at work. In one incident when he saw a boy he did not recognise wheeling a motorbike, Regard said his body began to have physical sensations in which the front of his chest began to shake. By analogy, he referred to this process as a state of possession in which he 'did not know himself again'. The boy, after a beating, confessed to stealing the motorbike. Regard told the boy: 'We do not spare a person of your type here.' The thief was taken to the youth chairman, who sent a message to the owner of the motorbike; this person in turn testified that this was indeed his own motorbike and that it had been stolen. On a quiet road leading away from the village, alongside a stream, the boy was put to death: a nail was knocked into his head, he was hacked with machetes and he was shot and burned. 'Nobody asked what happened to the boy,' Regard commented. 'Thieves are dangerous people because they prepare with powers.'

How the fear of the esoteric powers attributed to thieves contributes to the legitimacy of vigilante violence is further captured in understandings of the relationship between power and the body.

Bodies of power

At the time of writing (24 December 2007), the local state radio, Akwa Ibom Broadcasting Corporation (AKBC), had just announced the demise of two armed robbers in Etinan Local Government Area. They were shot by the police. One of the robbers was identified by the moniker 'MC' and was reported as the leader of a gang that had been operating with impunity. In itself this incident contributes just a small component of Nigeria's crime statistics: the country recorded 3,100 armed robbers killed by the police in 2004 (Human Rights Watch 2005). The radio report went on to note, however, that the bodies of the two robbers were publicly displayed at the central police station. The correspondent observed that witnesses to this spectacle were jubilant. Congratulating the police action, and urging them on to eradicate armed robbery completely, local residents exclaimed: 'We will now be able to sleep with both eyes closed.'

This account points to the popular legitimation given to the process whereby thieves and suspected thieves in Nigeria are subjected to forms of public humiliation and often much worse – extrajudicial detainment, torture and execution (Human Rights Watch 2005). The account also highlights a key aspect in vigilante practice, namely a fascination with bodies. In the following I will discuss aspects of the punishment of the body that form the central principles of vigilante practice and to which the vigilantes allude in their testimonies.

The analysis of this practice points to the importance of understanding the tacit cultural codes employed in defining and punishing deviants (Heald 1986). Here the thief is conceived of in embodied and discursive practices analogous to familiar representations of malevolent, non-human ancestral spirits in masquerade performance. Inflections of the aesthetics and politics of such former traditions not only shape the mode of contemporary Annang vigilantes but also provide a classificatory imperative for the punishment they dispense. The focus in this context is on the cultural construction of violence in which the classifications of purity and impurity, good and evil, are constituted cosmologically together with the reconstitution of a moral order of the world (Malkki 1995: 55–6).

Concepts of personhood and evaluations of a thief's character are captured in the routine performances of contemporary vigilantes when they catch a suspected thief. As indicated in Udom's account, the suspect, once apprehended or found guilty by an ordeal or by the vigilante's tribunal, is often beaten, stripped and rubbed with a mixture of charcoal and palm oil. The suspect is then tied at the waist using the rope of a palm-wine tapper and paraded around the village, usually to the market and the village head's compound, before being delivered to the police or, in less serious cases, to his father's compound. The thief will carry an item on his head to act as an exhibit of what he has stolen. On the way both the thief and the crowd which has gathered will sing a repertoire of shaming songs (*ikuo owo*, 'to sing a person').

This 'rough music' serves to humiliate the thief, and to reinforce the public role of young men of the vigilante group in defending the community (Alford 1959; Davis 1971; Thompson 1972, 1992). The public nature of this *charivari*-style practice indicates that there is also a moral imperative to reveal rather than conceal. As Fifty says, the practice is driven by a desire to demonstrate, in part, that bribes have not been taken secretly in order to release a thief. This revelatory logic applies in many familiar historical contexts, especially in confrontations with ambiguous and dangerous forces. For example, when a snake is killed it must be put in public view in order to show that no venom has been removed for purposes of poisoning an enemy. In former times such venom would be presented to the *akuku* (chief). Such a presentation – a tribute – also acknowledged the chief's position as the paramount public peace-keeper. In a dynamic and fluid political context, the popular recognition accorded to those who settled cases, mediated in conflicts and supervised the disposal of such poisons was a key index of power. The imperative of nonconcealment and public broadcast through parading is evident in many other forms of performance which involve transformation. Initiates into the *mbobo* women's fattening society[13] and the diviners' society (*idiong*) would be paraded around village markets before emerging from periods of seclusion. The parading of suspected thieves therefore reinforces an underlying understanding that these individuals have changed their status to that of a shameful and abject category.

Key elements of these performances are not only informed by a long historical trajectory of parading and shaming suspected thieves, but also offer clues to the legitimation of vigilante action. The visual representation of the thief in the village parade re-embodies the symbolism of masquerade performance, notably that of the ancestral masquerade (*ekpo*) and its use of beautiful and ugly masks. At harvest time each year the ancestors return to their lineages in the form of the *ekpo* masquerade. *Ekpo* is indigenous to speakers of languages of the Ibibio cluster and in its simulation of ancestral presence the masquerade represents Annang cosmology writ large. Members of the *ekpo* society wear carved wooden masks which are held to become possessed by the spirits of the ancestors. Beautiful masks representing good spirits (*mfon ekpo*) portray the face in human form and stress fertility, often by means of a series of smaller children's faces carved on the forehead. Ugly masks, in contrast, are painted in dark colours and have exaggerated and distorted features, and represent malevolent wandering spirits (*idiok ekpo*). These masks are usually smaller than the beautiful masks, with non-human features such as jagged teeth and sometimes represent disfigurement and skin diseases such as gangosa (Simmons 1957; Messenger 1973).

Malevolent ancestral spirits – those invoked by enemies or provoked by disregard – are potent, dangerous and unpredictable. This means that during the *ekpo* performance there is a strong emphasis on the physical control of the fiercest spirits represented by the masks. The most awesome and dangerous of the masks is that of the 'spirit of the ghosts' (*ekpo ndem*). Wearing this mask is a form of ordeal and only a descendant of the society's founder can don it without suffering misfortune. The initiate who wears the *ekpo ndem* mask must first sleep in the forest (*akai*) for seven nights, during which time he must not eat food cooked by a woman. He will pour libations on the graves of seven 'wicked' people (*idiok ilo*, literally 'ugly character'), and he will consume roots known as *adung abasi* ('root of god') that are said to make him feel like he is flying. His seclusion, invocations and consumptions each contribute to an enhanced state of malignant possession which is demonstrated during the masquerade in various symbolic forms, including the way the masked performer is tied at the waist with palm-wine tapper rope to prevent him from attacking onlookers, the way he circulates around the market clockwise, that is by the left-hand side, which demonstrates his malicious intent, and by the fact that he is prevented from bending down and hence from resolving a familiar set of high-to-low movements which are believed to make Annang rituals effective.[13]

As Udom's testimony illustrates, vigilantes openly recognise that the practice by which thieves are paraded with a rope at the waist and are daubed black with charcoal and oil draws on a striking aesthetic parallel with the masquerade representation of malevolent spirits. Just as *ekpo* masquerade players attempt to rub their bodies up against non-members, so as to shame them by dirtying their clothes, so the body of the thief is shamed by being marked with the same substance. Palm oil is commonly associated with moments of self-transformation, especially in rites of initiation. Hence, the use of palm oil on the thief not only designates shame but a shift of status from human to non-human. These aesthetics of alterity captured in vigilante performance exaggerate difference on the basis of symbolic oppositions: vigilante/thief; clean/dirty; right/left; truth/lie; beautiful/ugly; fertile/sterile; and innocent/guilty. These oppositions map onto conceptions of the person which distinguish between those of good spirits (*eti owo*) and those of bad (*idiok owo*), and in turn between those perpetrators whose infractions can be forgiven, with the perpetrator being reformed, and those perpetrators who are in Fifty's term 'natural blood criminals', and whose crimes demand retribution.

Indeed, as Regard's chilling bluntness concerning the fate of the motorbike thief illustrates, those criminals who are beyond reform are not spared. In Regard's words: 'Thieves are dangerous people because they prepare with powers.' He is referring here to the same kinds of medicinal and initiatory powers the vigilantes are believed to use to protect themselves. That the origin and strength of an armed robber's powers are unknowable and witch-like makes them especially to be feared (Pratten 2007b). An armed robber is killed for a number of reasons. Primarily, he belongs to an irremediable category of person: no amount of shame or reform will be possible since his 'type' of character cannot be changed. Also, to release an armed robber to the police or other authorities is to invite retribution since the latter may release the suspect in return for a bribe. Numerous tales, apocryphal perhaps, relate the lengths to which armed robbers will go to take revenge on those who can identify them.[15]

This fear of thieves is compounded by the possibility (as indicated in Fineboy's reference to MOPOL) that public security forces which would otherwise be called upon for protection are in fact implicated in the thieves' operations. As Taussig (2003: 202) suggests: 'There is something insufferably attractive about the margin of law where the state re-creates the very terror it is meant to combat.' In a situation where thieves wear police uniforms, and police officers are routinely arrested for themselves being thieves, vigilantes negotiate a landscape of 'radical uncertainty, unpredictability, and insecurity' (Mbembe & Nuttall 2004: 364). In this environment, the 'dead certainty' to which vigilante violence can lead may be seen in part to represent a popular resolution to the dislocations of trust, social identity and political sovereignty in the era of '419 fraud' (Apter 2000; Smith 2004, 2006), but more specifically to represent the inflection of localised logics of personhood and identity. To understand vigilantism as a mode of collective violence and the 'occult forensics' (Comaroff 2008) this entails, it is necessary to take account of the moral imperatives of vigilantism and to map the different moral and aesthetic evaluations people in different contexts make of their actions on the bodies of others (Spencer 2003: 1568).

Bodies of belonging

In contrast to thieves' bodies, which are marked in ways that serve to provide violent closure on a deviant other, the bodies of vigilantes are marked by a variety of practices of dissimulation. Given the evident danger inherent in vigilante operations – of moving in the dark, in the bush, at the village boundaries, and of being confronted by enemies, including armed robbers, witches and other malevolent forces – disguising one's body and one's intentions is an imperative. Most vigilantes disguise themselves by wearing dark clothes, usually black trousers and a black shirt. This disguise is referred to as *akpoho idem*, meaning 'changing the body'. Concealment of one's form is, however, also achieved in other ways. Weapons carried by vigilantes are completely concealed on the person. Machetes in particular have to be held upright and tight against the back of the arm so that in profile they cannot be seen.

As mentioned above, some vigilantes also disguise themselves by dressing as women. By wearing a kaftan and either a wig or a headtie, men like Fineboy transform their gendered appearance. At one level this transformation is a straightforward case of camouflage, since it is argued that no armed robber would expect a woman to be a vigilante.[16] Yet men dressing as women represents more than physical disguise. This cross-gendering conceals not only form but also intention. Men say that they cannot know how women think; hence to dress as a woman is to render oneself unknowable and secret to other men. While this cross-gendering operates as dissimulating disguise it also represents a set of positive connotations for the vigilantes and the villagers they protect. There are historical resonances to this transformation. Salmons (1985) argues that men once disguised themselves as women in order to cross into enemy territory during conflicts. During crucial stages of a woman's pre-marital fattening rite (*mbobo*), which is held to render her clean and fertile, young men of the *ekong* masquerade assume women's form in performances that endow the woman with spiritual protection.[17] Further ritual inversions are evident in the practices of the women's society called *iban isong* ('women of the soil'). When *iban isong* women lead a protest against a man and besiege his compound in support of an abused wife, they will wear ragged clothes, paint their faces blue or with charcoal, and dress somewhat like a man – wearing the legs and sleeves of men's clothes.[18] These inversions of male and female are believed to do two things: to denote danger and potency in the 'nonsensical' apparel, and to signify the crossing of domains. While male warriors dress as women to bless fattened women, so the women's forum dress as men when they bring war to a man's compound.

It is in this context that the mutual encompassment of male and female figures is a feature that is necessary for and complementary to the performance of perilous operations required for social reproduction and defence. The form of cross-dressing practiced by vigilantes may constitute, as Mary Moran argues in the case of Liberian rebels, an attempt to retrieve the power of the indigenous warrior (*ekong*; cf. Salmons 1985). Here, playing with gender identity concerns drawing power from the deliberate conflation of categories, to demonstrate that qualities of courage, strength, and supernatural prowess are not limited by biological endowment (Moran 1995: 80). Familiar aspects of vigilante membership – secrecy, protective medicines and the use of legitimated violence – constitute important aspects of masculinity, as locally understood. Men dressing as women further reinforces a representation of vigilantes as a force for fertility and hence a symbolic counterpoint to criminals who are represented as impediments to social reproduction.

In this context, vigilantism is not only a matter of the sort of physical tactics of manoeuvre that Fineboy describes or of the sartorial dissimulations discussed. Vigilantism is also a 'battle of powers', as the vigilantes would suggest. As each of the accounts confirms, vigilantes must protect their bodies in numerous ways beyond mere physical disguise. Bulletproof medicine and blessed bullets constitute the most familiar forms of protection in this context. It should be noted, however, that deploying supernatural registers of power in this way constitutes more than protection. When vigilantes recount the 'laws' of a medicinal protection they are also relating an ordeal through which they live every day and are enumerating potential infractions which could lead to their death. As such, these narratives should be interpreted in terms of a set of routine practices, disciplines of the self, mainly involving prohibitions against sex, which is at the same time an ontology of power and masculinity. The sequestered logics of bulletproof medicine and the like are invocations, 'local practices of re-enchanting tradition' (Mbembe 2002: 265), that constitute and renew subjectivities.

While vigilantism marks boundaries of inclusion and exclusion on the terrain of the body, so it also delineates frontiers of landscape and community. Fifty's comments concerning nocturnal security and his ability to sleep at home when the vigilantes are patrolling may be understood in terms of a familiar opposition between conducting socially productive activities within the community as opposed to nefarious and subversive activities outside, in the bush (cf. Jedrej 1986). I have discussed elsewhere the practices by which vigilante patrols re-territorialise spatial community boundaries during the curfew hours – after 10 o'clock at night (Pratten 2008). Vigilantes, in traversing a sequence of named markets, crossroads, squares and boundary paths, trace a topography that not only represents a physical space but also a landscape of names – a genealogical history (McCall 1995: 259; Ferme 2001: 23–48). These hidden, 'inward-turning' histories are productive of a temporal and spatial community in which young men are vested with the rights to exercise justice and are yet illegible to strangers and the state alike.

Practices by which vigilantes establish guilt also serve to configure the community's frontiers. Knowledge, truth and hence guilt in disputed cases are often ascertained through the processes of testing. In a context of highly personalised attributions of cause and effect the appeal of oaths (*mbiam*) and ordeals (*ukang*) lies in their invocation of forms of authority from the dead and the wild that transcend human experience. Oathing practices are therefore 'rituals of verification' by which truth, guilt and accountability are established through public spectacle; they constitute more than a guarantee of veracity, but also an ordeal through which oath-takers live or die. As Tonkin (2000) notes, they are 'dramas of truth'. In a recent case involving theft of medical equipment from the Ikot Akpa Nkuk health centre, for example, an oath specialist was hired to pour *mbiam* across each road leading to the village. A prime suspect, who protested his innocence, was compelled to undergo the ordeal of stepping over this buried substance which now serves as a general sanction to the community as a whole since the boundaries of the village are now delineated by the ordeal substance. As a generalised invocation the village is watching and waiting for someone to die from its effects which, since swollen legs are indicative of false oath-swearing, will again be indicated by bodily transformation. Within a generalised context of popular insecurity, compounded by an inherent mistrust of the police, we can appreciate the importance of those who have the capacity to distinguish order from disorder through familiar, if conservative, ways (Fields 1982). Similarly, Regard's initiation into the thief-finding cult and his 'diviner-detective' identity (Comaroff 2008) illustrate in a highly individualised and extraordinary fashion responses to crime and disorder that operate in both physical and metaphysical planes.

While some bodies are abjected by vigilantes, others are rehabilitated. In this light, the processes by which former suspected thieves from the village are reformed through incorporation into the vigilante group are apparently contradictory. The poacher-turned-gamekeeper scenario may also be seen as a familiar if precarious solution to problems of crime, but this process is multi-layered. As Fifty and Udom mentioned, those with criminal records (the 'bad boys') were incorporated into the vigilante group because they were indigenes of this community – 'sons of the soil'. Membership of the vigilante group therefore serves as a mark of indigeneity and stands in direct opposition to the violent closure meted out to thieves of non-indigenous origin. Opportunities for the young men of Ikot Akpa Nkuk who have strayed onto the wrong side of the law have taken two forms: inclusion within the circuits of accumulation that vigilante patrolling can offer, and sponsorship to support the learning and practising of a trade. The paternalistic imperatives to 'reform' bad influences from within the village draw on a discourse on poverty and youth unemployment. Within a familiar rhetoric of intergenerational tension, the vigilantes blame youth hardship and hence youth crime on the failings of patronage from fathers and elders, manifest in unsponsored and uncompleted education and apprenticeship. Perhaps most significantly, however, this practice may be interpreted in terms of patrimonial strategies by which the inclusion of known criminals within the vigilante group, who are under a constant threat of denunciation, serves to motivate a set of supporters for youth leaders whose own positions, as outlined below, are often challenged.

To hear from both sides

A key stated imperative for informal justice across southern Nigeria is to protect communities and individuals from being subjected to the perils associated with the formal judicial institutions of the state, especially the police. Pronouncements intended to stop individuals taking cases to the police before reporting them to an intermediary informal court or committee are commonplace, as is the practice of withdrawing cases from the police for settlement 'at home'. These practices attest to a powerful ideology of self-sufficiency and of protection from the predations of the state. They are borne out in numerous contexts that I have encountered, including the urban shantytowns of Port Harcourt where local patrons and hometown associations perform this role, and in the bylaws of the vigilante groups such as that of Ikot Akpa Nkuk. Vigilantes therefore must be seen beyond the night-patrols as one, albeit potentially violent, outlet within a legally pluralistic setting for dispute settlement. Alongside chiefs, lineage tribunals and churches, vigilante groups assert their own legitimate authority by calling for cases to be brought to them before the cases go to the formal state sector, and also provide a mode of arbitration that is popular, cheaper and quicker.

This brokerage between disputants and the formal legal system is persistent and effective because it enables individuals, chiefs, youth and others to insert themselves into the space of informal dispute settlement, with the authority, returns, knowledge and connections that come with it. These intermediary roles are politically productive. Two former vigilante leaders in Ikot Akpa Nkuk, for example, have now become village council elders, and their career trajectories have been accelerated precisely because of a reputation for providing effective justice, gained while they were powerful vigilante leaders. Underlying these trajectories, in fact, is a long-standing principle in Annang history of the capacity 'to hear from both sides', whereby effective judging of cases, dispute settlement and peacemaking, irrespective of the register of authority in which it is achieved, has proved to be a central feature of political power. And, while vigilantism has promoted some to political authority, financial benefits have also accrued from vigilante operations. The monthly returns from taxing business premises for night-time protection may be small, but annual lump sums (which some businesses prefer to pay) are not negligible. Neither are the returns from the provision of raw materials to external contractors working in the village for which the youth/vigilante committee routinely petition. Combined with fees and fines that are collected for settling cases and debt recovery, the turnover of the group is sufficient to warrant public accountability meetings and to generate complaints of misappropriation.

This intermediary role is therefore productive, but can also be precarious. Support from many constituencies, especially young people, chiefs and police, needs to be sustained at the same time. A succession of village youth committee leaders who have managed no more than a few months in office before being replaced points to the serial collapse in the ability to maintain this complex legitimacy. That the village vigilante group is constituted as the 'youth committee' carries significant weight. In contemporary Nigerian parlance, inflected as it is with popularised discourses from the Niger Delta militancy, 'youth' is a term that connotes claims for political and economic entitlement which are pronounced in increasingly vocal and violent discourses of disenfranchisement. Nevertheless, failure to make transparent account of the funds that accrue to the vigilantes ranks as the most significant cause for which youth chairmen are discharged. For the youth members of the vigilante movement, commensality and collective re-distribution are key principles underpinning their support. The consumption patterns of vigilante executives are watched keenly, often leading to petitions to account for funds at the village council. Where stories have emerged that leading vigilantes have acted alone – for example, by 'taxing' a business premises for purposes of individual gain – these individuals' popular support will wane. As Fifty outlined, other vigilante leaders have been replaced because they transgressed the bounds of traditional authority by calling on suspected thieves to swear *mbiam* oaths of innocence without reference to the village council. And from the perspective of the police, events in 2004, when several vigilante leaders from Ikot Akpa Nkuk were arrested and charged with possession of illegal firearms, illustrate the precarious status that requires vigilantes to monitor and maintain the relations of complicity in which they operate. In this case a local politician intervened to release the vigilantes on bail and an arrangement was subsequently brokered by which the vigilantes were able to retain weapons effectively licensed to them by the village council, and were issued with ID cards authorised by the police which keep a register of vigilante members.

Conclusion

For the 'inside story' on Nigerian vigilantes we must confront the messy, fractured, personal worlds of individuals, their biographies and motivations. It is important then to move beyond conventional approaches which emphasise the aggregated and abstracted two-dimensional 'institutionalised' view of vigilante violence. We cannot assume that vigilante groups are *a priori* 'genuine civil initiatives' charted on a course to progressive, democratic reform. They are entangled in complex personal biographies and historical narratives. A three-dimensional perspective surely allows one to understand that vigilantism does not simply represent the refracted relationship between society and the weaknesses of a state's policing. One needs to ask why patrolling, protection and punishment are embedded in people's daily, dangerous routines.

Following from this, it is a misreading to suggest that the practices and ideas of the vigilantes discussed here constitute a 'reversion to traditional institutions' (Meagher 2007: 90). The evidence presented concerns both the continuity and the contemporary contingency of a set of ideas and practices. It is therefore also wrong to assert that such a 'reversion' provides the 'key impetus behind violent vigilantism' (Meagher 2007: 90). The key impetus is a fear of armed robbers which is inevitably filtered through local cultural lenses. These same cultural lenses provide a context in which the moral economy of protection unfolds.

To account for the practice and persistence of vigilantes it is necessary to consider their own, inevitably self-legitimating, narratives. I hope to have demonstrated that these are not superficial ideologies which simply legitimate accumulation of wealth or criminality. The historical tenacity with which embodied semiotics of difference mark vigilantes from thieves along with practices that differentiate insider from outsider are not so easily dismissed. I also hope that the vigilante narratives have shown that there are critical, delegitimising discourses at work both within the vigilante group and among the various constituencies to which it relates. These serve to destabilise the group from time to time, just as fluctuations in perceived risks cause it to wax and wane, but they have not derailed the practice in the past 20 years.

It is important to stress, finally, that when viewed in this light popular justice is not merely popular but also productive. In the Nigerian context of endemic, 'radical' insecurity, to adopt Achille Mbembe's phrase, contemporary Annang vigilantism produces efforts to 'fix' representations of belonging, authority and selfhood that are otherwise in flux. The various practices of 'frontierism' and boundary formation, involving both closure and accommodation, for instance, serve to reinforce cognitive and spatial conceptions of indigeneity which link it to broader dynamics of what has been called 'new nativism' on the continent (Geschiere & Nyamnjoh 2000; Mbembe 2001). As a strategy by means of which forms of security and protection insert themselves into the power relations of state, chieftaincy and community, vigilantism offers a powerful space in which patrimonialism and rent-seeking can be legitimated. Hence it is here in the relations fostered by vigilant intermediaries that new forms of authority based on tactics from the margin – youth and violence – have emerged. And finally, as the vigilante voices discussed in this chapter suggest, night-guard practices constitute a powerful mode of subject formation based on practices of testing, discipline, disguise and protection. As Mbembe suggests, 'current African imaginations of the self are born out of disparate but often intersecting practices, the goal of which is not only to settle factual and moral disputes about the world but also to open the way for *self-styling'* (Mbembe 2002: 269). The cultural and historical contingencies of a process of self-styling among Annang vigilantes are evident in their attempts to re-formulate and fix those concepts and practices of masculinity, indigeneity and selfhood which are key to our understanding of contemporary vigilantism in Africa.

Notes

1 In 2002 the British and US governments launched substantially funded law-enforcement assistance programmes in collaboration with the Nigerian Police, with trials in community policing undertaken in Kaduna and Enugu states (Human Rights Watch 2005).

2 There are currently between 1,500 and 2,000 private security companies employing more than 100,000 people (Abrahamsen & Williams 2007).

3 To cite only the majority regional trends, crime-fighting in the Yoruba-speaking south-west has been led by the O'odua People's Congress (OPC; Akinyele 2001; Nolte 2007, 2004), in the eastern Igbo states by the Bakassi Boys (Baker 2002; Ukiwo 2002; Harnischfeger 2003; Smith 2004; Meagher 2007), and across the north by *shari'a* implementation committees, *hisba* (Casey 2007; Last 2008; Adamu 2008).

4 This research, aspects of which I have discussed elsewhere (Gore & Pratten 2003; Pratten 2006, 2007b, 2008), is based on fieldwork conducted in the village of Ikot Akpa Nkuk; this is headquarters of Ukanafun Local Government Area of Akwa Ibom state. The research was undertaken between 1997 and 2007 and has been generously supported by the UK's Economic and Social Research Council, the Nuffield Foundation and in two instances by the British Academy.

5 Cassava was introduced to the region within the first decades of colonial rule and quickly supplanted yam as the staple crop (Ohadike 1981; Pratten 2007a).

6 MSS Afr. S. 1505.6, Annual Report, Calabar Province, 1952.

7 Ukanafun Traditional Rulers' Council, Minutes of the Ukanafun Traditional Rulers' Council meeting, 20 September 1996.

8 Although normally I would cite individual's names openly, since this is considered appropriate recognition, on this occasion I have anonymised the names and 'guy-names' (nicknames) of the vigilante group members in order to protect their identities; with this in mind I have also chosen men who at time of writing are no longer active guards. The transcripts have been edited slightly for the sake of clarity.

9 Fineboy recalled seeing me at Ikot Essien market when I first witnessed *ekpo* in 1997. Ironically, many young men (re-)introduce themselves to me having taken part in the masquerade performance, but naturally I do not recognise them because during the performance they were masked.

10 Witnesses to an attack by gang of armed robbers on the compound of a politician returning for Christmas 2005 also reported hearing the robbers refer to themselves as 'MOPOL'.

11 The category of the strong and powerful (*okpochong owo*) refers to those who have suppressed a rival's power and who have overcome their rival's tests, trials and threats.

12 The expression 'to open the eyes' is commonly used in referring to initiation into esoteric secrets.

13 Women in *mbobo* would undergo a period of seclusion and deliberate fattening at the time of transition from adolescence to womanhood prior to marriage and childbirth. This could also constitute a means by which problems with infertility, headaches and

weight loss might be addressed.

14 Suspended objects, persons, spirits and gestures which have not resolved this high-low opposition – which broadly corresponds to a resolution between the sky deity (*abassi enyong*) and the spirits of the soil (*abassi ikpaisong*) – and which often includes items used in the preparation of medicines, are especially potent, transformative or malevolent.

15 This echoes a feature of national discourse on armed robbers. For discussion of a pivotal and infamous case see Marenin (1987).

16 Several women are in fact members of the vigilante group. However, they do not go on night patrol; instead they are tasked with listening out for gossip and punishing erring young women.

17 The earliest ethnographers documenting practices in this region also commented on the practice whereby Efik daughters would appear at burials dressed like men (Talbot 1914).

18 *Iban isong* also supervised the rites of widowhood (*ibid.*: 249). See also Ekpo (1995: 52–54). The most famous mobilisation of *iban isong* was in the 'Women's War' of 1929 (Van Allen 1972; Ifeka-Moller 1973).

References

Abrahams, R. 1996 'Vigilantism: Order and disorder on the frontiers of the state' in Harris, Olivia (ed.) 1996 *Inside and Outside the Law: Anthropological Studies of Authority and Ambiguity* (London: Routledge): 41–55

Abrahamsen, R. & Williams, M. C. 2007 'Introduction: The privatisation and globalisation of security in Africa' *International Relations* 21, 2, 131–41

Adamu, F. L. 2008 'Gender, *Hisbah* and the enforcement of morality in northern Nigeria' *Africa* 78, 1, 136–52

Akinyele, R. T. 2001 'Ethnic militancy and national stability in Nigeria: A case study of the Oodua People's Congress' *African Affairs* 100, 401, 623–40

Alford, V. 1959 'Rough music or charivari' *Folklore* 70, 4, 505–18

Anderson, R. G. (ed.) 1999 *Palm Wine and Leopard's Whiskers: Reminiscences of Eastern Nigeria* (Otago: National Libary of New Zealand)

Appadurai, A. 1998 'Dead certainty: Ethnic violence in the era of globalization' *Public Culture* 10, 2, 225–47

Apter, A. 2000 'Nigerian democracy and the politics of illusion' in Comaroff, J. L. & Comaroff, J. (eds) 2000 *Civil Society and the Political Imagination in Africa: Critical Perspectives* (Chicago IL: University of Chicago Press): 267–308

Austen, R. A. 1986 'Criminals and the African cultural imagination: Normative and deviant heroism in pre-colonial and modern narratives' *Africa* 56, 4, 385–98

Baker, B. 2002 'When the Bakassi Boys came: Eastern Nigeria confronts vigilantism' *Journal of Contemporary African Studies* 20, 2, 223–44

Buur, L. & Jensen, S. 2004 'Introduction: Vigilantism and the policing of everyday life in South Africa' *African Studies* 63, 2, 139–52

Casey, C. 2007 '"Policing" through violence: Fear, vigilantism, and the politics of Islam in northern Nigeria' in Pratten, D. & Sen, A. (eds) 2007 *Global Vigilantes: Perspectives on Justice and Violence* (London: Hurst & Co.): 93–126

Comaroff, J. 2008 'Detective fictions: In pursuit of sovereignty in the postcolony'. Annual Lecture, African Studies Centre, University of Oxford, 3 June

Davis, N. Z. 1971 'The reasons of misrule: Youth groups and charivaris in sixteenth-century france' *Past and Present* 50, 41–75

Ekpo, V. I. 1995 'Traditional symbolism of the Women's War of 1929' in Chike, Dike (ed.) 1995 *The Women's Revolt of 1929* (Lagos: NGA): 49–74

Eriksson Baaz, M. & Stern, M. 2008 'Making sense of violence: Voices of soldiers in the

Congo (DRC)' *Journal of Modern Afrian Studies* 46, 1, 57–86

Ferme, M. C. 2001 *The Underneath of Things: Violence, History, and the Everyday in Sierra Leone* (Berkeley CA: University of California Press)

Fields, K. E. 1982 'Political contingencies of witchcraft in colonial central Africa: Culture and the state in Marxist theory' *Canadian Journal of African Studies* 16, 3, 567–93

Fourchard, L. 2008 'A new name for an old practice: Vigilantes in south-western Nigeria' *Africa* 78, 1, 16–40

Geschiere, P. 1997 *The Modernity of Witchcraft: Politics and the Occult in Postcolonial Africa* (Charlottesville VA: University of Virginia)

Geschiere, P. & Nyamnjoh, F. 2000 'Capitalism and autochthony: The seesaw of mobility and belonging' *Public Culture* 12, 2, 423–52

Gore, C. & Pratten, D. 2003 'The politics of plunder: The rhetorics of order and disorder in southern Nigeria' *African Affairs* 102, 407, 211–40

Harnischfeger, J. 2003 'The Bakassi Boys: Fighting crime in Nigeria' *Journal of Modern African Studies* 41, 1, 23–49

Heald, S. 1986 'Witches and thieves: Deviant motivations in Gisu society' *Man* 21, 1, 65–78

Human Rights Watch 2005 *'Rest in Pieces': Police Torture and Deaths in Custody in Nigeria* 17, 11 (A) (New York: Human Rights Watch)

Ifeka-Moller, C. 1973 '"Sitting on a man: Colonialism and the lost political institutions of Igbo women. A reply to Judith van Allen' *Canadian Journal of African Studies* 7, 2, 317–18

Jedrej, M. C. 1986 'Cosmology and symbolism on the central Guinea coast' *Anthropos* 81, 497–515

Last, M. 2008 'The search for security in Muslim northern Nigeria' *Africa* 78, 1, 41–63

Malkki, L. H. 1995 *Purity and Exile: Violence, Memory, and National Cosmology among Hutu Refugees in Tanzania* (Chicago IL: University of Chicago Press)

Marenin, O. 1987 'The Anini saga: Armed robbery and the reproduction of ideology in Nigeria' *Journal of Modern African Studies* 25, 2, 259–81

Mbembe, A. 2001 'Ways of seeing: Beyond the new nativism. Introduction' *African Studies Review* 44, 2, 1–14

—— 2002 'African modes of self-writing' *Public Culture* 14, 1, 239–73

Mbembe, A. & Nuttall, S. 2004 'Writing the world from an African metropolis' *Public Culture* 16, 3, 347–72

McCall, J. C. 1995 'Rethinking ancestors in Africa' *Africa* 65, 2, 256–70

Meagher, K. 2007 'Hijacking civil society: The inside story of the Bakassi Boys vigilante group of south-eastern Nigeria' *Journal of Modern African Studies* 45, 1, 89–115

Messenger, J. C. 1973 'The carver in Anang society' in D'Azevedo, Walter L. 1973 (ed.) *The Traditional Artist in African Society* (Bloomington IN: Indiana University Press): 101–27

Moore, S. F. 1996 'Post-socialist micro-politics: Kilimanjaro, 1993' *Africa* 66, 4, 587–606

Moran, M. 1995 'Warriors or soldiers? Masculinity and ritual transvestism in the Liberian Civil War' in Sutton, Constance R. (ed.) 1995 *Feminism, Nationalism, and Militarism* (Arlington VA: Association for Feminist Anthropology): 73–88

Nolte, I. 2004 'Identity and violence: The politics of youth in Ijebu-Remo, Nigeria' *Journal of Modern African Studies* 42, 1, 61–89

—— 2007 'Ethnic vigilantes and the state: The Oodua People's Congress in south-western Nigeria' *International Relations* 21, 2, 217–35

Ohadike, D. C. 1981 'The influenza pandemic of 1918–1919 and the spread of cassava cultivation on the lower Niger: A study in historical linkages' *Journal of African History* 22, 3, 15–56

Olivier de Sardan, J. P. 1999 'A moral economy of corruption in Africa?' *Journal of Modern African Studies* 37, 1, 25–52

Peters, K. & Richards, P. 1998 '"Why we fight": Voices of youth combatants in Sierra Leone' *Africa* 68, 2, 183–210

Pratten, D. 2006 'The politics of vigilance in southeastern Nigeria' *Development and Change* 37, 4, 707–34

—— 2007a *The Man-Leopard Murders: History and Society in Colonial Nigeria* (Edinburgh/Bloomington IN: Edinburgh University Press/Indiana University Press, for International African Institute)

—— 2007b 'Singing thieves: History and practice in Nigerian popular justice' in Pratten & Sen 2007: 175–205

—— 2008 '"The thief eats his shame": Practice and power in Nigerian vigilantism' *Africa* 78, 1, 64–83

Pratten, D. & Sen, A. (eds) 2007 *Global Vigilantes: Perspectives on Justice and Violence* (London: Hurst & Co.)

Salmons, J. 1985 'Martial arts of the Annang' *African Arts* 19, 1, 57–63, 87–8

Shaw, M. 2000 'Crime and policing in transitional societies: Conference summary and overview'. Paper presented at Crime and Policing in Transitional Societies conference, University of the Witswatersrand, Johannesburg, South Africa

Simmons, D. C. 1957 'The depiction of gangosa on Efik-Ibibio masks' *Man* 57, 17–20

Smith, D. J. 2004 'The Bakassi Boys: Vigilantism, violence and political imagination in Nigeria' *Cultural Anthropology* 19, 3, 429–56

—— 2006 *A Culture of Corruption: Everyday Deception and Popular Discontent in Nigeria* (Princeton NJ: Princeton University Press)

Spencer, J. 2003 'Collective violence' in Das, Veena (ed.) 2003 *Oxford India Companion to Sociology and Social Anthropology* (New Delhi: Oxford University Press): 1564–80

Talbot, P. A. 1914 'Some Ibibio customs and beliefs' *Journal of the Royal African Society* 13, 51, 241–58

Taussig, M. 2003 *Law in a Lawless Land: Diary of a Limpieza in Colombia* (New York: New Press)

Thompson, E. P. 1972 'Rough music: Le charivari anglais' *Annales: Economies Societes Civilisations* 27, 2, 285–312

—— 1992 'Rough music reconsidered' *Folklore* 103, 1, 3–26

Tonkin, E. 2000 'Autonomous judges: African ordeals as dramas of power' *Ethnos: Journal of Anthropology* 65, 3, 366–86

Ukiwo, U. 2002 '*Deus ex machina* or Frankenstein monster: The changing roles of Bakassi Boys in eastern Nigeria' *Democracy and Development: A Journal of West African Affairs* 3, 1, 39–51

Van Allen, J. 1972 'Sitting on a man: Colonialism and the lost political institutions of Igbo women' *Canadian Journal of African Studies* 6, 2, 165–81

6

Violence in the Name of Democracy
Community Policing, Vigilante Action & Nation-Building in South Africa

THOMAS G. KIRSCH

Introduction

There is something disturbingly ironic about the fact that in recent decades sub-Saharan Africa has witnessed 'a remarkable number of transitions to democracy', while at the same time many 'societies on the African continent have experienced major crises of violent conflict, war and genocide' (Kaarsholm 2006: 1). Though the increase in vigilantism in many countries in Africa is not a new phenomenon, it forms a part of these developments. Pratten remarks, for example, that the 'emergence of night guards and vigilante groups as popular responses to theft and armed robbery has a long and varied history in Nigeria. Since the return to democracy in 1999, however, Nigeria has witnessed a proliferation of vigilantism' (2008: 1). In present-day South Africa too, where crime is widely considered to be a 'primary symptom of a new democratic era' (Hansen 2006: 280), for a number of years the transformation to an inclusive democratic system coincided with increased incidence of acts of popular justice which 'threaten[ed] the precarious South African miracle' (Jensen 2007: 48).[1]

However, the relationship between 'vigilantism' and 'democracy' certainly does not follow a unidimensional logic, since both notions are multifaceted and protean. The difficulties in defining 'vigilantism' have been discussed in the introduction to this volume and do not need to be recapitulated here. As regards the notion of 'democracy', on the other hand, Teresa Caldeira and James Holsten have pointed out that 'democracy entails a complexity of processes and institutions of citizenship, always becoming and unbecoming, often confusing and unstable', and that 'various and often contradictory sets of rules and games [are] in play in any democracy, at the same time and in the same space, some of which may be considerably less democratic than others' (Caldeira & Holsten 1999: 717–18). It is therefore crucial to show consideration of the variations in how vigilantism in Africa relates to (the promise of) democratic dispensations.

'Democracy' and its concomitant features in the politicolegal sphere do not always come off well in terms of how people in sub-Saharan Africa perceive them. This is due in part to the fact that, as Khehla Shubane has noted for post-apartheid South Africa, there is sometimes felt to be an 'excess of democracy' involving an 'excessive enthusiasm for human rights and freedom', which makes the government 'too concerned with the wellbeing of criminals rather than the rights of the victims of crime' (Shubane 2001: 192; see also Buur 2008). Similarly, Johannes Harnischfeger has argued that, in the eyes of many Nigerians, 'European principles of justice have ... become discredited' (2003: 23) and that, in their perception, 'the intricacies of an alien judicial system ... impede the quest for justice' (*ibid.*: 35). In such cases, 'democracy' has come to stand for politicolegal inefficiency and an excessively conciliatory approach, both of which vigilante groups believe to be in need of replacement by a more uncompromising (re)establishment of 'morality' and 'justice'.

But this critical attitude is sometimes also linked with people's experiences of discrepancies between, on the one hand, how 'democracy' is concretely *practised* and, on the other hand, what are held to be features of the *idea* of 'democracy', such as 'regular free and fair elections, universal suffrage, accountability of the state's administrative organs to the elected representatives, and effective guarantees for freedom of expression and association as well as protection against arbitrary state action' (Huber *et al.* 1997: 323). These discrepancies – constituting what has been called 'disjunctive democracy' (Caldeira & Holsten 1999) – yield the important observation that the existence of a formal political democracy in a given country is no guarantee that civil rights are being protected or that a democratic form of the rule of law is being followed. Seen in this light, vigilantism in Africa has been viewed as a disillusioned response to actual 'democratic' practice and to 'the failures of democracy to deliver expected political and economic dividends' (Smith 2006: 128).

At the same time, however, scholars investigating the relationship between 'vigilantism' and 'democracy' occasionally find themselves confronted by a configuration in which, paradoxically, vigilante action evidently violates 'democratic' principles while expressly being enacted in support of them. Such configurations are, for example, reflected in Ray Abrahams' perceptive observation that, '[a]lthough vigilantism supports the rights of individuals to band together in the fight to maintain order, it very often involves repression of individual rights to due legal process as laid down by the state' (Abrahams 1998: 17).

On the one hand, vigilante action tends to violate principles of 'democracy' in terms of political representativeness, transparency, accountability, rule of law and the equality of citizens. With respect to democratically constituted states, vigilante actions by citizens are commonly seen as undermining the politicolegal mandates and prerogatives of elected state representatives and, therefore, as threatening the sovereignty of the people. In turn, when such actions are commissioned by state representatives, whether officially or unofficially, they are usually considered to be an expression of authoritarianism and anti-democratic aspirations. No wonder, therefore, that there is a consensus among political commentators that 'vigilantism' and 'democracy' are positioned antithetically to each other and that 'no state wishing to claim to be fully democratic can allow vigilantism to be perpetrated and to thrive in a vacuum or the absence of state control' (Minnaar 2002: 130).

Yet, on the other hand, vigilantism in Africa is not always and necessarily anti-democratic. This is due to the fact that vigilante groups in several African countries have incorporated globally circulating discourses of 'democratisation' and started to use 'the language of democratic ideals' (Smith 2006: 128) in order to explain, legitimise and give direction to their acts of 'justice'. Such invocations of 'democratic' ideals by vigilante groups have been particularly well documented in the work of Lars Buur, who writes with regard to the *Amadlozi* vigilantes in post-apartheid South Africa that they 'did not intend the creation of a sovereign alternative ... nor did they attempt to undermine the new government. They saw themselves as the defenders of the new legal-political order; their aim was merely to assist the state and government against "the criminal elements that terrorized us"' (Buur 2006: 751). In doing so, the *Amadlozi* subscribed to 'notions of 'direct', 'radical' or 'popular' democracy [that also lay] at the heart of the people's courts of the 1980s' (Buur 2003: 26). It is with such empirical cases in mind that Lars Buur and Steffen Jensen conclude that vigilante action is 'constitutive of the democratic order and the rule of law by way of negatively identifying everything that law and order is not' (Buur & Jensen 2004: 140).

In this chapter, I look at the relationship between vigilante action and ideals of democracy in order to highlight a particular 'pas de deux in which norm and transgression, regulation and exception, redefine each other' (Comaroff & Comaroff 2006a: 5).[2] Generally speaking, I attempt to call the common antithetical depiction of vigilantism and democracy into question by dealing with a case in present-day South Africa that, in a telling and disturbing way, shows how adherence to democratic ideals by citizens can *produce* vigilante action. More particularly, this chapter combines a focus on vigilantism with approaches from the anthropology of public policy (Wedel *et al.* 2005) and the anthropology of democracy (Paley 2002) in order to address unintended and unforeseen consequences of state policies in post-apartheid South Africa that pertain to citizens' participation in crime prevention.

In South Africa, where 'the security of the person' was declared a constitutional right in 1996, continued high levels of crime are widely regarded as a threat to social peace, nation-building, reconciliation and socioeconomic development, while for some they also raise questions about the government's ability to act effectively as a sovereign power (see also Jensen 2001: 109). At the same time, state agencies engaged in crime prevention and law enforcement, such as the South African Police

Service (SAPS), are often overburdened and on occasion suspected of not having transformed themselves sufficiently since the end of apartheid (Brewer 1994; Brogden & Shearing 1993; Cawthra 1993; Marks 2000, 2005; Shaw 2002: 22–41). Given this situation, post-apartheid governments in South Africa have implemented policies aimed at enhancing the effectiveness of policing and the prevention of crime (including popular justice and vigilantism) while also reinforcing police accountability. An important aspect of these policies is the creation of formally institutionalised interfaces between the police and local 'communities', namely the so-called 'community policing forums' (CPFs). The CPFs are based on an organisational model of community policing that has been instituted in different versions in several countries worldwide (cf. Wisler & Onwudiwe 2008); their establishment in South Africa has been hailed as representing a shift from 'authoritarian' and 'reactive' policing to more 'democratic' and 'proactive' policing (cf. Davis *et al.* 2003), and thus as an expression of, as well as a catalyst for, post-apartheid transformations.[3] In fact, community policing was to 'become the fulcrum about which social transformation would turn' (Altbeker 2007: 27–8).

However, in the following I shall argue that, although this model of community policing is based on South African principles of participatory democracy, it nevertheless at times involves instances of vigilante action that occur not in spite of these principles but *because* of them. Thus, in contrast to other research in the field of political anthropology in Africa that deals with what have been called 'weak' or 'criminal' states (Chazan *et al.* 1999; Bayart *et al.* 1999), this chapter addresses the case of a state that in recent years has been treated by social scientists as a paradigmatic exemplar of successful democratic transition (Seidman 1999). Yet, instead of developing a critical review of the latter assessment – as has been put forward by, for example, Good (1997), Southall (1998) and Labuschagne (2004) – I shall concentrate on the controversial side-effects of the application of specific democratic principles in semiprivate associations concerned with crime prevention.

I develop my argument in several steps. First, I demonstrate that, as a particular structuration within sociopolitical practice, community policing forums in South Africa involve a twofold process. On the one hand, state agencies set an institutional framework within which 'civil society' is to constitute itself. Thus, contrary to approaches that consider civil society to exist beyond formal state structures, this is an example of state agencies interpellating a particular 'community subject' (Chesluk 2004: 251) by actively creating an institutionalised arena for entering into a dialogue with, making transparent and regulating 'civil society'. On the other hand, as my ethnographic fieldwork in South Africa has shown, those members of 'civil society' who involve themselves in this institutional framework constantly imagine and refer to 'the state' as a *conditio sine qua non* for encompassing morality and order. Thus, to a significant extent, it is through their discourses and actions that the image of 'the state' as the guarantor of an all-inclusive morality becomes constituted in local spheres of life (Hansen & Stepputat 2001).[4]

Second, I show that the CPF model is situated both at the centre *and* in the margins of the (envisioned) nation-state – the term 'margins' here being employed with reference to social, not territorial perimeters (Das & Poole 2004). CPFs are at the centre because they are involved in democratic strategies of post-apartheid nation-building through which attempts are made to overcome the legacies of apartheid segregation and thus previous divisions in society. In a sense, as a model of crime prevention, the CPF is being promoted as an arena for model citizens – that is, for law-abiding people who commit themselves to fighting crime in cooperation with state agencies and other citizens (no matter their background) in order to build a better society. As such, CPFs are modelled on concepts of peacefulness, openness, all-inclusiveness and transparency; they represent the vision of the 'new South Africa' *en miniature*. At the same time, however, CPFs programmatically aim at the margins (or even beyond the margins) of what visions of the nation-state define as lawful and legitimate, since they are concerned with social worlds that are characterised by violence, secrecy, exclusiveness and opacity.

Taken together, at first sight this looks like just another case of the familiar struggle of self-proclaimed 'good guys' against 'bad guys'. I want to suggest, however, that there are certain dilemmas entailed in this model which have to do with its role in nation-building. Since CPFs are founded on democratic principles of 'openness' and 'inclusiveness', any individual can participate in his or her neighbourhood CPF – no-one can be denied access to the CPF. And since CPFs are founded on the democratic principle of 'transparency', the activities of CPFs have to be public and transparent to anyone who wants to know about them – there is no room for secrecy or clandestine activities. However, in the final analysis all these features at times prove detrimental to what CPFs are supposed to accomplish, namely preventing crime. First, the principles of 'openness' and 'inclusiveness' actually expose CPFs to the participation of potential transgressors. Several cases have been documented of criminal networks infiltrating a local CPF. In such cases the CPF comes to be considered by outsiders as 'just another gang' (see, for example, Schärf 1996: 9–10, 2000: 13). Second, the principle of 'transparency' substantially restricts the range and success of CPF crime-prevention activities because once these activities become common knowledge, it is easier for others to take steps to circumvent them.

These two dimensions can be shown to be interlinked and to produce a dilemma: in order to build up public confidence in the morality and lawfulness of CPF members' 'principled practice' – which at times is questioned under the principles of 'openness' and 'inclusiveness' – CPF members have to demonstrate effectiveness in crime prevention. Only by successfully reducing crime can a CPF and its underlying policies attain legitimacy within its own neighbourhood. However, the means of

achieving this that the CPF has at its disposal, which include a commit-
ment to the principle of 'transparency', are more often than not inadequate
because, ironically, community policing forums are in a manner of speaking too public and too participatory to allow them to engage successfully
in crime prevention.

I argue that this constellation can lead to violent 'states of exception'
that are not proclaimed by formally instituted agencies of the state as the
nominal (and often effective) sovereign body, but by citizens who identify
with the principles of CPF policies and enact what I call 'civic states of
exception' in order to affirm CPF principles (and, by extension, the principle of participatory democracy in South Africa) by temporarily suspending them through vigilante action. I thus try to show how a democratic
ideal of public participation in crime prevention, though based on systematic features of a state-endorsed, principled model of crime prevention, has
the unforseen consequence that it produces instances of vigilantism through
which attemps are made to consolidate the politicolegal sovereignty of 'the
state' in local spheres of life.[5]

In the remainder of this chapter I shall first offer some remarks concerning the role of popular justice and vigilantism in South Africa. These
remarks will be brief because the history of vigilantism in South Africa
has already been discussed in more detail by Lars Buur, in his contribution to this volume. I then pursue an examination of several dimensions
of South African community policing policies before finally turning to an
ethnographic case-study of a 'civic state of exception' enacted by members
of a CPF in the Eastern Cape province.[6]

Non-state policing in South Africa

Popular justice, vigilantism and the state-endorsed involvement of non-
state actors in acts of policing have always been marked features of
South African history. Given the historical divisions within South
African society, vigilante groups served to control and suppress others,
while often also being an expression of the struggle for self-assertion in
the face of domination by oppressive social groupings or state agencies.
In general, these groups and their activities came into existence among
dominant *and* subaltern sections of society and have been framed in
ethnic, racial, political or territorial terms.[7] Some historical vigilante
groups among the white population, for instance, have understood their
actions to be a rightful and necessary informal supplement to the
activities of state agencies (Etherington 1988; Martens 2002; Murray
1989). In contrast to this, numerous legal self-help groups among the
South African black population have engaged in vigilantism as part of
the anti-apartheid struggle. In the latter cases, popular justice was
enacted as a strategy to resist and oppose state power by, on the one
hand, establishing an alternative politicolegal system, and on the other

hand, silencing (alleged) collaborators. Other South African vigilante groups have been shown to be part of a state-driven 'divide-and-rule' approach to politics whereby attempts were made to attain political continuity through the destabilisation of relationships between specific social groupings, such as members of the African National Congress (ANC) and the Inkatha Freedom Party (Adam & Moodley 1992; Harris 1989; Phillips 1989). Again, vigilante groups such as the organisation People against Crime and Gangsterism (PAGAD) conceive of themselves as a substitute for state organisations which are considered to be inefficient in crime prevention (Bangstadt 2005; Africa *et al.* 1998; Dixon & Johns 2001; Le Roux 1997; Pillay 2003). And lastly, in the wider history of South Africa, a large number of legal self-help groups had recourse to self-justice for the simple reason that there was no other alternative. In the early 1990s, some 80 percent of police stations were located in neighbourhoods populated by white people, even though the latter represented only ten percent of the overall population (Mufamadi 1994: 4). In the areas officially allocated to black and coloured (i.e. ostensibly mixed-race) people, by contrast, police forces were hardly seen – and when they were seen, their actions regularly involved indiscriminate killings, humiliations and gross human-rights violations (Brogden & Shearing 1993; Proudlock 1999).

This brief summary makes it clear that non-state policing has long been a systematic – and partly programmatic – constituent of the South African social and political environment. In this complex setting, what were repeatedly at stake were the interrelated questions of the legitimacy of the state, the legitimacy of means and ends in instituting and enforcing the law, and the legitimacy of the actors involved in the prevention and policing of crime. Taken together, legal self-help groups from various backgrounds all claimed to be establishing, maintaining or re-establishing social order. But how in particular this 'social order' was envisaged and how it should actually be achieved remained controversial. This was also because the different groupings – vigilante groups, neighbourhood watch groups, gangs, and different types of community court – had divergent understandings of the relationship between 'public good' and 'private benefit'. What was deemed desirable and legitimate by one group was often seen as undesirable and illegitimate by others. 'Transgression' was – and of course still is – a highly relativistic concept.

Against this background, the first democratic government elected in 1994 was faced with a series of critical challenges. It was confronted by a deeply divided society, citizens who mistrusted one another, and a public perception that crime was increasing drastically (cf. Comaroff & Comaroff 2006b: 214–21). It had to build on a state apparatus whose legitimacy had become highly questionable during the apartheid years. Finally, it had to face the existence of a variety of more or less informal groupings that engaged in whatever they themselves defined as 'crime prevention' (see also Lee & Seekings 2002).

Community policing as policy

The introduction of CPFs since the mid-1990s is an attempt to come to terms with all these challenges at once.[8] Broadly speaking, the basic idea of CPFs involves cooperation between police and 'communities' aimed at reducing crime. A CPF is associated with the police station local to its area and is composed of local police representatives, stakeholders and organisations within the local 'community', as well as anyone else who lives within the particular police precinct and is ready to become involved as a volunteer.[9]

Among other things, CPFs are intended to transform and bring together various *exclusive* legal self-help groups – such as those mentioned above – into one *inclusive* form of organisation that is officially endorsed and regulated by the state.[10] As such, it constitutes an attempt at 'reclaiming state sovereignty by domesticating unregulated forms of vigilantism and order-making' (Kyed 2007: 412). But CPF policies are also aimed at social integration more generally. By definition, the spatial boundaries of a CPF are identical with those of a given police station's jurisdiction. Since the end of apartheid the boundaries of many police precincts have in turn been re-demarcated so as to encompass previously segregated sections of society (rural/urban, black/white, affluent/poor).[11] Ideally, therefore, a CPF will include people from a variety of backgrounds who enter into dialogue with each other and – by pursuing a shared objective, namely crime prevention – develop spirit of cooperation, mutual trust and solidarity, which then forms the basis for the articulation of 'community' concerns and for reaching police accountability, while also making an important contribution to post-apartheid nation-building.

In present-day South Africa, where a 'language of crisis competes with the language of recovery' (Colvin 2003: 4), nation-building is described in hopeful words like 'rebuilding', 'reconstruction', 'reconciling', 'healing', 'forgiving', 'developing', 'transforming', 'redistributing' and 'recovering' (*ibid.*). A prominent instance of such hopeful optimism is the South African Truth and Reconciliation Commission (TRC), which programmatically aimed at creating a reconciled democratic future through the public acknowledgement of past violations. Yet, as Wilson (2001) has argued, the TRC did not so much reconstruct a historical record of the human impact of apartheid as stick to a vision of compromise and reconciliation while opting for a moral denunciation of apartheid as an evil *system*. By thus having recourse to a (Christian) narrative of the struggle of 'the good' against 'the bad', the TRC, according to Wilson, used an abstract and reified notion of 'morality' as the basis for nation-building. This, in turn, consolidated the legitimacy of the post-apartheid government which, by establishing the TRC, could publicly present itself as the guarantor of an all-inclusive morality in the new democratic South Africa. As we shall see below, CPFs similarly rely on a highly abstract notion of 'morality' as a basis for post-apartheid nation-building. And as I will demonstrate with regard to my case study, a view of 'the state' as a guarantor of 'morality' was also widespread among the CPF members I met.

According to the manual *Community Policing: Framework and Guidelines*, issued in April 1997 by the South African Department for Safety and Security for use by police officers, community policing is defined as a 'philosophy of or an approach to policing which recognizes the interdependence and shared responsibility of the police and the community in ensuring a safe and secure environment for all the people in the country' (South African Department for Safety and Security 1997: 6). The manual also specifies that police officers should:

> operate as information managers. This means 'interactive policing' – a routine exchange of information on a reciprocal basis with the community members through formal contacts and informal networks. These contacts allow the public to become more familiar with their local police service and the police to become more knowledgeable about their community. (*ibid.*: 8)

Besides this informational exchange with the police, CPF activities often include patrolling and conducting crime-awareness campaigns, and/or gathering crime-related information. Yet with regard to all these activities the CPF members' legal rights do *not* differ from those of other ordinary private persons. For example, like any other South African citizen a CPF member has the right to arrest another person, without a warrant, who 'commits or attempts to commit in his presence or whom he reasonably suspects of having committed' a so-called 'first-schedule' offence, such as murder, rape or robbery.[12] However, following the arrest the apprehended person has to be handed over to the police as soon as possible, otherwise the CPF member concerned would be liable to criminal charges and accusations of vigilantism.

As a basic principle, the South African CPF model relies on the idea that effective crime prevention is only possible through the involvement of members of 'the community' (cf. Crawford 1999). 'The community', in turn, is conceptualised as an autonomous sphere beyond 'the state' and thus as a (spatially bounded) unit of 'civil society'. At the same time, in South Africa – as in many other countries worldwide – since the early 1990s the idea has gained currency that 'a strong civil society is critical for a successful implantation of democracy' (Glaser 1997: 5).[13] The joint objectives of crime prevention and democratic nation-building in post-apartheid South Africa, mentioned above, are made possible by linking the notions of 'community' and 'civil society'.

Yet the duty of establishing a local CPF – that is, to initiate involvement by members of 'the community' (and, by metonymic extension, 'civil society') – is officially assigned to representatives of each police station. Among other things, police officers are called upon to collect data for a 'community profile' through demographic analyses and subsequently to 'consult with the various "communities of interest" in the area about the establishment and composition of a Community Police Forum. This is necessary to ensure that the CPF is indeed representative of the community' (South African Department for Safety and Security 1997: 52).

Thus, according to this policy document CPFs are constituted in three consecutive steps. First, state agencies investigate and classify spatially bounded units of the population. Second, these units are used as the basis for constituting a formally institutionalised arena for a dialogue between state agencies and those whom the state agencies identify as the units' representatives. And third, these spokespersons are expected *autonomously* to articulate the interests and concerns of 'the community'.

But how is the CPF's 'representativeness' attained? In dealing with this question, it is remarkable that such representativeness is *not* reached through democratic elections − other than in the case of each forum's executive committee, whose officeholders are indeed elected by that CPF's members − but via a thoroughly participatory process which allows anybody concerned to become a CPF member in his or her residential area. For example, one of the first steps in establishing a CPF consists in holding a meeting of community representatives at which it is 'important that *all* community groups should be represented' (South African Department for Safety and Security 1997: 53; emphasis added). In a draft version of the manual, from September 1996, the logic of this inclusiveness is explained by stating that 'a formal election of representatives ... is not practical' for the following reasons:

> Firstly, it should be noted that crime is a dynamic social phenomenon and that the CPF will have to be able to co-opt different 'communities of interest' and service providers as the crime problem changes. Secondly, we belief that formal elections will result in an exclusion of important minority interests. Thirdly, we wish to point out that representatives of the various structures of the National Peace Accord (NPA) were not formally elected. The bodies were structured to reflect the needs of the particular communities. The same should apply in the case of the CPFs. (SADSS 1997)

In the final instance, this principle of 'inclusiveness' implies that *anybody* can participate in the community policing forum local to his or her residential area.

Moreover, in line with general democratic ideals (see, for example, Taylor 2007: 124), it is expected that the workings of a CPF will be characterised by 'transparency' − that is, open sharing of information, as opposed to opacity and the clandestine operations associated with illegal or antisocial activities. According to this approach, the role of a CPF is to deal with 'community' affairs which, by definition, are 'public' and 'accessible'. CPF activities are thus contrasted with 'private' activities that do not concern 'the community' or are secretive and directed against members of 'the community'. The principle of 'transparency' therefore promises to ensure lawfulness on the part of 'the community' and accountability on the part of the police.[14]

Community policing as principled practice

However, as we shall see below, some of the foregoing principles involve paradoxes and lead to dilemmas for those who, as CPF members, try to act within their spirit. These dilemmas most clearly come to the fore when CPF members are faced with the expectations and imaginations of non-members. This is because CPFs, more than ten years after their introduction, remain a hotly debated issue. Many people simply have no interest in participating in CPFs, and the model is rejected by some because of its origins in and alleged connections with ANC party politics. Several of those who refuse to participate in CPFs suspect forum members of being partial and of pursuing political or even criminal agendas. For others, CPFs represent a morally questionable collaboration with the state; these individuals accuse CPF members of spying on neighbours, fomenting distrust between people and indulging in denunciations. Here, paradoxically, public participation in crime prevention is felt to be a transgression in itself.[15]

Despite their status as officially recognised bodies, CPFs therefore have to struggle to gain public acceptance. In general, the principles of 'inclusiveness' and 'transparency' do provide some legitimacy. Yet, these principles can have unintended consequences, since they often prove detrimental to another important aspect of the CPF's legitimacy, namely *visible effectiveness* in crime prevention.[16] As indicated above, this is because, first, the principle of 'inclusiveness' exposes the forum to the participation of actual or potential transgressors, and second, the CPF's effectiveness at preventing crime is restricted because of the application of the principle of 'transparency'. Yet for a CPF, demonstrating effectiveness in crime prevention is the most important way of demonstrating that it is committed to an overarching morality, despite the principle of 'inclusiveness'. Thus, taken together, CPF members are caught in a dilemma whenever they try to translate policies into practice.

Turning now to the examination of a particular CPF case, in South Africa's Eastern Cape province, I argue that this dilemma is at times solved by 'civic states of exception' – that is, by the active *disregarding* of CPF principles in order, paradoxically, to *affirm* them publicly.

Community policing in Trenton[17]

The community policing forum in Trenton, the municipal area in which I conducted part of my ethnographic fieldwork, came into existence in the late 1990s after certain residents had been asked by representatives of the responsible police station to help in establishing one. The CPF was launched at a publicly advertised general assembly to which all Trenton's residents were invited. This was also the occasion at which the forum's executive board was elected by participants in the assembly.

In subsequent years meetings were usually held once a week. In the course of these meetings, members of the CPF – that is, those attending the meetings – communicated with one another and discussed crime-related information. This information had often been obtained through so-called 'street managers' – that is, residents who were cooperating more or less officially with the CPF by monitoring their own streets. After the discussion, occasionally a request would be made to the attending community police officer to deal with a particular matter, with CPF members at times even specifying how they felt it should be dealt with. In other cases, CPF members debated on which legal instruments and bylaws could best be employed in order to get rid of what they had previously identified as 'unwanted' and 'potentially crime-conducive' activities. In some instances, the CPF then contacted and called for the cooperation of state agencies other than the police, such as the Liquor Board or municipal departments responsible for local infrastructure.

Police forces and other state agencies, aware that complaints from the CPF could have disadvantageous consequences for them, were generally eager to cooperate with the forum. In fact, the police were constantly under pressure to demonstrate good working relationships with 'the community'. For example, when in 2005 police officers in Trenton were preparing for the public launch of a provincial vehicle safety campaign, they were desperate to find CPF members to join them. The absence of any 'community' representatives would have caused the police to be seen in a negative light and would most likely have generated admonishments from the Department for Safety and Liaison – the state agency responsible for devising and implementing CPF policies at provincial level – in Bhisho, the capital of Eastern Cape province.

Desegregation, diversity and nation-building

In 2004, the community policing forum in Trenton was seen by the police and provincial Department for Safety and Liaison as a positive role-model for others. Trenton was a racially desegregated and economically diversified municipal area, and the CPF had succeeded in attracting a number of continuously active members from all sorts of backgrounds.

For example, the CPF was led by an elderly man who had earlier been involved in the anti-apartheid struggle but had then fallen into political disgrace; he described his involvement in the CPF as an attempt to gain symbolic rehabilitation. Belonging as he did to the left wing of the ANC, he subscribed to communist ideals when addressing the crime problem. Another member was a teacher who had lost her elder brother in the anti-apartheid struggle and had decided to continue her brother's vision by fighting what she considered to be the only remaining impediment to the formation of a truly new South Africa, namely crime. Having previously lived in the township of Mdantsane, she was well aquainted with the working of 'street committees', and she tried to make this knowledge productive in post-apartheid crime prevention. However, there was also a former soldier who, after dismissal from the South African Defence Force in the mid-1990s, had fearfully isolated himself, had subsequently acted as a night patrolman in a private neighbourhood watch scheme, and now saw the CPF as providing an opportunity to move freely again: nobody, he said, could attack him because now he was genuinely serving society. Yet another member was a pastor in an African Pentecostal church; for him, praying for peace and becoming involved in the CPF represented two sides of the same coin – they were different and yet complementary strategies in the fight of the righteous against evil. His Christian perspective was shared by another member, a woman who worked as the housekeeper of a hostel for young people and who argued that the consumption of alcohol constituted the main cause of criminal behaviour.

As this sketch illustrates, those actively engaged in the CPF in Trenton had diverse backgrounds and different personal agendas for becoming involved in it. But they also differed in many other respects: for example, in the racial category to which they had been assigned under apartheid (some of them 'Black', others 'White' or 'Coloured'), in their political affiliations, in their relationship with religion, and in their experiences with other forms of crime prevention. Similarly, CPF members had markedly divergent definitions of 'crime', different explanations for the causes of crime and different ideas about how crime could be fought most effectively.

Yet at the same time the CPF members in Trenton agreed with each other that the CPF represented an extra-political space in which differences should be disregarded by everyone engaging in nation-building through crime prevention. During CPF meetings the members became aware of the differences between them and were proud of the fact that they were able to collaborate in spite of them. Thus, on the one hand, they considered themselves to be a community-based exemplar of sucessful nation-building; on the other hand, they also realised that nation-building was something that still needed to be accomplished – after all, they said, there were still many 'criminals' around who were hampering the thorough transformation of South Africa. For them, accordingly, the CPF represented evidence for the given reality of a democratically transformed South Africa *and* a foundation which, in the future, would make South Africa's democratic transformation possible.

Principled practice

Given the latter point, CPF members in Trenton identified to a great degree with South African policies on the forums. Many members were acquainted with official policy documents and were determined to apply their knowledge in crime prevention. In doing this, not all of them were satisfied with the concrete performance of state agencies and the general political situation in South Africa; several were actually quite critical of government representatives and the local police. But the majority did subscribe to the basic principles of CPF policies, such as 'inclusiveness' and 'transparency'. As ideals, they asserted in conversations with me, these principles were above party politics, government programmes or the workings of state agencies. Their dealings were thus abstracted from concrete political configurations by envisaging and acting towards a reified nation-state for which, in turn, they considered 'the state', as an overarching guarantor of morality, to be the *conditio sine qua non*. Generally speaking, the members of the CPF accordingly engaged in the 'discursive construction of the state' (Gupta 1995: 375), a process whereby 'the 'periphery' [reached] toward the centre to embrace the nation as much as (if not more than) the center [reached] out to the periphery' (Nugent 1997: 322).

It is with the above 'state-idea' (Abrams 1988: 58) in mind that the members of the CPF interacted with other residents in Trenton. Some of the members being well versed in legal frameworks concerning crime and policing, they counselled other residents on request, occasionally specifically advising them on how to deal with the police. In this role as knowledge-brokers with regard to safety and security (cf. Ericson 1994), they implicitly conveyed the image of 'the state', described above, to others. It is in this sense that 'the state' came to be constituted as a principled moral entity through CPF activities in local spheres of life.

As became clear in the course of my fieldwork, CPF members defended these principles by any means at their disposal. In late 2004 the view that alcohol represented the primary cause of criminal behaviour, as mentioned above, unexpectedly triggered a series of events which led to a crisis within the CPF and to an attempt to (re)gain its legitimacy in Trenton – and, more generally, of South African CPF principles – through vigilante action.

Civic states of exception

Close to the hostel in which one of the CPF members acted as housekeeper was a so-called 'tavern' – that is, a drinking place that was mainly used by young black males. The coloured housekeeper of the hostel, whom I shall here call 'Sally', insisted that something should be done about this tavern because of noise pollution, instances of illicit behaviour – such as oral sex taking place on the pavement in front of the tavern – and the likelihood that stolen goods were being sold on its premises.

Knowing that Sally's attitude towards the tavern was to a large extent informed by her Christian beliefs, the other members of the CPF were initially reluctant to do anything about the matter. But eventually they wrote a letter to the relevant municipal authorities to the effect that – according to the wishes of the CPF as a 'representative body of the community' – the tavern's licence should not be extended. Some time later the municipal authorities promised to examine the case and indicated that they were generally supportive of the interests of 'the community'.

The tavern owner first reacted by complaining in local ANC branch meetings. He argued that the CPF's and especially Sally's attitude were racist because no such complaints had been raised in relation to nearby drinking establishments that were frequented by whites. Since the CPF's chairperson was also a member of the ANC branch, he was then placed under pressure from other party members. He struggled to defend the steps taken by the CPF, but was increasingly forced to acknowledge that this affair seriously called into question the legitimacy of the CPF as a ('racially') inclusive organisation. This influenced his later actions and demonstrates that although CPFs are conceptualised as extra-political spaces, party politics do play a role in their actual workings.

Then something surprising happened. The tavern owner started attending CPF meetings. Nobody could stop him doing so because of the CPF principle of 'inclusiveness', mentioned above. The chairperson and some other CPF members actually welcomed his attendance as clear evidence of the CPF's success in building up a comprehensive 'moral community'. Yet for several others – members of the CPF and other residents – his participation appeared unacceptable because he was seen as belonging to the 'unlawful' sections of society. Sally, for example, told me that his participation opened the CPF up to the public in a way that conflicted with its aims. For her and others it was like inviting criminals to meetings concerned with questions of crime prevention. Thus again, the legitimacy of the CPF was called into question – this time not because of its alleged racist exclusiveness, but because of its 'inclusiveness' and 'transparency'. In the following days Sally stopped attending CPF meetings. Other residents verbally attacked CPF members in the street and expressed their irritation over the new developments.

In turn, the tavern owner, knowing that his continued economic existence depended to some degree on the CPF, struggled to demonstrate to the other forum members that he was indeed a law-abiding person. Moreover, he did this by offering to provide the CPF with specific knowledge he had acquired and access to networks he had developed while running the tavern. In contrast to all the other CPF members, he was well acquainted with methods involved in selling stolen goods and other illicit activities, and he knew who in the neighbourhood was involved in burglaries, drug-dealing, and so on.

As it eventually turned out, the CPF willingly accepted his offer so as to regain its own legitimacy. After a debate how the tavern-owner's knowledge could be used, it was decided that he and several others would form a 'task team' which would act independently of the CPF, yet whose (hopefully anticipated) efficiency in crime control would be ascribed to the

CPF (cf. Buur 2003: 30, 2005: 201). The tavern-owner was given a free hand in establishing this task team, and only a few CPF members learned who had joined it and what it actually did. The task team thus represented an exclusive association and adopted a non-public and secretive approach. In addition, as it turned out, the methods applied by the task team resembled those of vigilante groups in that it isolated suspects and in some cases obtained confessions by force (see also Hansen 2006: 289).

Shortly after the tavern-owner had joined the CPF, the forum in Trenton arrested suspects in a major crime. This would not have been possible without the knowledge and connections of the tavern-owner. The fact that the existence of the task team contradicted the principles of 'inclusiveness' and 'transparency' for many CPF members was more than compensated for by its obvious success. And the fact that the suspects had been threatened and beaten during the search for more culprits and stolen goods also seemed quite acceptable to them, given that the CPF and its underlying democratic principles had now proved effective and thus legitimate – at least for the time being.

Concluding remarks

In a contribution to the anthropology of public policy, Wedel and co-authors have drawn attention to research that builds upon the semantic association of the term 'policy' with 'policing' in demonstrating 'how policy aids the state in shaping, controlling, and regulating heterogeneous populations through classificatory schemes that homogenize diversity, render the subject transparent to the state, and implement legal and spatial boundaries between different categories of subjects' (Wedel *et al.* 2005: 35). However, these reserachers caution that the 'point here is not that policy dictates the behavior of its target population but rather that it imposes an ideal type of what a 'normal' citizen should be. Individuals of a population must contend with, measure up to, subvert, manipulate, or simply internalise these ideal types as part of their own identity' (*ibid.:* 37–8). Making and implementing public policy should therefore be considered not as 'a linear process with a predetermined outcome', but rather as a process that encounters 'unforeseen variables, which are frequently combined in unforeseen ways and with unforeseen consequences' (*ibid.:* 39).

This chapter has dealt with unintended and unforeseen consequences in relation to a set of state policies in post-apartheid South Africa that concern citizens' participation in crime prevention. The case examined is an example of how the principles of participatory democracy in community policing can produce dilemmas for those who engage in it, eventually leading to configurations where 'the line between community police and vigilante groups is blurring' (Fourchard 2008: 17).

In this chapter I have demonstrated how the members of a community policing forum engaged in vigilante action in order to provide their organisation with legitimacy as a law-abiding, morally righteous and principled association. Here, a temporary 'civic state of exception' was enacted by people who self-consciously identified with what they envisaged to be 'the state' and who found themselves facing paradoxical constellations of factors when they tried to act in its spirit. This civic state of exception came into being not because of socioeconomic problems, nor because law-enforcing state agencies were absent, nor because people generally subscribed to local 'values and practices other than human rights and due process' (Buur 2003: 35). Quite on the contrary: it came into existence when citizens assumed the position of 'the state' and transgressed sovereign state law in order to legitimise and corroborate basic principles of the sovereignty of 'the state'.

The events described above have their own specific features. Not all of those who engage in community policing would subscribe to visions of post-apartheid nation-building. I have met members of CPFs who are nothing but cynical about the state of the nation in South Africa, others who have become heavy-hearted because of the lack of efficacy of the crime prevention measures they have instituted, and still others who, in skilful ways, exploit the idiom of community policing for their personal benefit. Nevertheless, I would suggest that the anthropological study of 'idealists' can help us highlight some of the general dynamics that inform the well-documented 'paradox that vigilantes often see themselves as breaking the law in order to respect it' (Abrahams 1998: 153). After all, if it is true, as Appadurai (2007: 29) has noted, that 'democracy rests on a vision' and that 'all visions require hope', then such study can provide tentative answers as to why for some, unfortunately, hopeful visions of democracy require violence.

Notes

1 The arguments put forward in this chapter were previously presented at the joint seminar of the Department of Social Anthropology, University of Cape Town, and the Department of Anthropology and Sociology, University of the Western Cape, South Africa, and at seminars at: the Department of Social Anthropology, University of Halle, Germany; the Department of Sociology and Social Anthropology, Stellenbosch University, South Africa; the African Studies Centre, University of Leiden, the Netherlands; the Department of Anthropology and African Studies, University of Mainz, Germany; the Department of Anthropology at Goldsmiths College, London, United Kingdom; and the African Studies Centre at Oxford University, United Kingdom. I thank participants in all these seminars for their helpful comments. Any errors are my own.

2 Up to this point in my argument I have put the words 'vigilantism' and 'democracy' in scare quotes in cases where the sociocultural and theoretical relativity of these terms needs to be stressed. Subsequent uses of these words will dispense with the scare quotes.

3 More recently, South Africa's policy of using community policing forums has been supplemented by 'sector policing' – an even more decentralised approach to policing;

see, for example, Dixon (2000, 2007), Dixon & Rauch (2004), Maroga (2003) and Steinberg (2004). Moreover, since the early 1990s, 'a host of community structures have emerged to mobilise against crime. They include anti-crime forums, anti-crime committees, neighbourhood watches, vigilantes, ... community safety forums, residents' liaison committees, disciplinary committees, Mothers Against Crime, and many others' (Schärf *et al.* 2001: 65–6). However, in this chapter I will deal exclusively with policies, discourses and practices relating to CPFs.

4 In the following, the term 'state' is put in scare quotes when referring to 'the state' as an imagined and discursively constructed entity; without scare quotes, the terms state, state agencies and government are used in relation to existing political structures, actors and processes.

5 Thus, in a way, this chapter deals with an aspect of what Mann (2004: 2) has called the 'dark side of democracy'. He argues that 'democracy has always carried with it the possibility that the majority might tyrannize minorities'. On the other hand, S. Tambiah (1996) has suggested that the competitiveness inherent in democratic elections is a major contributor to collective violence.

6 Fieldwork in South Africa was conducted over a total period of 13 months between 2003 and 2009, and was funded by the German Research Foundation (DFG) and the Volkswagen Foundation. The data presented here were collected during prolonged periods of participant observation among various CPF and during interviews and informal conversations, as well as through analysis of South African CPF policy documents.

7 For general overviews of non-state policing and popular justice in apartheid and post-apartheid South Africa see, for example, Baker (2002), Buur (2003), Minnaar (2002), Schärf & Nina (2001), Shaw (2002) and Steinberg (2001).

8 The South African model of community policing is informed by experiences elsewhere in the world where similar forms of public participation in crime prevention have been employed – for instance, in Brazil, Canada, Haiti, Kenya, Mozambique, the Netherlands, Sierra Leone, Uganda, the United Kingdom, several Scandinavian countries and the United States (see, for example, Baker 2008; Davis *et al.* 2003; Kyed 2009; Ruteere & Pommerolle 2003). The South African CPF model therefore represents the outcome of the transnational diffusion of conceptions of community-based crime prevention that have become increasingly influential in the course of neo-liberal globalisation (Brogden 2004, 2005). At the same time, CPFs in South Africa can be said to have precursors in the ANC's model of 'street committees', which under apartheid served as an alternative politicolegal structure in the townships (Stemmet & Barnard 2003; see also Suttner 2003). The groundwork for CPFs in South Africa was laid already before the 1994 elections in the National Peace Accord of 1991, which was signed by the then ruling government, the ANC and the Inkatha Freedom Party after protracted and largely contentious negotiations. This document, among other things, stated that '[t]he police shall be guided by the belief that they are accountable to society in rendering their policing services and shall therefore conduct themselves so as to secure and retain the respect and approval of the public' (Section 3.1.3). Two years later, the Interim Constitution (1993) specified the form of this co-operation by mandating that an Act of Parliament was to 'provide for the establishment of community-police forums in respect of police stations' – provisions that eventually came to be included in, for instance, the South African Police Service Act (1995), the National Crime Prevention Strategy (1996), the White Paper on Safety and Security (1998), and the SAPS Interim Regulations for Community Police Forums and Boards (2001), which formally established and detailed the functioning of CPFs.

9 For analyses of community policing in South Africa see, for example, Bénit-Gbaffou (2006, 2008), Brogden (2002), Clapper & König (1998), Dixon (2004), Gordon (2001), Jagwanth (1994), Mbhele (1998), Pelser (1999), Pelser *et al.* (2002), Sarre (1994), Schärf (2000), and Comaroff & Comaroff (2007). For works on community

policing in Europe and the USA see, for example, Greene & Mastrofski (1988), Friedmann (1992), and Lyons (1999).

10 For general discussions of crime policies in post-apartheid South Africa, see Du Plessis & Louw (2005) and Van der Spuy (2000).

11 In post-apartheid South Africa, a similar strategy of nation-building and political and economic consolidation has been pursued through the spatial reordering of politico-administrative units. For example, one initiative aimed at integrated development was the creation of the municipality of Buffalo City in the Eastern Cape. This encompasses urban and rural areas, formerly 'white' and 'black' residential spaces, and two major urban areas – East London and Mdantsane – that had previously belonged respectively to the apartheid-era Republic of South Africa and the 'homeland' of Ciskei. On the normative ordering of police territoriality, see for example Herbert (1996, 1997).

12 According to the South African Criminal Procedure Act (Section 42).

13 In this regard, discourse on CPFs shares certain aspects with contemporary discourse on NGOs which, according to Fisher, 'relies upon several key terms – participation, empowerment, local, and community – each of which has been given a variety of meanings and linked in different ways to ... perceptions of the origins, capacities, objectives, and impacts of NGOs' (Fisher 1997: 442). For analyses of the role of 'civil society' and what are called 'civic organisations', 'civic associations' or simply 'civics' in South Africa, see for example Adler & Steinberg (2000), Friedman (1991), Glaser (1997), James (2004), Mafunisa (2004), Neocosmos (1996), Seekings (1992) and Swilling (1993).

14 Nevertheless, the police have followed this principle of 'transparency' only partially. As I was able to observe, the liaising community police officer expected CPF members to make their information publicly accessible, while at the same time disclosing publicly only certain information concerning planned police operations (see Ericson 1989).

15 For other problems surrounding CPFs and criticisms of them, see Brogden (2002), Mbhele (1998), Mottiar & White (2003: 10–11) and Samara (2003: 290).

16 In this regard CPFs are no different from other forms of 'democratic policing' which always require 'a high degree of visibility' (Hansen 2006: 283).

17 The name of the municiple area has been kept anonymous.

References

Abrahams, Ray 1998 *Vigilant Citizens: Vigilantism and the State* (Cambridge: Polity)

Abrams, Philip 1988 'Notes on the difficulty of studying the state' *Journal of Historical Sociology* 1, 1, 58–89

Adam, Heribert & Moodley, Kogila 1992 'Political violence, "Tribalism", and Inkatha' *Journal of Modern African Studies* 30, 3, 485–510

Adler, Glenn & Steinberg, Jonny 2000 *From Comrades to Citizens: The South African Civics Movement and the Transition to Democracy* (Houndmills: Palgrave Macmillan)

Africa, Cherrel; Christie, Jennifer; Mattes, Robert; Roefs, Marlene & Taylor, Helen 1998 *Crime and Community Action: Pagad and the Cape Flats, 1996–1997* (Cape Town: IDASA)

Altbeker, Antony 2007 *A Country at War With Itself: South Africa's Crisis of Crime* (Johannesburg: Jonathan Ball)

Appadurai, Arjun 2007 'Hope and democracy' *Public Culture* 19, 1, 29–34

Baker, Bruce 2002 'Living with non-state policing in South Africa: The issues and dilemmas' *Journal of Modern African Studies* 40, 1, 29–53

—— 2008 'Community policing in Freetown, Sierra Leone: Foreign import or local solution?' *Journal of Intervention and Statebuilding* 2, 1, 23–42

Bangstad, Sindre 2005 'Hydra's heads: PAGAD and responses to the PAGAD phenomenon in a Cape Muslim community' *Journal of Southern African Studies* 31, 1, 187–208

Bayart, Jean-François; Hibou, Beatrice & Ellis, Stephen 1999 *The Criminalization of the State in Africa* (Oxford: James Currey)

Bénit-Gbaffou, Claire 2006 'Police–community partnerships in responses to crime: Lessons from Yeoville and Observatory, Johannesburg' *Urban Forum* 17, 4, 7–32

—— 2008 'Community policing and disputed norms for local social control in post-apartheid Johannesburg' *Journal of Southern African Studies* 34, 1, 93–109

Brewer, John D. 1994 *Black and Blue: Policing in South Africa* (Oxford: Clarendon Press)

Brogden, Mike 2002 'Implanting community policing in South Africa: A failure of history, of context, and of theory' *Liverpool Law Review* 24, 157–79

—— 2004 'Community policing: A panacea from the West' *African Affairs* 103, 413, 635–49

—— 2005 '"Horses for courses" and "thin blue lines": Community policing in transitional society' *Police Quarterly* 8, 1, 64–98

Brogden, Mike & Shearing, Clifford 1993 *Policing for a New South Africa* (London: Routledge)

Buur, Lars 2003 'Crime and punishment on the margins of the postapartheid state' *Anthropology and Humanism* 28, 1, 23–42

—— 2005 'The sovereign outsourced: Local justice and violence in Port Elizabeth' in Hansen, Thomas Blom & Stepputat, Finn (eds) 2005 *Sovereign Bodies: Citizens, Migrants, and States in the Postcolonial World* (Princeton NJ: Princeton University Press): 192–217

—— 2006 'Reordering society: Vigilantism and expressions of sovereignty in Port Elizabeth's townships' *Development and Change* 37 4, 735–57

—— 2008 'Democracy and its discontent: Vigilantism, sovereignty and human rights in South Africa' *Review of African Political Economy* 35, 118, 571–84

Buur, Lars & Jensen, Steffen 2004 'Introduction: Vigilantism and the policing of everyday life in South Africa' *African Studies* 63, 2, 139–52

Caldeira, Teresa & Holston, James 1999 'Democracy and violence in Brazil' *Comparative Studies in Society and History* 41, 4, 691–729

Cawthra, Gavin 1993 *Policing South Africa: The South African police and the transition from apartheid* (London: Zed Books)

Chazan, Naomi; Mortimer, Robert; Ravenhill, John & Rothchild, Donald 1999 *Politics and Society in Contemporary Africa* (Boulder CO: Lynne Rienner)

Chesluk, Benjamin 2004 '"Visible signs of a city out of control": Community policing in New York City' *Cultural Anthropology* 19, 2, 250–75

Clapper, Vailant A. & König, Deon 1998 'Citizen participation through small group activities: The possibilities for community policing in South Africa' *Africanus* 28, 1, 49–65

Colvin, Christopher J. 2003 'Contingency and creativity: South Africa after apartheid' *Anthropology and Humanism* 28, 1, 3–7

Comaroff, John L. & Comaroff, Jean 2006a 'Law and disorder in the postcolony: An introduction' in Comaroff, Jean & Comaroff, John L. (eds) 2006 *Law and Disorder in the Postcolony* (Chicago: University of Chicago Press): 1–56

—— 2006b 'Figuring crime: Quantifacts and the production of the un/real' *Public Culture* 18, 1, 209–46

—— 2007 'Popular justice in the new South Africa: Policing the boundaries of freedom' in Tyler, Tom R. (ed.) 2007 *Legitimacy and Criminal Justice: International Perspectives* (New York: Russell Sage Foundation Publications): 215–37

Crawford, Adam 1999 *The Local Governance of Crime: Appeals to Community and Partnerships* (Oxford: Oxford University Press)

Das, Veena & Poole, Deborah (eds) 2004 *Anthropology in the Margins of the State* (Oxford: Oxford University Press)

Davis, Robert C.; Henderson, Nicole J. & Merrick, Cybele 2003 'Community policing: Variations of the Western models in the developing world' *Police Practice and Research* 4, 3, 285–300

Dixon, Bill 2000 'Sector policing: Go forth and multiply' *Crime and Conflict* 19, 16–20
—— 2004 'Community policing: "Cherry pie" or *melktert? Society in Transition* 35, 2, 251–72
—— 2007 'Globalising the local: A genealogy of sector policing in South Africa' *International Relations* 21, 2, 163–82
Dixon, Bill & Johns, Lisa-Marie 2001 *Gangs, Pagad and the State: Vigilantism and Revenge Violence in the Western Cape* (Johannesburg: Centre for the Study of Violence and Reconciliation)
Dixon, Bill & Rauch, Janine 2004 *Sector Policing: Origins and Prospects* (Pretoria: Institute for Security Studies)
Du Plessis, Anton & Louw, Antoinette 2005 *Crime and Crime Prevention in South Africa: 10 Years After* (Pretoria: Institute for Security Studies)
Ericson, Richard V. 1989 'Patrolling the facts: Secrecy and publicity in police work' *British Journal of Sociology* 40, 2, 205–26
—— 1994 'The division of expert knowledge in policing and security' *British Journal of Sociology* 45, 2, 149–75
Etherington, Norman 1988 'Natal's black rape scare of the 1870s' *Journal of Southern African Studies* 15, 1, 36–53
Feenan, Dermot (ed.) 2002 *Informal Criminal Justice* (Aldershot: Ashgate)
Fisher, William F. 1997 'Doing good? The politics and antipolitics of NGO practices' *Annual Review of Anthropology* 26, 439–64
Fourchard, Laurent 2008 'A new name for an old practice: Vigilantes in south-western Nigeria' *Africa* 78, 1, 16–40
Friedman, Steven 1991 'An unlikely utopia: State and civil society in South Africa' *Politikon* 19, 1, 5–19
Friedmann, Robert R. 1992 *Community Policing: Comparative Perspectives and Prospects* (New York: St Martin's Press)
Glaser, Daryl 1997 'South Africa and the limits of civil society' *Journal of Southern African Studies* 23, 1, 5–25
Good, Kenneth 1997 'Accountable to themselves: Predominance in southern Africa' *Journal of Modern African Studies* 35, 4, 547–73
Gordon, Diana R. 2001 'Democratic consolidation and community policing: Conflicting imperatives in South Africa' *Policing and Society* 11, 121–50
Greene, Jack R. & Mastrofski, Stephen D. 1988 *Community Policing: Rhetoric or Reality?* (New York: Praeger)
Gupta, Akhil 1995 'Blurred boundaries: The discourse of corruption, the culture of politics, and the imagined state' *American Ethnologist* 22, 2, 375–402
Hansen, Thomas Blom 2006 'Performers of sovereignty: On the privatization of security in urban South Africa' *Critique of Anthropology* 26, 3, 279–95
Hansen, Thomas Blom & Stepputat, Finn (eds) 2001 *States of Imagination: Ethnographic Explorations of the Postcolonial State* (Durham NC: Duke University Press)
Harnischfeger, Johannes 2003 'The Bakassi Boys: Fighting crime in Nigeria' *Journal of Modern African Studies* 41, 1, 23–49
Harris, Peter 1989 'The role of right-wing vigilantes in South Africa' in Kirkwood, Mike (ed.) 1989 *States of Terror: Death Squads or Development?* (London: Catholic Institute for International Relations): 112–29
Herbert, Steve 1996 'The normative ordering of police territoriality: Making and marking space with the Los Angeles Police Department' *Annals of the Association of American Geographers* 86, 3, 567–82
—— (ed.) 1997 *Policing Space: Territoriality and the Los Angeles Police Department* (Minneapolis MN: University of Minnesota Press)
Huber, Evelyne; Rueschemeyer, Dietrich & Stephens, John D. 1997 'The paradoxes of contemporary democracy: Formal, participatory, and social dimensions' *Comparative Politics* 29, 3, 323–42
Jagwanth, Saras 1994 'Defining community policing in South Africa' *South African Journal*

of Criminology 7, 2, 165–76

James, Deborah 2004 'Civil society in South Africa' in Glasius, Marlies; Lewis, David & Seckinelgin, Hakan (eds) 2004 *Exploring Civil Society: Political and Cultural Contexts* (London: Routledge): 149–53

Jensen, Steffen 2001 'The battlefield and the price: ANC's bid to reform the South African state' in Hansen & Stepputat 2001: 97–120

—— 2007 'Policing Nkomazi: Crime, masculinity and generational conflicts' in Pratten & Sen 2007: 47–68

Kaarsholm, Preben 2006 'States of failure, societies in collapse? Understandings of violent conflicts in Africa' in Kaarsholm, Preben (ed.) 2006 *Violence, Political Culture and Development in Africa* (Oxford: James Currey): 1–24

Kyed, Helene Maria 2007 'State vigilantes and political community on the margins in post-war Mozambique' in Pratten & Sen 2007: 393–415

—— 2009 'Community policing in post-war Mozambique' *Policing and Society* 19, 4, 354–71

Labuschagne, Pieter 2004 'The doctrine of separation of powers and its application in South Africa' *Politeia* 23, 3, 84–102

Lee, Rebekah & Seekings, Jeremy 2002 'Vigilantism and popular justice after apartheid' in Feenan 2002: 99–115

Le Roux, Cornelius J. B. 1997 'People Against Gangsterism and Drugs (PAGAD)' *Journal for Contemporary History* 22, 1, 51–80

Lyons, William 1999 *The Politics of Community Policing: Rearranging the Power to Punish* (Ann Arbor MI: University of Michigan Press)

Mafunisa, Mutuwafhethu John 2004 'The role of civil society in promoting good governance in the Republic of South Africa' *International Review of Administrative Sciences* 70, 3, 489–96

Mann, Michael 2004 *The Dark Side of Democracy: Explaining Ethnic Cleansing* (Cambridge: Cambridge University Press)

Marks, Monique 2000 'Transforming police organizations from within' *British Journal of Criminology* 40, 557–73

—— 2005 *Transforming the Robocops: Changing Police in South Africa* (Scottsville: University of Kwazulu-Natal Press)

Maroga, Millicent 2003 'Two sides of the same coin? Sector policing and community policing forums' *SA Crime Quarterly* 6: 13–16

Martens, Jeremy C. 2002 'Settler homes, manhood and "houseboys": An analysis of Natal's rape scare of 1886' *Journal of Southern African Studies* 28, 2, 379–400

Mbhele, Wilfred Themba 1998 'Community policing forums: Why aren't they working?' *Crime and Conflict* 14, 9–13

Minnaar, Anthony 2002 'The "new" vigilantism in post-April 1994 South Africa: Searching for explanations' in Feenan 2002: 117–34

Mottiar, Shauna & White, Fiona 2003 *Co-Production as a Form of Service Delivery: Community Policing in Alexandra Township* (Johannesburg: Centre for Policy Studies)

Mufamadi, Sydney 1994 *Statement by the Minister of Safety and Security: 'A Programme to Address Violent Crime Including the Killing of Police Personell'* (Pretoria: Ministry of Safety and Security)

Murray, Martin J. 1989 '"The natives are always stealing": White vigilantes and the "reign of terror" in the Orange Free State, 1918–24' *Journal of African History* 30, 1, 107–23

Neocosmos, Michael 1996 'From people's politics to state politics: Aspects of national liberation in South Africa, 1984–1994' *Politeia* 15, 3, 73–119

Nugent, David 1997 *Modernity at the Edge of Empire: State, Individual and Nation in the Northern Peruvian Andes, 1885–1935* (Stanford CA: Stanford University Press)

Paley, Julia 2002 'Toward an anthropology of democracy' *Annual Review of Anthropology* 31, 469–96

Pelser, Eric 1999 *The Challenges of Community Policing in South Africa* (Pretoria: Institute for Security Studies)

Pelser, Eric; Schnetler, Johann & Louw, Antoinette 2002 *Not Everybody's Business: Community Policing in the SAPS' Priority Areas* (Pretoria: Institute for Security Studies)

Phillips, Mark 1989 'Divide and repress: Vigilantes and state objectives in Crossroads' in Kirkwood, Mike (ed.) 1989 *States of Terror: Death Squads or Development?* (London: Catholic Institute for International Relations): 15–36

Pillay, Suren 2003 'Problematising the making of good and evil: Gangs and PAGAD' *Critical Arts* 16, 2, 38–75

Pratten, David 2008 'The politics of protection: Perspectives on vigilantism in Nigeria' *Africa* 78, 1, 1–15

Pratten, David & Sen, Atreyee (eds) 2007 *Global Vigilantes: Perspectives on Justice and Violence* (London: Hurst & Co.)

Proudlock, Paula 1999 'Licence to kill: Police use of force' *Crime and Conflict* 15, 28–32

Ruteere, Mutuma & Pommerolle, Marie-Emmanuelle 2003 'Democratizing security or decentralising repression? The ambiguities of community policing in Kenya' *African Affairs* 102, 4, 587–604

SADSS 1997 = South African Department for Safety and Security 1997 *Community Policing: Framework and Guidelines* (Pretoria: South African Department for Safety and Security)

Samara, Tony Roshan 2003 'State security in transition: The war on crime in post-apartheid South Africa' *Social Identities* 9, 2, 277–312

Sarre, Rick 1994 'Community policing: Themes for South Africa' *Acta Criminologica* 10, 1, 5–10

Schärf, Wilfried 1996 'Community policing: A preliminary critical analysis'. Paper presented at Workshop on Community Policing, Technikon SA, South Africa

—— 2000 'Community justice and community policing in post-apartheid South Africa'. Paper presented at Workshop on the Rule of Law and Development, Institute for Development Studies, University of Sussex, United Kingdom

Schärf, Wilfried & Nina, Daniel (eds) 2001 *The Other Law* (Lansdown: Juta)

Schärf, Wilfried; Saban, Gaironesa & Hauck, Maria 2001 'Local communities and crime prevention: Two experiments in partnership policing' in Steinberg 2001: 65–85

Seekings, Jeremy 1992 'Civic organisation in South African townships' *South African Review Service* 6, 216–38

Seidman, Gay W. 1999 'Is South Africa different? Sociological comparisons and theoretical Contributions from the land of apartheid' *Annual Review of Sociology* 25, 419–40

Shaw, Mark 2002 *Crime and Policing in Post-Apartheid South Africa: Transformation Under Fire* (Cape Town: David Philip)

Shubane, Khehla 2001 'A question of balance: Crime-fighting in a new democracy' in Steinberg 2001: 186–202

Smith, Daniel Jordan 2006 'Violent vigilantism and the state in Nigeria: The case of the Bakassi Boys' in Bay, Edna G. & Donham, Donald L. (eds) 2006 *States of Violence: Politics, Youth and Memory in Contemporary Africa* (Charlottesville VA: University of Virginia Press): 125–47

Southall, Roger 1998 'The centralization and fragmentation of South Africa's dominant party system' *African Affairs* 97, 389, 443–69

Steinberg, Jonny (ed.) 2001 *Crime Wave: The South African Underworld and its Foes* (Johannesburg: Witwatersrand University Press)

—— 2004 *Sector Policing on the West Rand: Three Case Studies* (Pretoria: Institute for Security Studies)

Stemmet, Jan-Ad & Barnard, Leo S. 2003 'Committees, tyres and teenagers: '"people's power" and "alternative structures" as part of the strategy of the ANC to render the country ungovernable during the 1980s' *Journal for Contemporary History* 28, 1, 92–109

Suttner, Raymond 2003 'The African National Congress (ANC) underground: From the M-Plan to Rivonia' *South African Historical Journal* 49, 123–46

Swilling, Mark 1993 'Civic associations in South Africa' *Urban Forum* 4, 2, 15–36

Tambiah, Stanley 1996 *Leveling Crowds: Ethnonationalist Conflicts and Collective Violence in South Asia* (Berkeley CA: University of California Press)

Taylor, Charles 2007 'Cultures of democracy and citizen efficacy' *Public Culture* 19, 1, 117–50

Van der Spuy, Elrena 2000 'Crime and its discontent: Recent South African responses and policies' in Shaw, Mark (ed.) 2000 *Crime and Policing in Transitional Societies* (Johannesburg: Konrad-Adenauer-Stiftung): 167–75

Wedel, Janine R.; Shore, Cris; Feldman, Gregory & Lathrop, Stacy 2005 'Toward an anthropology of public policy' *Annals of the American Academy of Political and Social Science* 600, 1, 30–51

Wilson, Richard 2001 *The Politics of Truth and Reconciliation in South Africa: Legitimizing the Post-Apartheid State* (Cambridge: Cambridge University Press)

Wisler, Dominique & Onwudiwe, Ihekwoaba D. 2008 'Community policing in comparison' *Police Quarterly* 11, 4, 427–46

Index